Business
Commu
Today

Business Communication Today

A guide to effective communication techniques

Sue Smithson, BA (Hons), MEd
Senior Lecturer in Communication,
Farnborough College of Technology

ICSA Publishing · Cambridge

First published in 1984 by ICSA Publishing Ltd
Fitzwilliam House, 32 Trumpington Street, Cambridge CB2 1QY, England
and
51 Washington Street, Dover, NH 03820, USA

ISBN 0 902197 20 7 (Cased)
ISBN 0 902197 21 5 (Paper)

Library of Congress Cataloging in Publication Data
Smithson, Sue.
   Business Communication Today.
   Bibliography: P.
   Includes Index.
   1. Communication in Management.
   I. Title.
HF5718.S635   1984   658.4/5   84-17235
ISBN 0-902197-20-7
ISBN 0-902197-21-5 (pbk.)

Designed by Ron Jones

Typeset by Communitype, Leicester

Printed in Great Britain by St Edmundsbury Press,
Bury St Edmunds, Suffolk

Contents

Introduction   vii

Part 1   An introduction to communication and its effective planning
  1   Communication – a management problem   3
  2   Planning communication – note-taking and note-making
     as invaluable aids   14

**Part 2   Written communication – the preparation and construction of
business documents**
  3   Daily paperwork – forms, memoranda, written instruc-
     tions and notices   27
  4   Reports – an essential basis for decision-making   42
  5   Letter writing – an essential element in public relations 62
  6   The discussion paper – a problem of construction   77
  7   The essay – writing answers for examinations or
     assignments   81

**Part 3   Oral communication – the need for effective techniques in a
variety of business situations**
  8   Oral presentations – instructing, reporting and giving talks   95
  9   Meetings – using valuable time   111
  10   Interviews – assessment techniques   138
  11   Telephone and reception techniques – a public relations
     function   160

**Part 4   New directions in business communication – the expansion of
information technology and its implications**
  12   The rapid revolution – a review of the techniques now
     available for business communication   171
  13   The human factor – the need to prepare for technological
     change   183

Contents

Part 5 The use of English
    Appendix A   The parts of speech   197
    Appendix B   Syntax and the use of vocabulary   209
    Appendix C   Punctuation   215

Notes to the text   223

Further reading   225

Index   226

Introduction

This book aims to be a comprehensive guide to the techniques that are essential for effective communication in any business situation today. It was written because there are an increasing number of complaints about weaknesses concerning communication within business organisations, and an increasing number of fundamental errors by professional people. Examining bodies have recognised the problems, and now demand an ability to communicate well at any level. They have attempted to meet this contingency, either by introducing a module, or examination paper, which explores the whole subject of communication, or by setting question papers in their own areas of technical expertise. These tests require a mastery of that field, and the ability to communicate it to anyone. Examiners for the Institute of Bankers, the Institute of Pension Management, the Institute of Chartered Secretaries and Administrators, and the Business/Technician Education Council (BTEC), have already adopted this approach.

It is hoped that a wide variety of readers will find this book useful; however, it is aimed specifically at those studying to gain a qualification in any of the fields mentioned above, and at those who feel that their communication skills need improvement because they have just been, or are about to be, promoted to a position where they are involved with managing people. Anyone in an administrative or managerial role, and anyone who intends to enter either of these areas in the immediate future, will find some helpful guidelines here.

For this reason, the text and the exercises have been approached from an adult viewpoint, and have taken account of the fact that attendance at classes may not be possible. Any activities or assignments set are based, therefore, on self-evaluation. In addition, knowing that many people whose first language is not English are now studying for professional qualifications, or practising in management and administration within the United Kingdom, a supplement, giving guidelines on grammar and English usage, has been provided.

This book is concerned with the major problems and techniques that affect the communication process in the contemporary world. The first part gives an overview of the problems particularly related to effective management, and of the principles and planning needed to overcome them. The second part deals with written communication and gives guidance on all kinds of business documentation. The third part deals with oral communication, the face-to-face interaction process which at first seems easy but which can be fraught with misunderstanding. The fourth part gives an outline of the new advances made in communication with the advent of information technology and discusses the the possible progress, and the inevitable limitations, of such innovations. Finally, a supplement is given to assist anyone who may need a reminder of the basic rules of English grammar and usage. Although this was prepared with foreign students in mind, it has been planned deliberately to provide a revision course for those who may have left formal education some time ago.

This book is dedicated, therefore, to all those who, whether studying formally or not, have been brave enough to continue their 'education' or to undertake self-improvement. Communication is a critical, as well as a much criticised, area. The future of any enterprise depends on its effectiveness, so it is with great sincerity that I wish you every success.

Acknowledgements

I would like to thank the following people for their advice, encouragement and practical help in compiling this book: my colleagues in the Business Behavioural Resources Unit at Farnborough College of Technology, Michael and Patricia Cresdee, Mrs Sheelagh Trice and Mrs Betty Root.

Sue Smithson
Reading
May 1984

Part 1 | An introduction to communication and its effective planning

1 | Communication - a management problem

The importance of management communication

Two perennial complaints within businesses concern communication and management, yet it is hard to define either term precisely. If you ask anyone what communication is, you will probably receive a rather vague answer like: 'Getting yourself understood, I suppose', which addresses only part of the problem. Even more hazy are most employees' ideas of what their managers do all day. Having asked many groups this question, I get the impression that the answer is 'remarkably little!' Most managers would dispute this, but the significant fact here is that employees are not informed about the day-to-day company business. Today, as the business world becomes increasingly complex and multinational, and as technological advances in communication techniques accelerate, it is vital that the essential nature of both management and communication is clearly understood and that both are carried out effectively.

The survival of any enterprise depends upon its effectiveness. If communication and management are weak, the inevitable consequences will be falling morale, low productivity and financial disaster – a catastrophic chain of events for any business. It is necessary, therefore, to begin by defining the factors that are fundamental to any act of communication or management at any level.

Good communication has two objectives. The first is to obtain total understanding when any message is passed from one individual (or group) to another. The second objective, which is more difficult, is to obtain the response that is required. This is central to the communication process. The first objective can be achieved relatively easily if the individual chooses the most appropriate medium and the most suitable language, whereas the second objective requires the correct *approach*. This latter objective is ignored often, much to the detriment of human relations and productivity.

A successful manager must be a competent communicator, as management at any level can be defined as 'implementing decisions through others' or, more simply, 'getting things done by other people'. Management and communication are interdependent, and are necessary in order to execute

3

management tasks effectively. Henri Fayol described these comprehensively as 'planning, commanding, controlling and co-ordinating'.[1] If any one of these tasks is to be performed well, clear communication is crucial.

Complaints about communication within businesses

At first, the requirements for good communication seem simple to put into practice; after all, we have all been attempting to communicate actively since birth, first by gesture, look or cry, and later through the more sophisticated technique of speech. We have had to learn ways of obtaining what we required from family, friends, colleagues and the community as a whole. We should be experts at this, and often think that we are. Why then, should dissatisfaction about communication still be so widely found? (I have even seen a poster on an office wall showing some mushrooms muttering that they are constantly kept in the dark!) How does such a situation arise, and why do so many employees feel that their managers treat them in this way? There are a number of answers to this. I will start by asking the reader a direct question.

Are you a good communicator?

At this stage, before reading on, you will have concluded, probably, that you *are* a good communicator on the whole (and therefore have no need of this book!), however, the number of complaints continues to grow. The problem lies partly in our own self-perception – Burns was wise when he wished for the power 'to see ourselves as others see us'.[2] We are guilty often of self-delusion, as recognising our own faults means that our ego and status become impaired. No one ever believes that they are bad drivers or bad lovers, similarly that they are bad managers or bad communicators – it is always other people!

How often have we been guilty of not checking our instructions before attempting to put them into practice or interpreting them to others? If our instructions are not carried out in the way we intended, we try to cover this up, not wishing to appear foolish (just as the courtiers wouldn't admit to not being able to see the Emperor's new clothes![3]). Unfortunately, this unwillingness to face our inadequacies has resulted in them being perpetuated. We never think to seek help in order to improve our techniques.

The situation has not been assisted by the fact that help, in the form of training, has been available only relatively recently in this country. Whilst Harvard was founded in the United States of America in the nineteenth century, Britain had to wait until 1947 for its first management college, and it wasn't until the 1960s that the two business schools (at London and Manchester), and most other management training, really got underway. Apart from a strong non-vocational bias in our academic traditions, two powerful myths were largely responsible for this neglect which left us far behind the USA and Germany. These were the myth of the 'resourceful amateur'[4] and the mystique of 'experience'. The trouble with both of these, in terms of our management record, is that the results have been far from magical, and 'experience' has often meant that the same mistakes have been repeated every year!

The result is that most people in managerial positions have received very little general management training or guidance in communication. In 1983 the estimate was that only 40 per cent of managers had been given the opportunity to improve themselves. Although expert at their professions when promoted, these managers are liable to fail to 'implement their decisions through others'. What Dr L. J. Peter has called the 'Peter Principle'[5] – that people are 'promoted to their level of incompetence' – is the inevitable result, and nowhere is that incompetence felt more than in poor communication.

We can all improve our techniques and the first step (apart from *recognising* that we can do this) is to identify some of the major problems and to see how they may be overcome.

Identification of some major problem areas in communication

Lack of forethought and objective-setting

The initial problem in attempting to communicate well is the clear definition of the objective. This is a management problem, too. It became evident, in a survey of managers' work carried out at Oxford,[6] that most had 'butterfly minds' and had failed to set – and therefore to achieve – the objectives which were essential to adequate planning. Although it sounds obvious to say that we should decide what we want to do before we do it, many people *do* need to 'engage brain box before opening mouth'. Failure to do so can often arouse resentment or aggression, which means that the 'required response' will not be forthcoming.

When setting objectives for communication, the nature of the message, and the characteristics of the receiving individual or group, must be taken into account. It is very easy, when the objective should be persuasion, to adopt an approach which will result in confrontation. When the nature of the message involves, for example, the introduction of change, this error is likely to result in sabotage of the intended innovation. It is necessary to use our knowledge of the receiving parties (their attitudes, vocabulary, etc.) to condition the methods used and the approach adopted. Amazingly, this simple principle is often ignored. In 1977 the *Sunday Times* carried an article called 'The art of gobbledegook',[7] which included a letter sent to British Leyland workers by management. This was written in extremely complex language and was threatening in tone. Not surprisingly, it had resulted in a stoppage. Alongside this letter, the *Sunday Times* had printed a version of it which had short, basic vocabulary and no threats. It was therefore concise, comprehensible and neutral in tone. This is a classic example of a misunderstanding occurring through poor communication. It is vital, particularly with industrial relations in the car industry, to have clear definitions of objectives and to make sure that they are communicated in the right way.

Problems that have derived from perception and attitudes

Every human being amasses individual attitudes from early childhood. Ideologists have not been slow to recognise that this is a particularly influential period. 'Give me a child when he is seven, and I will give you the man' was always the claim of the Jesuits. Our attitudes come from our experience with our families, friends and contemporaries, as well as from our geographical, cultural and educational backgrounds.

If we compare, for example, a young, university-educated manager from the south of England, who takes over a northern factory, and a 50-year-old shop steward, who has been brought up locally and trained as a craft apprentice, we will see that they both have different attitudes which are bound to be obstacles if any change of policy is proposed. Its implementation will be difficult and could lead to a confrontation, but it will be *inevitable* if *no* cognizance is taken of the differing attitudes and perceptions (or view of events) of the two men. If we take the attitudes and perceptions of others into account, and try to condition our approach accordingly, it will be easier to gain acceptance.

A good illustration of this was shown in a television series on the introduction of micro technology.[8] A local authority was going to be computerised, and it was very much in favour of this taking place as soon as possible. As it wryly commented, the one thing that was forgotten was the people – the unions. What the management *perceived* as a more efficient system was perceived by the work-force not only as a difficult innovation involving re-learning, but also as a move towards redundancies. The problem was exacerbated by the style – the management *imposed* the system without *consultation*. Needless to say, the change was blocked by the people who should have operated it. The story had a happy ending, for the management realised its mistake and suspended the system. They consulted and negotiated with the work-force; the result was acceptance and co-operation.

Policy documents
Memoranda
Circulars
Notices
Reports
Forms
Meetings and meeting documentation
Interviews
Internal telephone
Tannoy/'bleepers'/paging systems
CCTV
Word processors
Teleprinters
Computer links and data output

Fig. 1   Internal media.

Problems concerning the wrong choice of medium/method

There are basically four communication methods from which to choose. There are oral methods (the spoken word), written methods, visual methods and audio (or sound) methods. These can be relayed through a variety of media – voice, documents, pictures, diagrams, graphs, radio, television, electronic systems, etc. (see Figs. 1 and 3). The choice of the most appropriate combination of method and medium depends upon the nature of the message and the likely characteristics and/or reactions of the individual or group destined to receive it.

To take a very simple example, if a message is informative and the receiving group is a mass audience, which includes a number of levels of intelligence and language, and may be multi-cultural, the best method will be visual. Signs at international airports, traffic lights and road signs rely heavily on visual messages therefore.

On the other hand, if confirmation and records are needed, written methods are vital. Contracts – and even the memorandum which confirms an oral request for action – must be conveyed in writing. If the message requires a reaction or some feedback, this method will not be the most appropriate – in fact, memos that have attempted to convey messages without previous oral communication have been known to get 'lost' or to be found in waste-paper baskets! Again, all this is to do with *response* – obtaining the reaction you

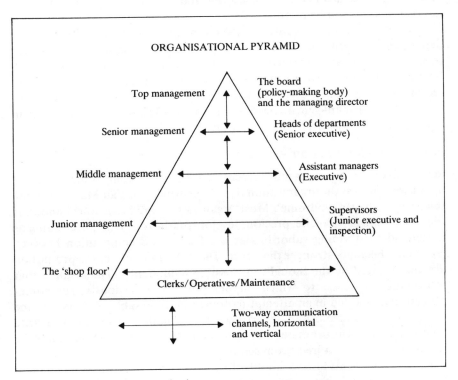

Fig. 2   Internal lines of communication.

require – and is connected with the 'approach' element of the original objectives and planning.

Today, the range of *media* is great and the techniques are increasing in number and sophistication. Facsimile has promoted the fast communication and recording of contracts; television, the radio and videos now reach a mass audience previously undreamed of. The Open University has taken advantage of this, and 'distance learning' is likely to increase. Computers, particularly the micro/portable ones, could make offices and international travel outdated and unnecessary. More than ever before, the correct choice of *method* needs to be tied in with the appropriate medium. The best choice of method and medium, however, is linked with further problems which are bound to affect the success of communication.

Problems deriving from the organisational environment

The environment in which people work is bound to create a series of constraints. If, for example, the environment is a noisy one – the factory floor, the open plan office and the street outside can create this – and one which is full of visual distraction, there will be minimal concentration on the message being conveyed, particularly at the beginning and end of the message. This problem is increased if the method chosen is oral. In these circumstances, therefore, extra care needs to be taken to arouse and maintain attention and to check that what has been said has been understood. (Confirmation using another method will be useful.)

If an organisation is separated geographically – split sites, branches or departments – then the individual groups will not communicate with each other. (They may have a vested interest in not doing so, if their objective is to 'empire build' at the expense of others.) Very special care needs to be taken to see that information is disseminated equally, otherwise intense resentment may occur. Top management needs to take a specific lead in co-ordination, in order to avoid divisions in the organisation.

Withholding information – secrecy, its cause and effects

Secrecy in offices produces much resentment and many complaints. What are its causes? There is the organisational problem which Alastair Mant[9] calls 'the thwarted manager syndrome'. Most organisations are hierarchical and thus there is not much room, i.e. precious few jobs, at the top. What often happens is that talented young subordinates are feared and competition between colleagues becomes stronger than ever. The difficulties of limited promotion are complicated by the thought of possible redundancy. The result is that information – access to which implies power – is jealously, sometimes obsessively, guarded in an attempt to appear indispensable. (In one extreme case, a manager memorised departmental information and refused to write anything down. Unfortunately, he died suddenly and his section had to be scrapped and restructured 'from scratch'.)

Rival departments also withhold information from each other. When there is fierce competition between departments, either for resources – most often in

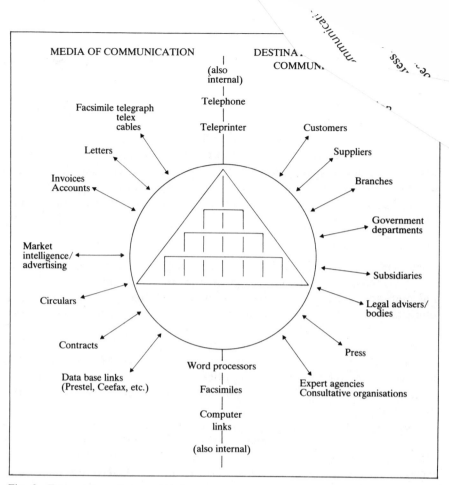

Fig. 3 External lines of communication.

the public sector – or for power, the differing objectives, personalities and backgrounds of the major protagonists add to the strife. Accountancy departments and sales staff often compete with each other, as do research and development and production staff. In one firm, R & D failed to communicate with Marketing, and vice versa, because the two heads were locked in strife. The inevitable result was, of course, detrimental to sales!

This kind of secrecy has two effects – one is the fall in productivity or efficiency, the other is the pernicious growth of the grapevine. People starved of information will create explanations for themselves. For example, if a new machine is installed, and the staff aren't fully informed about it, rumours of people losing their jobs could start. Openness, full briefing, the supply of information to those who need it, the continual attention to both horizontal communication (or liaison) and vertical communication (see Fig. 2) are vital, therefore, but are neglected frequently.

The third reason for withholding information often goes unnoticed until too late. It concerns feedback. If something goes wrong, people often fail to

Herewith a feasibility study in semantics which may indicate at this present point in time a jumping-off ground from grass roots to a fully integrated sentence structurisation. That it is arranged alphabetically is for the convenience of readers who may wish to increase its potentiality.

Between ourselves — Between you, me and the rest of the world.

Can I help you? — What the hell are you doing here? Go away.

Carefully considered — I've not had time to read it.

Computerised — Abolished.

Correct me if I'm wrong — Don't contradict.

Diversion — Add 10 miles.

Everyone's entitled to their own opinion — You don't know what you're talking about.

Far be it from me — I know better.

Free — Fully charged for in the price.

Fully guaranteed — Guaranteed by whom? For what? And for how long?

I'd be grateful if — You'd better do it or else.

I don't mind constructive criticism but — Mind your own business.

I have been instructed — I have not been instructed but am clearing some papers off my desk.

I'll get in touch — you won't be hearing from me.

I'm sure you're right — I'm sure you're wrong.

Improvements — Destroying things that get in the way of lorries.

I must have got it wrong — I'm right but there's no point in arguing.

I regard this honour as a tribute to the whole team — It was all my own doing.

I won't be a minute — I could be here indefinitely.

In depth — Too long.

We must have lunch sometime — I can't face seeing you just yet, if ever.

Of course you know best — Of course I know best.

Off the record — I've told 20 people.

Strictly off the record — I've told hundreds of people.

To be perfectly frank — Don't believe a word I'm going to say.

Unfortunately — Luckily.

We're taking care of it — I don't know what you're talking about.

With due respect — Thinking very little of you as I do.

You and I both know — You don't know but I'm telling you.

You will appreciate that — You will not like the fact that.

Fig. 4   Sir John Betjeman's 'ABC of double-talk' (courtesy of *Punch*).

Morris (author of *The Naked Ape*) has written a fascinating book on non-verbal communication entitled *Man-Watching*.[13] Gestures, we learn, are not universal and can be responsible for misinterpretation between nations, sometimes leading to physical aggression! Interviews, as we will see later, often rely heavily on non-verbal evidence of a candidate's suitability.

Words alone are not enough – tone, expression and gesture all give us further clues. Sir John Betjeman[14] has humorously demonstrated this. His list (see Fig. 4) shows how words can mislead and that sometimes we need more than one method in order to communicate adequately, or divine the true meaning of someone else's thoughts!

Finally, there are those curious words which become 'coloured' by our perceptions and attitudes, or those of others, and are therefore liable to be misused or misinterpreted. They are usually words used to identify human groups. Minority groups are subject to this form of identification and reaction in particular. Test yourself by considering words like 'student' or 'woman driver'. What images do they conjure up?

We are at best irrational, and should be aware that our perceptions are *not* those of others – if there is any doubt at all, there is a need to explain and clarify. Above all we should avoid using those terms which can produce emotional, rather than rational, reactions – in a working situation, even the term 'worker' can be seen as discriminating!

Conclusion – some basic principles to be observed in all methods of communication

It is hoped that this chapter has served to introduce some of the problems of communication and to demonstrate why it is not the simple process it might seem. I have attempted to identify the many areas of difficulty and to point out why effective communication is essential to successful management and business. In conclusion, it may be helpful to formulate some fundamental principles which need to be applied to communication techniques.

The major principles which should precede any act of communication, oral, written or visual (and the necessary questions that need to be asked in relation to each) are as follows:

1. *Set the objective* If you are the communicator, are you informing, questioning or persuading? If you are receiving instructions from others, are you positive as to what is required of you? What methods of clarification/investigation do you need to use?

2. *Define the requirements* What is the nature of the message? Who are the receiving groups? Connected with this, who needs to know, and who should know on an 'information basis'? Who needs to be consulted, and about what? What are the likely reactions to the message of the people concerned? What approach will be most fruitful, therefore?

3. *Choose the most appropriate methods and media in order to gain comprehension and co-operation* Once the questions listed under the first two major principles have been answered, what methods of communication are best – oral, written, aural or visual? Which media can convey the message in the least offensive way and will be guaranteed to gain as much understanding and co-operation as is required?

4. *Select the language to suit the recipient* This applies if the method chosen is oral, written or audio. What is the level of technical knowledge on the subject? What is the usual vocabulary range? What words should be avoided specifically because they may have emotive connotations which arouse resentment? What words need definition? What can be said in a simpler and more economic way?

5. *Plan the sequence* Logical ordering is particularly vital when giving instructions or commands. What order of words is needed to gain optimal understanding, fastest learning, highest productivity and lowest error? The latter can sometimes affect cost and, perhaps more personally important, safety! (This is given more attention later in the book when written instructions are discussed at length.) All I need say here is that in areas such as instruction and report writing, the right sequence of words is essential for proper communication.

6. *Attract attention* 'Switch on' or attract the attention of your recipients before continuing with your carefully planned communication. Are they listening or concentrating? Are their thoughts really on your objective? How can you focus their minds on the matter in hand? Is there an initial question or statement which will help? (Most people do not respond or concentrate

immediately – the act of asking them a question, or making a statement that requires them to think about the immediate matter, helps considerably to avoid part of the message being lost.)

7. *Check and confirm the effects of any act of communication* What has been the outcome? Have people understood? Have people acted in the way that you expected? Have there been any unwelcome or unexpected delays or outcomes? If there have, whose fault was it, and at what stage did these occur? Without these questions (which may uncover unwelcome news and which are essentially self-critical), we cannot evaluate either our own performance as a communicator or the real effect of our attempt to communicate.

8. *Review the feedback and modify, where necessary* When the effects have been assessed (including those which were not expected), how successful was your communication? In retrospect, what would you do to improve the situation? How would you use this learning experience – for this is what the review process is – in your future communication activity? This last process is important, for, without undertaking this honestly, we cannot analyse mistakes and rectify them. It is quite evident that this is the only way to make real progress and true improvement for the future, although it can be painful as it means that we have to swallow our pride and examine our own performances.

Before I discuss the various techniques of communication, I have set some questions which are designed to show you some of the problems and principles outlined in this chapter.

* * *

Suggested activity for interest

Compare reports of the same story in *The Times* and *The Sun*. Which newpaper uses the most Latinised forms?

Suggested activities for self-evaluation

1. How would you choose to communicate the following: news of a redundancy, progress within a department, a change of working method, a reprimand over a minor matter, company accounts, and new legislation affecting employees? Give reasons.

2. Can you express the following ideas more clearly?

'It is generally believed in the department that an improvement in production can be effected by the abolition of restrictive practices.'

'The cost may be upwards of a figure rather below £10m.'

'It is regretted that this point was not made clear in our communication and that as a consequence delay has resulted.'

2 | Planning communication– note-taking and note- making as invaluable aids

The principles that apply to any form of communication must also be applied to any planning process. Unfortunately, even people who are normally methodical in other aspects of their work often fail to adopt the systematic approach, which is essential if communication is to be really effective, and to achieve the two fundamental objectives, which have been previously stated – to gain complete understanding *and* the required response. The many problems which were discussed in the first chapter are not easy to solve. They need to be recognised clearly and a conscious effort must be made to overcome them. Careful forethought and planning are essential prerequisites for an effective communicator, therefore.

Notes as a preparation for communication

There are a number of techniques which can assist in planning and these can usually be applied in specific situations, such as preparing for meetings and composing reports or instructions. (These will be discussed in detail under their respective headings in subsequent chapters.) However, one basic and invaluable aid for all situations is the ability to *take* good notes if you are attempting to condense, select and comprehend information from other sources, and to *make* clear notes when composing your own communications.

It is therefore extremely useful at this stage to look at the need for good notes, to distinguish between the uses of note-making and note-taking and to give some guidance which will help to improve these techniques which are of primary importance when planning any form of communication.

The need for good notes

We *take* notes in a variety of situations for three important reasons. The first is that we cannot remember everything. Many of us have poor short-term memories but, even if we do not, the difficulties tend to increase with the amount to be learned, or with advancing age. We need 'reminders' therefore – even the infallible computer needs the right cue to 'jog its electronic memory' and retrieve the right information. Furthermore, it is not enough to be reminded of what was written, what was said or what occurred, for we may need, at some time in the future, an accurate and permanent record to which we can refer at a later date. This, then, is the second need; we must be able to take notes in such a way that we can still understand precisely what was meant after a period of time. Finally, much of the information which we receive is complex and bulky; some of it is irrelevant to our objectives. Good note-taking can reduce this information, by summarising it to manageable proportions.

We *make* notes also – or should do so – to prepare any communication in advance. This has two main purposes. The first is to aid *analysis* of the problems and requirements of the particular circumstances in which the communication is taking place. It is at this stage that the principles are best applied – the noting of specific aims and objectives, the planning of the most logical sequence, and so on. The second is to assist in composing any written or oral communication, in order that it is presented well. All this is crucial if we are to achieve the objectives of communication – gaining understanding and the desired response from the reader or audience. If we adopt a competent approach, it looks very professional.

Note-taking and note-making are vital to ensure that the many forms of communication are effective. It will be useful to identify the functions and techniques of both these invaluable aids. Before doing this, however, I will comment on the different arrangements of notes.

Arrangement of notes

Whether note-taking or note-making, two possible arrangements are common in order to identify key themes and the points dependent upon them. Perhaps the most usual arrangement (and one which is most familiar from our school days) is the 'ladder' layout (see Fig. 5). An alternative structure, however, and one which has much to recommend it, is the 'star' layout. Here, the central

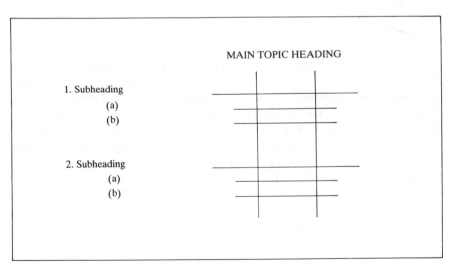

Fig. 5   The 'ladder' layout.

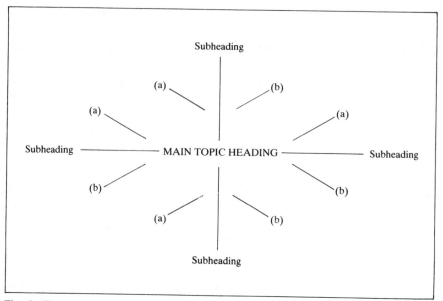

Fig. 6   The 'star' layout.

theme is placed at the centre and the dependent points 'radiate' from it, like the rays of the sun (see Fig. 6).

Whatever the arrangement initially chosen, it is wise to review the notes and re-arrange, index and file them, otherwise loss, forgetfulness, and all the frustrations that stem from mislaid or misunderstood notes, are likely to occur!

The functions and techniques of note-taking and note-making are slightly different, and I will now distinguish between the two.

Note-taking

Functions

The functions of note-taking are to aid recall, ensure accurate records and produce cogent summaries in the following situations: attendance at conferences, training courses, seminars or lectures; face to face oral exchanges, such as interviews for selection, appraisal, counselling or disciplinary purposes; attendance at meetings, both formal and informal; participation in telephone conversations, or any other 'distance' exchange; and condensing information from a variety of sources, such as legal documents, reports, surveys, text books or the mass media.

Techniques – note-taking whilst listening

Many of the functions identified above require note-taking whilst listening. I shall identify the main problems here and suggest some techniques to overcome them.

Communciation research has shown that we spend 80 per cent of our waking time communicating and that about half of that time is spent listening, yet our education concentrates on reading and writing, rather than listening, skills. We know that it may not be safe to assume that we listen well and that lack of concentration either results in work having to be done again or in errors being made – obviously frustrating to the individual and costly to the organisation.

Listening is the main way in which we learn about facts, people, problems and events. It has implications for every aspect of business – if we do not listen with commitment and understanding, we cannot expect success in marketing, production, employee relations or anything else.

In fact there are *four elements* to listening, and the process of *hearing* is only one of these. When we hear we are using a natural sense, but, quite often, what is heard does not 'penetrate'. In today's world where there is so much background noise – muzak in supermarkets and pubs, traffic outside, and telephones in the open plan office – it is *usual* for us to exclude the sounds around us. We must make a conscious effort to exclude such distractions and reach *beyond* hearing to listening, which aids *concentration*.

It is necessary to *focus our attention* on the speaker in order to concentrate well. Some speakers are better than others, so we must not be passive – and wait for our attention to be captured – but consciously give our thoughts to the speaker and look carefully at the value of what is being said. In addition, *note-taking* is extremely valuable in aiding this concentration process. It is noticeable that poor listeners tend to invite and create distractions and that they rarely take notes. As one training officer (who was running a managerial course in response to a recognised need for listening skills) succinctly put it: 'Take note: notes make good listeners!'

A second element of listening is *interpretation* or *clarification*. If you listen for themes and ideas, as well as for facts, they will give you the framework of the material and direct you towards the 'signposts' under which the facts can be listed. In terms of note-taking, they will give you the subheadings to which facts need to be related. Another aspect of clarification is checking that nothing has been misheard or misunderstood. We have to overcome our usual reserve and our natural tendency not to wish to appear foolish, because, if we misunderstand or omit something important, we are likely to make serious mistakes and make worse fools of ourselves! This applies to courses and conferences, as well as to interviews or telephone conversations. In the latter case, for example, it is essential to note the pertinent facts, whether for our own reference later, or for someone else. It is easy to mishear on the telephone – numbers like 30 and 13 are often confused – and the results could be disastrous!

This leads to the third element of listening which is *responding* – both to what is said and to the manner in which it is conveyed. Sometimes, a speaker's delivery or mannerisms can be irritating or annoying (this can be the result of our own perception or prejudice – more will be said about this when we look at interviewing in Chapter 10). It is necessary to look for the content and ignore the distractions of the speaker's style. An acute response is needed.

Responding to the speaker means adjusting your note-taking to his or her way of organising material, ideas and facts. Some speakers are very systematic and give clear cues, such as: 'Now I will deal with...', 'firstly...secondly', and 'to conclude...'. With speakers like this, it is easy to recognise the 'signposts' and to derive good subheadings. If their speeches are very condensed you will need to take a lot of notes. Other speakers need more time to make each point and may give many examples; they may digress, too, or indulge in reminiscences which may not be pertinent (or even interesting!). With such speakers it is necessary to select the main points, perhaps noting briefly one example which best recalls that fact for you. There will be fewer notes in this case. Some speakers may not be clear or systematic and you will need to listen attentively for emphasis in tone of voice, or repeated points, in order to detect the major themes and facts.

In some listening and note-taking situations – like interviews – you may need to reduce your note-taking in order to interact and respond in a more positive way. Brief notes can be expanded later. In any case, it is important to *review* any notes you make because, although they may appear clear at the time of writing, they may be misunderstood later.

The fourth element in the listening process is *evaluation* and this, too, needs reviewing afterwards. Here you are *judging* what is said, in terms of how far you agree, whether there is any evidence to the contrary, how you can utilise the information or ideas given, and how much is relevant and important to you. This involves selection and critical appraisal; both will help to make your notes more concise, comprehensible and usable. One pitfall to avoid is having your evaluation of a particular argument conditioned by an emotional response of some kind. A speaker may use an emotive word or phrase to which you may react, and which may colour your judgement and confuse the issue. If you take the minutes of a meeting you should record the main points of discussion, and the major decisions made, and should *not* include irrational reactions! Sometimes, too, we react quickly to an idea expressed and our minds race ahead, pre-occupied with our own line of thought, ignoring the speaker.

The two important rules are to keep *listening*, forcing yourself to note what is actually said, and to *review* your notes afterwards when you can 'recollect in tranquillity'.[15] This review process, as already mentioned, helps to clarify, systematise, rationalise and reinforce. It also provides a useful *checking* process – did you omit anything you would now like to include? Did you include anything not relevant which you can now delete? Did you use standard abbreviations or have you written anything which you won't be able to interpret later? Re-writing may be necessary – do this while you still remember what happened!

In conclusion, listening in order to take notes involves hearing, interpretation, clarification, responding and evaluation. To take good notes we need to increase concentration, avoid distraction, respond to the speaker, look for the main ideas, facts and signposts, and review our notes systematically afterwards. These should have clear subheadings, numbered facts, be comprehensible after a period of time and should provide an accurate and concise record.

Techniques – note-taking whilst reading

Taking notes whilst reading is easier than taking them whilst listening, as the material can be read again if it is not understood the first time.

There are four different ways of *reading* for information (for study purposes or for composing complex documents, such as reports and contracts). Each requires a slightly different approach. They are scanning, skimming, recording for study and critical reading.

Scanning means looking for key words in dictionaries or encyclopaedias. *Skimming* means looking for the broad outline of a passage. This is equivalent to the technique of searching for a framework when listening. When reading, the reader needs to pay particular attention to subheadings or, if there are none, to the first sentence of each paragraph, which is often known as the 'topic sentence'. (Paragraphs, by the way, rarely include more than three points.)

Reading for study means taking notes, and assessing what you have read at intervals. (It is very easy to continue reading without taking in the facts!) This aids concentration and avoids the time-consuming process of re-reading.

Critical reading is connected with reading for study in particular, although it is also relevant to reading for the preparation of a report. When reading critically, the reader is attempting to evaluate and appraise the text. This is a complex process, demanding an 'instant' gathering and application of the previously known facts to the written material being assessed. It enables the reader to judge the valuable process of selection – in terms of what is perceived to be nearest the truth, and in terms of what is relevant to the reader's present purpose.

To conclude, note-taking when reading is more straightforward than note-taking when listening. Both are required in business. It is significant that many professional examinations now ask candidates to summarise a passage in note form. This is a marked breakaway from précis writing and recognises the value of the brief, concise, but accurate, note-form summary, whether this is for the recipient's future use or for others.

As this technique is now demanded in many examinations, I will now give some guidelines for would-be candidates faced with such an exercise.

Techniques – note-form summaries

The *objectives* should be kept clearly in the mind – to summarise the original material as briefly as possible, but include all the main points, and to make sure that the note is understandable, after a period of time, to any interested party. Use the following sequence:

1. Read the original carefully, trying to grasp the main themes and arguments.

2. Write down a theme sentence/title for each passage – this helps you to keep to the point and to identify the notes later.

3. Re-read, underlining the main points, and note appropriate headings for each paragraph, using the 'topic sentence' to assist you.

4. Write out your summary from this, using the topic subheadings identified, and group the related numbered points beneath them.

5. Check the *balance* of the passage – you should not give undue weight to one section at the expense of another. You should omit detailed examples and illustrations. As emphasised earlier, a useful check here is that a paragraph rarely contains more than three main ideas, facts or arguments.

6. Check the *consistency* of your summary in terms of numbering and indentation.

7. If the summary is prepared for examination purposes, check the number of words required, reduce them, if necessary, and write the total at the end. It helps to use the third person, past tense and reported speech.

8. Whether the summary is prepared for an examination, or for other people's reference, check the basics (spelling, punctuation and grammar) but *above all* ensure that it presents the main points of the original in a form that is easily understood and is completely clear to those who have *not* seen the original.

9. Use plenty of space. Where you have used subheadings, indent – it is much clearer to the reader. The final notes should be a 'skeleton' of what was read, but should be able to stand alone. The summary should be a concise and precise record, presented in a form that anyone can understand.

Preservation of notes

Before we leave note-taking, it is worth emphasising that, as notes are often taken for study or reference purposes, and will be needed at a later date, they should be filed and organised systematically, otherwise time will be wasted in trying to find them, or in trying to fit them into a context long forgotten. To preserve a permanent record in a logical sequence, it is helpful to give a title, date and page number so that quick, accurate reference can be made. If there are many notes, indexing is invaluable. An efficient filing system, kept in this way, is the only method of ensuring that notes can be retrieved immediately when needed.

The subject under which they are filed needs careful choice, bearing in mind future recollection. Subject references need to be logical – everyone must be able to follow them. This is true of notes you have taken and of notes you have made in order to prepare for a task. It is to the latter which we now turn.

Note-making

Functions

Note-making is important to the preparation process. You must make notes before you compose a written communication, or do any public speaking, as in the following situations: giving oral or written instructions, or briefing subordinates; participating, by presenting an oral or written report at a meeting; reporting, orally or in writing, to a superior, or to colleagues (as part of project or team work); composing a memorandum, letter or any other form of business document; preparing for an interview by anticipating questions and composing answers; and making a speech or giving a talk, for example, at a conference.

Techniques – defining objectives, constraints and parameters

As in preparing any act of communication, it is essential to begin by examining the objectives carefully. For example, if you are preparing oral or written instructions, your main objective will be to make sure that the receivers can carry them out accurately. If you are instructing orally, demonstrations can be given, and questions asked, if your instructions need clarification. It is more difficult to prepare written material for an unknown mass audience with a wide range of intelligence. If you are preparing a report, you have to decide whether your objective is to impart information *only* or whether you wish your recommendations to be accepted. In the latter case, an element of persuasion becomes one of the objectives.

The definition of constraints and parameters is also crucial at this stage. For example, questions need to be asked and answered about how much time is available to prepare and/or conduct your communication, what your recipients' knowledge of your subject will be, what their level of interest may be, and whether their attitudes to what you are trying to accomplish are favourable, unfavourable or indifferent. This will influence *what* you will say or write, in what sequence, in what language, and what approach you will use to achieve your objective. All this needs to be noted in advance.

Techniques – random data collection and note-making

The collection of the necessary data to make a knowledgeable and professional oral or written presentation is the second priority. There are many sources of information – written or otherwise – and many different 'slants' on any given subject. Your task is collection, selection and collation. Decide on what sources you need to consult first – this is often done in 'magpie' fashion as each possible source occurs to you. Note, in a random way, anything which seems to relate to the topic on which you are working. The 'star' formation, mentioned earlier, is useful here. Thoughts and arguments, too, may come to you at random and should be added to the picture as soon as possible. A small notebook helps enormously here.

Techniques – grouping of notes, and selection and sequence of material

As note-making is a prerequisite of effective presentation, the next stage must be to select the random notes and put them in a sequence that suits the objectives and the parameters. First, group the random notes under topic headings, making sure that these do not overlap and are not repetitive, then look back at the objectives and parameters of the task and eliminate those notes which are irrelevant or inappropriate. This ruthless process of selection is extraordinarily difficult, as people are reluctant to abandon information

21

which they have unearthed, however irrelevant or inappropriate it is. The selection process is essential if we are to meet the set objectives.

Secondly, write out the selected notes in the best sequence possible – this will relate to the objectives and recipients you have identified, paricularly the latter. Your recipients need to build on their existing knowledge in a logical way, so the introduction of your presentation should relate to this, and the rest should progress from there, concluding with a summary and suggestions for future actions or trends.

Techniques – heading and numbering for reference planning

As already stated, notes need to be headed and numbered logically, in order that you can refer to them easily and quickly. Ideally, they should give an outline of the final report or talk to be produced and should thus be a working document. For this reason, it is probably better to use the 'ladder' approach, once you have selected the relevant topic headings and facts to fit your particular objectives. It is particularly important that the numbering pattern which you use is consistent, and that subheadings are clear and underlined. Indentation assists the reader to pick out new sections quickly. This is particularly important in making notes for a talk, or preparing notes for other people.

Techniques – making notes for a talk

Talks include meetings, oral reports, interviews and training sessions. Some people find public speaking a frightening experience. Good notes made in advance help to boost and maintain confidence; they promote the image of the speaker also. A structured presentation, which conveys a message quickly, shows that a speaker thinks clearly, whereas a rambling presentation demonstrates that the speaker is unprepared.

There are some further points to bear in mind when preparing an oral presentation. Firstly, it is important to maintain eye contact with the audience. This demonstrates an interest in and awareness of them as a group, and is likely to sustain interest and gain a positive response. For this reason, notes for a talk need to be in the form of 'prompters' or 'cue cards' and should not be written out in full as the tendency to read them produces an extremely dull delivery. A good technique is to write large headings in felt pen on cards which can be seen easily and which can be manipulated easily in front of the group. In this way, quick reference can be made and eye contact maintained. This is also important in order to obtain some 'feedback' from the audience – their faces and eyes communicate to the speaker whether they have understood and whether or not they are interested. The speaker needs to adjust to these signals – actors know how important this interaction is for an effective performance.

Secondly, it is important to arouse and maintain attention. Thought needs to be given at the note-making stage as to the best way to introduce the subject. Notes should indicate the aims of the speaker and how he will organise his talk. In this way, the audience will find an obvious starting point and will have some idea of the structure which will help them in following what is to be said and in taking notes.

Thirdly, the sequence must be logical and clear – points should lead on from one another and arguments should be lucid and balanced, with all the pros and cons indicated. This requires careful note-making in advance.

Finally, the 'summing up' or conclusion should give a concise summary or 'recap' of the main points made, and perhaps indicate future trends, since it is more interesting for an audience if they are left with some guide-lines for conjecture and further thought.

Techniques – making notes for other people

The technique of making notes for other people has already been mentioned and the note-form summary discussed earlier gives some guide-lines. It is most important that these notes should be comprehensible to someone who was not present at the meeting, talk or whatever. As these notes will be used as a reference document by others, they should be presented professionally and have a clear title, a date, a reference as to why they were initiated or requested, and subheadings which are guides to the topic. The points should be numbered consistently and sources should be given, as well as some indication as to who may be contacted if any further information is required. In other words, every consideration needs to be given to other readers and every effort made to present notes which can stand alone and be immediately understood.

* * *

Suggested activities for self-evaluation and interest

1. Summarise a television interview or talk. Read your summary through a week later *or* give it to someone else to read. How much of it is recorded accurately? How much of it makes sense?

2. Prepare notes for a verbal presentation to a training group on one topic/area of work familiar to you. If you can, tape the subsequent performance and evaluate it.

3. Carry out the same exercise as the first activity listed above, this time for an article in a paper or professional journal.

Note: These exercises can be done with a colleague; you can then evaluate each others' work.

Part 2 | Written communication - the preparation and construction of business documents

3 | Daily paperwork – forms, memoranda, written instructions and notices

The form and the image of a company

Perhaps the most common method of communication within any organisation is the form; it is one that creates much frustration if care is not taken with its design and wording, and if the number of forms which an individual has to fill in is not taken into account. As mentioned earlier, some people who need to claim social security benefits get so put off by the forms that they don't fill them in, even though there is a monetary incentive to do so. Robert Townsend, in his amusing, provocative book, *Up the Organisation*,[16] suggests that the application forms designed by most personnel departments actually *prevent* most good candidates from applying – they take one look at the form and don't want to know about the company that produced it! Here the form is failing in its first function – to give the new employee his first good impression of the company. Order forms have other functions and are fundamental to the management, information and communication systems of firms. They *should* aim to simplify and standardise the recording, receiving and arrangement of information for all those who need to refer to them. They have a close bearing on efficiency, as, without forms, information would be given in a very haphazard way.

Forms within organisations are used for a wide range of functions, from simple computerised stock control to complex appraisal forms. They have in common, however, the systematic and direct methods by which they record and communicate necessary data to all levels of a company. Good design and control of forms is therefore vital to the efficiency of communication within and between companies. To understand the problems and principles here, we will look at the three major functions of the form – firstly, the form as an important instrument of public relations; secondly, the form as a method of control and planning; and, thirdly, the form as a basis for assessment.

The form as a PR exercise

The first impression that most people gain of a company comes from the forms which it issues – the application form, the order form, the invoice, or the range of forms to be found in the foyer of a bank. Those who design them need

Farnborough College of Technology

Hampshire Education Committee

APPLICATION FOR THE POST OF ....

PERSONAL PARTICULARS

Full Name	Marital Status	Address
Maiden Name (if applicable)	D.E.S./No. Ref.	Tel. No. ....
Date of Birth / Age		Ages of Children

PRESENT APPOINTMENT

College or Firm	Date of Appointment	Position Held
Address		Subjects taught with stage
	Present Salary	
Notice Required		

EDUCATION AND QUALIFICATIONS (in chronological order)*

Name of School, College or University	Date From D M Y	To D M Y	F/T or P/T	Date of Award	Name of Award (with Class, Division, subjects)

PROFESSIONAL QUALIFICATIONS

Professional Membership	Date of Election	By Examination or Not

PREVIOUS EXPERIENCE (in chronological order, include apprenticeships if any)*

Name of Previous College or Employer	Date From D M Y	To D M Y	F/T or P/T	Position held (subjects taught and stage if applicable)

Please leave no gaps in these chronological records

Fig. 7   An application form (courtesy of Farnborough College of Technology).

NAMES OF TWO PERSONS WHO HAVE AGREED TO ACT AS REFEREES

Name	Name
Address..	Address..
....	....
Position Held	Position Held

SUPERANNUATION SCHEMES

Give brief details of any superannuation scheme, other than the Teachers' Superannuation Scheme in which you have participated

FOR APPLICANTS FOR PART-TIME POSITIONS ONLY

State periods (morning, afternoon and evening) and days when you are normally free to accept appointment, together with subjects you wish to offer

LETTER OF APPLICATION

Include any further information, such as details of research, publications, special interests or responsibilities, courses attended, sports, hobbies, etc.

....

....

....

....

....

....

....

....

....

....

Date ....   Signed ....

(Continue on a separate sheet if necessary. A recent testimonial may be attached if you so wish).

REGISTERED DISABLED	**FOR OFFICE USE ONLY**
Are you a Registered Disabled Person Yes/No	College Department ....
Nature of Disability	Post and Grade ....
Registration No.	Date of Commencement ....
PARTICULARS OF ADVERTISEMENT	Succeeds ....
In which Paper/Journal seen?	Industrial increments recommended ....
....	**APPOINTMENT RECOMMENDED**
Post Reference No.	Date Signed
	....
	Principal.

Note:

Canvassing disqualifies and a candidate who is found after appointment to have supplied false or incomplete information knowingly will be liable to dismissal.

Fig. 7   (Continued)

to keep two major purposes in mind – that the forms should give a good image of the organisation from which they come (badly designed and presented application forms and order forms are likely to put off would-be employees and customers respectively) and that they should facilitate the recording of all useful and relevant information.

Application forms need to be clear and should ask for specific information which will help in compiling a short list of appropriate candidates (see Fig. 7). Instructions and headings should not be ambiguous, and attention should be given to space – the spaces allowed for addresses, qualifications and job experience are often too small. An application form needs several different sections. The first is for personal data - name, address, age, nationality, etc. (Information such as number and ages of children, medical record, or anything which may affect the candidate's ability to perform the job well, is often recorded here too.) Some people resent questions about background and family history, so the application form should state *why* such questions are needed. The second section usually concerns education and qualifications. Here some selectivity should be used; for instance, it is not relevant to ask an adult candidate about his primary school education. Dates are important here, for sometimes an unexplained 'gap' becomes evident which may have to be 'probed' at the interview stage! The third section is usually devoted to job experience and special responsibilities. There is often a section for recording other interests – a useful key to finding out what sort of personality a candidate has. (He may indicate whether he is good at teamwork or concentrated activity on his own.) Referees are usually asked for, and, finally, there is a space where the candidate has to say why he thinks he is right for the job.

Order forms also provide the first impressions of an organisation. We are all familiar with the irritations of filling in forms which are not clear – the lack of space for the exact description of the goods and the ambiguities relating to what catalogue numbers should be recorded where. Order forms need to record the method of payment, in order that this can be checked and cleared later. Some are computerised; if not, access to the order, by anyone who needs to refer to it, is vital and this means everyone concerned needs a copy. Carbon copies (of different colours) may be taken, although, as we will see later, modern technology may render this method obsolete. Meanwhile, the older manual systems remain – and are often the cheapest method for some small firms.

Forms should be easy to read. Some are printed in such small letters, and are so cramped, that they are neither legible nor easy to fill in; others are printed very faintly. In order to promote an acceptable public image, the form needs to be simple, clear, legible, easy to fill in and polite. It is a sort of 'salesman' and its success will depend on its design and the approach made. Its aim should be two-fold – to obtain the precise information required *and* to create a favourable reaction. (You might like to take a critical look at the application forms issued by your own company/organisation!)

The form as a method of control and planning

Forms are a prerequisite of recording data systematically – and, therefore, of good planning. Attention must be given to the *design* and to the *control* of forms if they are to be effective. Proper management control is essential to ensure that forms are efficient and economical in design, as well as in use. Much attention has been given to this in recent years. A form should be designed to suit the work for which it is used and to keep the clerical cost of using it as low as is consistent with efficiency.

Some central control is required in order to avoid the proliferation of forms. All forms should be recorded in a central register and specimens of them should be filed; a new form should be authorised only when it has been ascertained that its purpose is not already served by an existing form. Forms in use should be investigated to see whether any can be eliminated, combined with others or improved. Where separate entries exist on a number of forms, it may be possible to reorganise the system to include information on one set of forms which can be produced simultaneously. Alternatively, if a form is circulated, this does away with the need of sending out several identical copies. Standardisation is an important factor; it is often possible to standardise features, such as size and colour, to facilitate filing and reference.

We can summarise the *purposes* of the control of forms as being:

1. To retain and use necessary forms only.
2. To ensure that the necessary ones are well designed and achieve the most at the lowest costs.
3. To produce forms by the most appropriate and economical method.
4. To distribute copies of forms only to those who have justifiable reasons for having them.
5. To study proposed new forms, or revise old ones, to ensure that they are essential.
6. To review all forms in use periodically, in order to keep them in line with the system requirements of the office.
7. To evaluate the amount of time required to fill forms in and use them.

The benefits of form control can be seen in terms of economics, motivation and efficiency. Economies may be achieved in several ways – for example, in time spent in unnecessary form filling; handling and filing can be reduced; printing, paper and other reproduction costs can be saved; and so can storage and filing space. Frustration, and the sense of futility experienced by those faced with unnecessary numbers of forms, will be avoided, work will become simplified, errors will be reduced because instructions will be better understood, and better communication will result.

The form as the basis for assessment

The form is used as a first screening in assessing personnel, whether this is part of recruitment or of a continuous appraisal system. In terms of selection, the application form mentioned earlier is the first insight into the candidate's history, experience and personality. It is important that the form should assess candidates accurately, as short lists of those to be interviewed have to be made.

Appraisal forms can be badly designed, too. These cause problems which can have catastrophic effects in terms of cost. Human resources are great assets when used well but they can cause significant drawbacks if they are neglected, misdirected or demotivated. It is, therefore, crucial to the efficient operation of a company that employees should be recruited and assessed with care. (To quote Townsend[17] again, he sees the 'mahogany curtain' of a manager's door as the single biggest barrier to 'knowing the people'. Giving his own brand of advice, he states the necessity of being able to lock the door, sack the secretary, get his mail from the mailbox, and answer it by photocopying each letter, and posting it back, with his answer written on it, and to spend the rest of the time getting to know the 'good guys' – who you pay – and the 'lemons' who you sack or 'pay to stay at home'!) A more usual way of attempting to ensure that the right people stay with a company, and get paid what they deserve, is the appraisal system. Yet appraisal forms are often designed so poorly that they give only quite meaningless information – and are therefore quite useless. In order to illustrate this, I will give an example. Figure 8 shows an extract from an appraisal form used to assess the performance of girls selling advertising space over the telephone. Before you read the

	Below	Average	Above
1. Personal qualities			
Enthusiasm.			
Honesty.			
Initiative.			
Self-discipline.			
Perception.			
Ambition.			
Loyalty.			
Sincerity.			
2. Sales qualities			
Number of calls per day.			
Number of contacts per day.			
Revenue per call/contact/per day.			
3. General			
(a) General appearance and manner.			
(b) Is confidence up to standard required?			
(c) Is physical condition up to standard? (Check sick absence record.)			
(d) Is employee punctual in attendance at work?			

Fig. 8 An example of a useless form.

following comments on it, perhaps you might like to assess what is wrong with it yourself!

1. The headings at the top of the three columns are completely inappropriate to the qualities they attempt to assess in number 1. (What is 'average enthusiasm'? Is 'average honesty' stealing the paperclips but not the typewriters?)
2. In number 3, 'General appearance' is also impossible to assess on an 'average' basis. The other questions are direct ones which require a yes/no answer, not a rating.
3. The only part of the form that is relevant and useful is number 2. The others would be completely meaningless and would be useless in helping to make any assessment.

The 'merit rating' type of appraisal or assessment forms, which give a continuum of ability or performance which must be marked by the assessor, are not ideal either (see Fig. 9). The tendency here is to mark the middle three columns and to leave the others – people are unwilling to praise or condemn, but see everyone as 'fair'. (This is characteristic of school reports too!)

Perhaps the best kind of appraisal form, and the one that gives the most adequate and accurate information, is the one that includes clearly indicated ratings and gives space for comments from both the appraiser and the appraised. It would achieve the objective of reaching a fair assessment of the individual's performance, potential and needs in a reasonable way.

To summarise, a great deal of care needs to be given to the design of forms if they are to give the precise data. They are, after all, a basis for information and ultimately managerial decision-making. Forms which affect people, whether they are customers or employees, need more attention paid to them, in order to avoid lost orders or the misuse of expensive human resources.

---

1. **Work quality:** the reliability, accuracy, and neatness of work produced.
   O Exceptional   O Very good   O Competent   O Acceptable   O Unacceptable

2. **Work quantity:** the amount or volume of work turned out.
   O Exceptional   O Very good   O Competent   O Acceptable   O Unacceptable

3. **Judgement:** the ability to make well-reasoned, sound decisions which affect work performance.
   O Exceptional   O Very good   O Competent   O Acceptable   O Unacceptable

4. **Initiative:** the combination of job interest, dedication and willingness to extend oneself to complete assigned tasks.
   O Exceptional   O Very good   O Competent   O Acceptable   O Unacceptable

5. **Teamwork:** the working relationship established with fellow employees in the working environment.
   O Exceptional   O Very good   O Competent   O Acceptable   O Unacceptable

6. **Dependability:** the reliance which can be placed on an employee to persevere and carry through to completion any task assigned. This also applies to attendance and punctuality.
   O Exceptional   O Very good   O Competent   O Acceptable   O Unacceptable

---

Fig. 9   Another example of a useless form.

Memoranda – the case for brevity and care

Memoranda are another common form of inter-organisational communication that are not planned well. This is unfortunate, since this means that we do not get much feedback from them – we do know that many are ignored, lost, mislaid, or arouse hostile reactions. It is important, therefore, to set objectives and plan the approach and content of the memorandum in order to obtain the feedback you require.

The functions of memoranda

Memoranda, like forms, have a variety of functions. As the name suggests, they act as a reminder of action to be taken. They can also give information on policy, plans or procedures, and in this case are likely to be longer and more complex than the brief 'memory jogger'. They are a medium for conveying orders and instructions, and as such need careful thought and composition. An important function is to confirm oral agreements – people often do not remember what was said during an informal meeting, and a memorandum provides a written reference for all parties concerned.

The design of memoranda

The memorandum is used mostly for brief communications, although these can be quite long. Two forms are usually provided within companies, one for very short memos, and one for more complex ones. Both should be written as concisely as possible. Memos usually contain the date, the name and/or position of the receiver, the circulation list of the intended receivers, a subject heading to identify the topic, and a reference number. It is particularly important that all this should be accurately recorded. As memoranda arrive in crowded in-trays, topics and dates are essential for the receiver's reference and planning purposes, while a complete circulation list promotes the speed and efficiency of the communication process.

The composition of memoranda

If memoranda are to achieve the two objectives of good communication – to ensure clear understanding and to obtain the required response – they must be carefully composed. The approach and tone of the memo need to be chosen with your purpose in mind – are you simply informing or reminding, are you persuading someone to accept change, or are you instructing? If you convey your message successfully, you will elicit the right response.

In addition, where memoranda are of the longer, more complex type, it is a good idea to subdivide the details of information given, or action required, into numbered points, as this makes them easier to refer to. If this is done, it is helpful to add two further paragraphs – an introduction, stating the objective or intention of the memorandum, and describing any background information necessary to the situation requiring attention (this helps focus the reader's attention on the matter – to start him thinking before the action or information details are given), and a conclusion, either reiterating the specific action required by the receiver, and stating by what date it should be carried out, or giving further information concerning the next step to be taken, as initiated by the memo. The receiver should be left in no doubt as to what is required next. It is also necessary to check on the results of the memorandum, particularly as feedback will be either delayed or, in some cases, non-existent!

Memoranda have considerable advantages as a method of communication; they allow time for the sender to plan his communication logically and to take into account what his approach should be – often not done with a spoken request. The fact that a memo is read means that the receiver can give it his full attention whereas he may be distracted by noise with a verbal communication. It means, too, that more than one person can be contacted without time being wasted on telephone calls or discussions. Perhaps most important, memos provide permanent written evidence of intention for the reference of both receiver(s) and sender, and are especially important when conveying detailed information or requests.

However, memos have disadvantages, of which we should all be aware if we are to use them in the most effective way, and avoid their weaknesses. The sender has no immediate way of gauging the receiver's reaction, therefore careful planning and approach are essential. The sender has no way of knowing whether the memo has been received or read, so careful checks are needed to ensure that it has been read, understood and acted upon in the required way. For this reason, memoranda are best used to confirm information or requests originally given orally.

There are two major problems associated with style – one is abruptness and the other is verbosity. The former can lead to resentment. The one line memo which says 'Please come and see me immediately' is an example of this. The tone is a bit rude and autocratic, in spite of the 'please'. This sort of memo is liable to arouse anxiety and defensiveness – not the best combination if you are trying to enlist someone's co-operation or find out the truth about something. Finally, it gives no reason for the request (or command). People like to be given reasons, and work better as a result. In this case, there is no indication as to what the memo is about so the receiver can't prepare for the meeting. Of course, this may be intentional and be an unfair strategy in what has come to be known as 'memo warfare'! It is scarcely the most effective way to achieve the objectives of communication.

Verbosity appears to be particularly characteristic of bureaucratic organisations, such as government departments. I once saw a government memo which consisted of seven closely-written paragraphs, with ten references, by numbered sub-sections, to other documents. It also gave no indication of what was required by its receiver and was a suitable case for waste-paper basket treatment!

Figure 10 gives a suggested layout for a clear, concise memorandum which can be easily understood. You might like, in the light of this section, to examine critically some of the memoranda which you receive. You will be asked to compose a memo in the self-evaluation exercise at the end of this chapter.

```
┌─────────────────────────────────────────────────────────────────────┐
│                                                                       │
│                         Name of organisation                          │
│                                                                       │
│                            MEMORANDUM                                 │
│                            ──────────                                 │
│                                                                       │
├─────────────────────────────────────────────────────────────────────┤
│    From:   (name and position)          Date:   (in full)             │
│                                                                       │
│    To:     (name/s and position/s)      Reference:  (if relevant)     │
│                                                                       │
├─────────────────────────────────────────────────────────────────────┤
│              Subject: (topic heading)                                 │
├─────────────────────────────────────────────────────────────────────┤
│     Introductory sentence giving aim, intention, background information│
│     or reason for present situation.                                  │
│                                                                       │
│        1.  Numbered details of information required or given.          │
│        2.                                                             │
│        3.                                                             │
│                                                                       │
│     Concluding sentence defining action required of receiver or next  │
│     step in process initiated.                                        │
│                                                                       │
│                                          Initials of                  │
│                                          sender                       │
│                                                                       │
│                                                                       │
└─────────────────────────────────────────────────────────────────────┘
```

Fig. 10   A memorandum, showing layout and principles of planning/composition.

Written instructions

Written instructions are often ignored or misunderstood. Instructions on manufactured goods are often misleading – particularly with imports where there are translation errors on the label! Manufacturers and trainers now tend to *precede* written instructions by initial explanation or demonstration, where possible, hence the increase in demonstrations of new products in chain stores, and, of course, in training courses. Anyone in the modern technology field, for example, will emphasise the importance of personal instruction, followed by 'hands-on' experience, before reference is made to the written instruction. If possible, written instructions, like the memorandum, should be used only as a *confirmation* of an oral explanation or a visual demonstration. The following principles need to be borne in mind when writing instructions:

1. *Define your objectives* What are you hoping to achieve during the period of time? In terms of previous knowledge, qualifications, intelligence and present performance, for what kind of receiver are you writing?
2. *The best sequence* Once you have defined your objectives, decide on the order in which you write your instructions. For example, there is not much point in issuing this instruction for defusing a bomb: 'Push the red button but you must disconnect the blue wire first'.
3. *Stress all safety factors* This is required by law, as a result of the Health and

Safety at Work Act and the Employee Protection Act. In an industrial environment, this means wearing safety clothing, not neglecting dangerous debris and paying due attention to ventilation and heating. In a commercial environment it often means paying attention to minor points which could be hazardous, such as drawers left open, trailing wires, unsafe sockets and top-heavy cabinets. In every case, the potenial dangers, and regulations to prevent them, need to be stressed, so it is necessary, when preparing written instructions, to include them in your plan.

4. *Make your meaning clear* The need for clarity in written instructions is of paramount importance. Language that can be understood by everyone must be chosen. The sequence of the instruction needs to be logical for maximum understanding, no matter what the starting point of the receiver's knowledge. It can be helpful to include diagrams, tables, pictures, charts, or other visual methods of communication, to illustrate what is being explained in words. Such illustrations must be clear, otherwise they can mislead or confuse.

5. *Monitor and check what you have written* In an organisational setting, the same problems often occur and a new entrant is placed frequently in a situation where he/she has had the minimum possible instruction and induction on joining the organisation, and is then expected to cope by watching – or doing the job. The inevitable results are costly errors and a wastage of time, declining confidence, increasing unhappiness in the individual and frustration from other members of the work-force whose performance is dependent upon that of the recruit. Here, carefully prepared, well-written instructions, with clear pictorial or diagrammatic illustrations, can help enormously to avoid these problems. In addition, if the immediate superior cannot always be available, someone needs to be assigned to a 'tutoring' role. If the newcomer feels there is a person to whom he can refer directly if in doubt, and that this person is likely to react kindly and helpfully, rather than abruptly and superciliously, the original instruction is supported and reinforced. Even more important, errors are reduced and competence (and, inevitably, self-confidence) increased.

This tactic also helps to create a method for monitoring and checking whether the instructions issued are, in fact, comprehensible; it helps to overcome the basic problem of having no feedback, which is the usual one in written instructions. Otherwise, with a mass-produced consumer product, for example, other forms of checking need to be carried out. A constant assessment of the number and types of complaints is useful, as some form of modification to the original instructions may be needed. Without some kind of checking or feedback system, things could go disastrously wrong, to the ultimate detriment of the organisation's productivity and profitability.

The following checklist gives some guidelines for planning written instructions:

1. *Define your objectives* When doing this, take into account what you want the receiver to do, how many receivers there are, and their previous knowledge, vocabulary level, etc.

2. *Choose your media* Are written words enough, or will you need diagrams, pictures? Do you have the opportunity to provide verbal/demonstrated instructions first? Do you have the opportunity to provide *someone* who can help in the event of confusion?

3. *Plan a logical sequence* When doing this, take into account all the details necessary for the employee/customer to carry out the task you require, and how you wish the task to be carried out. Make sure that all the necessary technical details are included and are defined in a clear way. Ensure that all the illustrations and diagrams are clear and self-explanatory. Ascertain also *who* the employee or customer may approach if he needs to query anything about the operation, and *why* the task needs to be carried out. (Giving reasons makes for a more intelligent and co-operative approach.)

4. *Check your written instructions* Ensure that safety and health hazards are emphasised. Identify possible areas of breakdown, with possible remedies or personnel to whom reference may be made. Make sure the instructions have clear subheadings and numbered points. Are they *simple* as well as *comprehensive*? Are there any reiterated difficulties or complaints? If so, does the fault lie in the instructions? If this is so, how can it be remedied?

5. *Modify what you have done* Change any aspects which have proved unsatisfactory. This review process, and willingness to modify, is the only way to improve on any weakness.

Written instructions, whether they appear in a memorandum, instruction manual, or consumer's leaflet, can be extremely careless, leading to misuse, frustration and, possibly, accidents, which will result in complaints, dissatisfaction and loss of custom or recruits. If enterprises wish to achieve and maintain success and a good public image they need to devote more thought and time to them.

Notices – a subject for neglect

The problems previously discussed with memoranda – of remaining unread, being ignored, arousing unknown resentment – are even more evident when it comes to notices; yet they remain one of the most favoured, if most ineffectual, methods of communication. Most organisations are just beginning to realise that notices should be reinforced with another method of communication, such as memoranda, circulars, letters in paypackets and announcements over the Tannoy. It is worth examining why the general effect of notices is so poor and if anything can be done to avoid their weaknesses.

Notices remaining unread

This appears to be for three reasons, two of which are connected with where the notices are placed. Firstly, notice-boards are often poorly sited – for example, in a dark corridor where they can be passed without anyone remarking that they are there, or where they can be read only with difficulty; or in an area where they are not even seen by many members of departments who have no cause to pass through. Secondly, notice-boards are often neglected and not cleared of outdated material. This is partly because no one has the responsibility for clearing them. The third reason why notices remain unread is lack of 'eye-attraction'. If the notice is recent, who is to tell? If it is in small type, who is going to bother to stop? In both cases, no one's attention will be caught.

Notices arousing unpredictable reactions – lack of feedback: good and bad examples

Notices, like memos, suffer from the limitations of being a one-way communication; it is very difficult for the notice writer to know what reactions the passer-by may have. It is worth noting, however, that some notices have obviously been prepared by people who have given no attention at all to the second objective of communication – to obtain the required response. Look at Fig. 11, an example of a notice seen on a building site. Perhaps you might like to consider what is wrong with it, especially in terms of the objective I have just mentioned, before reading the following comments:

1. The notice begins by discriminating against a particular group of workers, enhancing the 'them' and 'us' aspects, and probably arousing initial resentment from that group. It is also a direct order, and is abrupt and very autocratic.
2. The notice gives no *reason* as to *why* people should not pass beyond the yellow line, thus arousing curiosity and posing a challenge.
3. The likely effect is that someone will take up that challenge, impelled by the combination of anger and inquisitiveness.

This notice will therefore elicit the opposite response from that required. Figure 12 shows a notice which has a better approach. It will obtain more widespread co-operation.

NO CASUAL LABOURERS
TO PASS BEYOND THIS
YELLOW LINE

Fig. 11 The wrong way to word a notice.

> # CASUAL EMPLOYEES ARE ASKED NOT TO CROSS THE YELLOW LINE AS ENGINEERING WORK IS IN PROGRESS AND SUBSIDENCE IS LIKELY

Fig. 12   The same notice as that on page 39, worded more diplomatically.

A checklist for notice display and composition:

1. *Display* Notices should be sited in a well lit place (through which all concerned will pass), or should be near a point where they are needed. For example, the sign: 'Have you remembered the guards?' should be placed *on* the machine being used. Notice-boards should be cleared regularly of old information. Notices should be on coloured paper or have coloured headings to attract attention. Key words or phrases need to be underlined, or be in capitals. 'Poster' techniques should be adopted if it is very important to attract attention.

2. *Type of notice* If it is essential that certain people should read a notice, then a circular note, personally addressed, should be sent to them as well. This is particularly true of Notices of Meeting (to be discussed in Chapter 9).

3. *Composition of the notice* Display techniques should be used to attract attention; a large clear heading is essential. The objectives should be clear – is the notice informing, telling or persuading people to co-operate? Notices should contain material which can be conveyed briefly and clearly; more complex information is best conveyed by memo. Complex language must be avoided as the receivers' levels will vary according to their intelligence, knowledge and vocabulary. Short words and phrases should be used and the message should be simple and concise. Particular attention should be paid to tone and approach, in order to avoid undetected resentment. If instructions are given, *reasons* can help to promote the desired response.

Conclusions

All the types of communication discussed in this section are extremely common; they form part of the daily routine, yet those who prepare them are often guilty of the most cardinal errors, as we have seen. It is hoped that the guidelines given will enable the worst faults, which we have all observed, to be avoided and that the suggestions for improvement given will be beneficial for the morale and productivity of any enterprise.

* * *

Suggested activities for interest

Within your own organisation, carry out the following critical surveys:

1. Survey the notice-boards and evaluate their usage.
2. Analyse any routine form at present in use and suggest improvements.

Suggested activity for self-evaluation

You are an office manager working for a large production company which has many departments and you have responsibility for the secretarial staff, the general administrative section and internal/exernal communications. You are therefore responsible for the switchboard operator, who also acts as receptionist. This member of staff is Mrs Jackson; she has been with the firm for a number of years, and has one son in college and a daughter who has just become engaged.

Lately there have been a number of complaints that telephone calls have been cut off abruptly, that customers have received very brusque treatment, and that, on one or two occasions, Mrs Jackson has been rude to important callers. The managing director is a personal friend of one of these and has now asked you to deal with the situation.

You call in Mrs Jackson, who initially insists that nothing is wrong, but finally tells you that she has been feeling unwell, that her son has failed his first year examinations and that her mother has been widowed and has come to live with her. In addition, she has to prepare for her daughter's wedding. She has found that the increasing work load with the reception area and the telephone has been extremely difficult to cope with efficiently. Decide what action you would like to take and write an advisory memorandum to the managing director.

4 | Reports – an essential basis for decision-making

The functions of reports and their importance to the management process

Reports are vital to the management process, whether their content concerns a commercial organisation, a public institution or the government of a nation. If management, at the apex of any of these, is concerned with long-term planning and overall policy, then it must be informed fully about the effects of the decisions it has made. Only in this way can past errors be remedied and the necessary modifications be made to ensure survival and success. Equally, it is in this way that progress can be monitored and measured. Any minor problems uncovered in the process can be detected quickly and investigated immediately. The instrument which makes this full feedback possible is the report.

The standard of report writing, however, is constantly criticised, notably by employers in high technology who complain of poor planning, inarticulate expression, incoherence, carelessness, verbosity and, worst of all, inaccuracy. They state that this is even true of those who are deliberately recruited with grooming for management in mind. It would seem that education, not least at the higher level, neglects the training of this extremely important aspect of management communication. Increasingly, report writing has been included in in-house, often post-graduate, management trainee schemes, and examiners of professional bodies have set questions as reports, only to criticise the answers severely. It would seem that much more attention needs to be given to the techniques of good, cogent report writing, if management information is to be precise and to form a reliable basis for future decision-making. Let us consider first the objectives of reports.

The objectives of report writing

Perhaps the first and most obvious objective – yet one which is often ignored by the report writer – is to ensure that the report is *read* and *understood*. This is least likely to happen if it is wordy or full of incomprehensible technical jargon or if it is poorly presented. Such a document, or one with little fact and much superfluous 'padding', tends to arouse immediate impatience, boredom and, possibly, even contempt for the writer – not exactly the ideal motivation to read on. On the other hand, a professionally presented report, with helpful subheadings, a logical sequence and concise factual information, presented in good, clear English, with any technical terms defined, will be likely to elicit an immediate respect for the competence and intelligence of the writer, which means that the reader will want to read it fully and attentively. It will also ensure an understanding of the subject, even if it is a technical one.

The second objective is to give adequate and accurate information to all concerned, whether they are colleagues or superiors. If a report is to provide the facts on the basis of which decision-making and planning must take place, it is essential that there should be no omissions of 'uncomfortable' results or occurrences, or any other manipulation of the truth which the writer may see as politic at the time. Unfortunately, as we will see when we come to identify the major problems of report writing, the temptation to give a palatable version of the facts often perverts, first, the truth itself, and, second, the ability to decide on an appropriate policy.

The third objective is to process information for others. This requires a clear analysis of the information available, as well as the ability to summarise concisely yet comprehensively. *All* the vital information needs to be present in a brief, logical form which others can grasp quickly and refer to. They may need, for example, to select one particular section for their own purposes, or for discussion at a meeting. A quick point, clearly made and numbered under a subheading, is invaluable here. Essentially, the report is a reference document and this should be recognised in its composition.

Finally, the report is usually an advisory document; its objectives are to advise and inform and, sometimes, to persuade. The recommendations made at the end of a report are therefore a priority for both the reader's and writer's attention. They must respond to the objectives of both parties. For example, if costs are the main consideration of the person requesting the report, but increased budgets for research are that of the writer, the recommendations must be diplomatic in tone and be seen to grow logically from the methods and analysis contained in the main body of the report. Only in this way is the case likely to be considered in an unbiased and impartial way. Persuasion is a delicate matter and must be seen to rest on sound evidence and clear argument if it is to stand a chance of acceptance. Keeping both sets of objectives in mind helps the writer to adopt the correct approach, to direct his planning and to make proposals which are based on clear thinking. Not all reports, of course, contain recommendations, so it is useful to categorise the different types of report.

Types of report and their uses

Routine reports on forms

These are reports which are required so frequently that a set form is designed; the objectives here are to make the information contained in the report easy to record and easy to classify. Examples of such reports are those required for public safety – accident reports for the police, insurance companies or factory inspectors; those required for selection or assessment of personnel, such as the appraisal reports mentioned earlier; and those required to record procedures or work progress. Although they would seem to be the most systematic and accurate, they are often not so, as we shall see when we identify some of the problems later in this chapter.

Information reports

As the name suggests, these are reports which condense information for others. They do not normally include any recommendations, although they may suggest areas in which further studies could be valuable, or suggest items for the attention of readers. If they are very brief, they usually appear on the longer memorandum form, but contain specific headings to guide the receiver. If they are long, they appear as a separate document with a title page.

Examples of this kind of report might include reports describing a training course, conference or exhibition which others have been unable to attend; a summary of numerical data, such as statistics identifying major trends, variations and possible conclusions for those who have not had the opportunity to study them, yet who are directly or indirectly affected; and information on what has occurred as a result of a recent change in procedure or recent work progress where this has been exceptional rather than routine.

Investigation reports

These are perhaps the most complex of all. They are used, as their name suggests, to report the results of a full scale investigation to all parties. They may be brief, or they may be as long as those prepared by a Royal Commission. They may investigate matters of public or social concern, or look into long-term scientific or technological problems. They may enquire into matters of interest to one company in any of the functional areas – marketing a new product, for example, or a proposed change in flexitime. They may look at methods which would affect economies for a firm or for a nation. Whatever the length or subject, this kind of report usually ends with proposals or recommendations. These are often used as a foundation for decision-making by the body or authority which requested the report, so essentially they are advisory rather than executive.

Technical reports

These type of reports either give information on progress in a technical area or investigate a difficult technological problem at some length. As such, they are likely to fall into one of the two categories already discussed. Certainly their layout will have much in common with these. The differences are minor – they are likely to include much more diagrammatic or numerical material which can often pose problems of presentation. Sometimes, too, style can be a stumbling block for those untrained to write at length and more used to practical activity.

Projects

Projects can be narrative or investigatory, but normally fall into the latter category. They are usually an in-depth study of one area or problem, which is important to the writer and to the authority requesting the report, and are sometimes used as a bridge between training and work experience. As such, their relevance to both parties is of paramount importance. In terms of layout, they most resemble the long investigation report. As with technical reports, they have presentation problems since they often contain a great deal of diagrammatic or illustrative material.

Projects normally give proposals for the consideration of the authority which requested them and can cover a very wide variety of topics, organisational, technological, economic, social or any other area of interest to those concerned.

All the categories of reports mentioned here exhibit various problems which can hinder the achievement of their objectives. Let us now identify some of these in the hope that they may be conscientiously avoided and that the standards of report writing be improved, for, as we have already seen, weaknesses here can lead to unfortunate results for management information and therefore for policy-making.

Some major problems in report writing

The first problem – poor form design – affects routine reports only. (This has already been discussed at length in Chapter 3.) The second problem concerns the accident report, which is an eyewitness narrative of events. There are two difficulties here – one is connected with our ability, or inability, to recall accurately. The other, perhaps more alarming, results from the way in which we organise what we see (often not what actually occurred), or our *perception* of events. If we witness an accident or a crime, our memory of the actual happening is often very vivid, but this is not so with what occurred immediately prior to the crucial moment. Our inability to be exact may alter considerably what *caused* the event – where someone was standing, what position two cars were in, what the conditions of work or weather were, for example. Futhermore, our perception of events is often at fault.

During a training session on perception, a lecturer conducted an interesting experiment on the differing perceptions of a simple event. He arranged for his lecture to be interrupted by people in duffle coats, anoraks and scarves who overturned furniture and disrupted proceedings. He then asked his audience how many people there had been, of what sex they were, and of what age. The audience said there were between four and seven people (in fact there were five), only one person saw a female (in fact there were three), and everyone put their ages under 30 (in fact two were over 40). An interesting, if worrying, demonstration of how role stereotype (aggression – male; anoraks and scarves – young) affects our perception. Perhaps these problems are unavoidable; but careful observation and notes made immediately after the occurrence help accuracy considerably – as any policeman knows.

You write	You mean
It can be proved that . . .	I hope it can be proved that . . .
It is generally acknowledged that . . .	I once heard someone say that . . .
It can be shown that . . .	You figure it out, I can't be bothered.
It is clear that . . .	It's not clear, but I'm shaming you into taking it for granted.
Did not operate as well as had been predicted.	The equipment burst into flames.
After considerable experimentation, a solution was found.	We fiddled about until it came right.
A typical sample.	The only sample which did what we wanted.
If instability results, appropriate remedial action will suggest itself.	If instability results you will have to think of something, Jack.
It is technically feasible, but there are practical problems.	It cost ten times as much as we estimated.
Transient tests were carried out.	The fuses blew every time we switched on.
The equation was solved numerically.	We averaged eight different answers.
This value is a first approximation.	This value is flagrant guesswork . . .
It should be possible to improve the method.	Nothing worked.
The fundamental principles will now be described in detail.	We mugged the following from a text book.
It is of interest to compare . . .	It isn't but I'm going to all the same.
There are certain practical difficulties in realising the gain figures.	All the transistors burn out simultaneously.
Some reservations must be placed on these figures.	These figures are quite useless.
The most promising approach is . . .	We couldn't think of another way to do it.
The author wishes to thank Mr . . . for a number of significant comments.	The group leader insisted on poking his nose in.
It can be construed that . . .	Any guess is valid.

Fig. 13   The 'no problem syndrome' – phrases, used in technical reports, which mean something else.

The third problem is much easier to solve with effort and the application of careful planning. This is the problem of poor layouts and illogical sequences which still bedevil most reports. (The systematic layout of reports and the proper planning of sequence will be discussed in some detail later.) All I need to say here is that effort should be made to analyse material thoroughly, to group the material into topics or a chronological sequence and to give clear subheadings throughout to guide the reader.

The fourth problem is that of inadequate methodology. The success of any report in terms of accuracy – which, as has been stated, is the paramount consideration – depends on the correct choice of methods, that is, those best suited to researching the material and analysing it. A variety of methods are available to the report writer, as we will see later, and much thought should be given to deciding initially what is the most appropriate method.

Finally, there is the insidious problem of careless inaccuracy or, more seriously, deliberately misleading information. This is the outcome of what could be called the 'no-problem' syndrome – a deliberate attempt to justify the actions of the writer, or his status and competence, in the eyes of his superiors or colleagues (see Fig. 13). In any report, the first aim must be accuracy if the decisions to be made as a result are to be sound. Neither a superior or colleagues will thank a report writer who misled them. Systematic planning and methodical stucture, so that the report can be easily read, understood and used as reference, are therefore vital.

Constructing good reports – techniques and layouts

Preparation and methodology

Preparation and methodology are relatively simple in routine reports. The major needs are careful observation, clear and immediate note-making and reviewing, and concise recording. These needs apply whether the report required concerns an accident, work progress or the continuous assessment prior to appraisal, and Chapter 2 on notes is a useful aid here.

In information reports, the major needs would be observation and note-taking. For example, if the report is about attendance at a conference, course or trade exhibition, careful review immediately after the event, and a summary under clear subheads, together with the careful collation of any relevant illustrative material or costs, will be essential to its correct planning. The information report may, however, use the methods which are also common to investigation reports, projects and technical reports.

The most complex reports may use any of the following sources of information and methods of research and investigation:

1. *Sources of information* Depending on the subject of the report, these might include: published information, including text books; legislation; official memoranda; notes taken at conferences, seminars or during training; articles; surveys carried out by other organisations; research carried out by others; files and records; policy or administrative documents; lists of costs; statistical data; computer data; and rules and regulations.
2. *Methods of investigation* These might include: observation, either personal and informal, or resulting from a work study or organisation and methods project; questionnaires and surveys conducted by the writer; interviews or informal discussions; meetings; calculations; experiments and testing following a hypothesis, i.e. scientific methods; and pilot programmes.

Of course, there are others too, as each report will be unique in demanding a different selection of sources and methods, but the ones listed above give those which are most commonly used.

The next stage is to collate the information and to organise it, selecting *only* what is relevant to your objective and discarding that which is not. Only then can the information be analysed, conclusions drawn and, if necessary, recommendations made. It is very useful at this stage to employ systematic note-taking techniques, grouping the material under subject headings as indicated in Chapter 2. This will help with the eventual composition of the report, where the material needs to be grouped first under the major headings demanded by the particular type of report required and then be subdivided in a logical, subheaded sequence which is appropriate to the subject.

It will be helpful, at this point, to discuss the different layouts (in terms of major sections) which are typical of each category of the longer and more complex reports. Routine reports on forms, and short reports on memoranda are not discussed here since memos have been dealt with in Chapter 3.

Sections of information reports – major subheading system and contents

The following framework is the most common for the information report:

1. *Title page* This will include the subject of the report, the name and position of the writer and the name and position of the requesting individual or authority. It includes the date of submission also. If the report is so brief as to appear on a memorandum form, then details will, of course, be recorded in the appropriate spaces given on the printed heading.

2. *Index or contents page* This will include a list of the major subheadings (and sometimes the subdivisions), alongside the relevant page numbers. This helps the reader to select instantly and is particularly useful for reference if the document is, for example, to be discussed later by a number of interested parties.

3. *Introduction and terms of reference* This normally includes the following:
(a) The authority and/or position of the person or body requesting the report and the reasons for this request.
(b) The objectives and purpose of the report.
(c) The scope of the report, i.e. whether there is a requirement for any proposals – sometimes information reports do give these.
(d) The position of the person compiling the report.
(e) Any other relevant background information necessary to that particular report, for example, if it is to report on a conference, course or exhibition – dates, venues, names and numbers of those attending; if is is to summarise numerical data – the sources of these.

4. *Analysis of information* This section gives a summary of the facts and information derived from the events attended or sources mentioned in the previous section. It is here that the material needs to be grouped under subsection headings appropriate to the subject and that the most attention needs to be given to logical sequence and consistent numbering, as this is obviously the longest major section of this kind of report. It will also state initially any problems or priorities for the attention of the reader.

5. *Appendices* If there is any bulky illustrative material, lists of costs or other

core chemicals plc

Memorandum

From: C J Gray   Date: 19 May 1984
       Clerical Office Supervisor

To: R W Grainger
       Administration Manager

Subject: Training in Word Processing Techniques

In answer to your request of 18 May 1984, I have enquired about external courses available in the local area which might be suitable for retraining personnel in this office.

Information received:

1. Courses: These are available at:

    (a) Barnborough College of Further Education: one day per week beginning 26 September 1984, duration 12 weeks. Cost: £75. Distance from office: 5 miles, bus service available.
    (b) Curzon College of Technology: two evenings per week beginning 26 September 1984, duration 12 weeks. Cost: £85. Distance from office: ½ mile.
    (c) Skills Centre: three weeks' short course, beginning 4 June 1984. Cost: 'uncertain – grants are available; probably minimal' (Job Centre official).

2. Additional factors:

    (a) Only six employees are at present engaged in this office, and the present manual system needs at least five to operate efficiently at minimum productivity.
    (b) Because of booked holidays, there will be a shortage of staff in June.
    (c) All six employees are female and either have family commitments in the evening or social ones.

Conclusion:

It would seem that (a) might be the most suitable for your consideration, though this will depend on the time scale envisaged for automation.

                                                          CJG

Fig. 14   A short information report written on a memorandum form.

lengthy data, these may be included in numbered appendices at the end. For example, attendance at an exhibition may produce a number of glossy brochures or price lists, to which reference may be made in the 'Analysis' section, but which need to be included separately, so as not to interrupt the reading process.

6. *Acknowledgements and/or bibliography* Any acknowledgements to individuals who assisted in compiling the report, or lists of published information (bibliography), need to be given at the end of the report.

Fig. 14 shows an example of a short information report.

Sections of investigation reports – major subheading system and contents

The title page, contents and terms of reference/introduction section will include the same data and layout as for the information report. After that, however, the layout will be slightly different, therefore the major sections and their contents in this case will be:

1. *Title page* This is the same as that for the information report.
2. *Contents page* This will include the major sections, subsections and appendices with the relevant page numbers.
3. *Terms of reference* These will be the same as those for the information report, except that this time they are likely to include, in the scope of the report, the fact that recommendations are required.
4. *Methods of investigation and/or sources of information* Sometimes this section is also known as *Procedure*. In this section, the methods of investigation chosen and the sources of information used should be listed. As stressed earlier, it is particularly important that those most suitable for the purpose, and most likely to give *specific* information required for the objectives set in the terms of reference, are given.
5. *Analysis of information* This is also known as *Findings*. As the title implies, it is here that all the information, which has been derived from the methods and sources, is summarised and analysed. Again, it is likely to be the most lengthy of the sections, and requires careful attention to the grouping of topics, as well as a logical sequence and clear guide subheadings. Furthermore, it is often useful to refer back to the 'Methods' section, so that the reader can see clearly how the findings *are* derived. This is called 'cross reference' and is a great help to the reader in following the thought processes of the writer and in recognising the evidence on which they have developed. For example, if two of the methods listed have been interviews with the supervisors and the analysis of documents now constituting the work load of the office, then from this, the two first subheadings in the Analysis section might be: 'Interviews with supervisors – from these it was found that ...' and 'Analysis of documents – this showed that ...'.

The analysis section is, in many ways, the most important and the most in need of clear organisation because of its length and complexity. It is central to the report, linking the briefly summarised objectives and sources with the conclusions and recommendations. These should also be fairly short because, if the analysis has been adequate, they will, after all, grow naturally from the facts summarised there. In other words, a logical development should be clear to the reader from the objectives through to the recommendations.

6. *Conclusions* This section summarises and evaluates the problems, priorities and evidence, which deserve the main attention of the reader, before going on to recommend what should be done in each case – what should be pursued or studied further, what requires immediate action or long-term planning, what changes might be necessary and where the status quo is acceptable. It weighs alternatives and gives comparisons of these before ultimate action is proposed.

7. *Recommendations* This section gives suggested lines of action to meet the requirements of each of the priorities or problems identified in the previous two sections. Essentially, these proposals are advisory and the initiating authority makes the final decision as to whether they should be implemented.

It is worth noting here that the proposals stand a better chance of being put into practice if they are viable and if they take into account the original objectives of the report, as laid down by that authority, as well as the constraints which may prevent them from being carried out. For example, it is unlikely that a report would recommend that the Government should spend an extra X million on, let us say, the Health Service, if immediate expenditure is needed for something else – for instance, the outbreak of a war or rising unemployment payments. Of course, at that level, too, constraints would exist and priorities would need to be decided upon. If an election was imminent, these might change. So the *feasibility* of the recommendations, given the objectives and the circumstances in response to which the report was written, is important to both reader and writer.

8. *Appendices* These fulfil the same role as that discussed for the information report, except that they might include a wider variety of material. For example, if a questionnaire method has been used, then a sample might appear here; so might the detailed statistical analysis, leaving the 'Analysis' section of the report free to identify trends and priorities by reference, thus keeping it more concise and consequently quicker and easier to read.

9. *Acknowledgements and bibliography* This section fulfils exactly the same function as for the information report.

Figure 15 (on pages 53–57) shows an example of an investigation report.

Sections of technical reports – major subheading system and contents

These reports combine some of the layout characteristics of the information report with some from the investigation report. However, there are certain headings specific to them. Of course, the word 'technical' could be taken to cover any area which demands specialist knowledge. The major consideration to be kept in mind when writing any technical report is the reader's level of knowledge. This will dictate the starting point and will determine whether a section on background is to be included and how much it will contain, and what terminology can be used without definition. If there is any doubt, it is always better to suppose less knowledge than a great deal. The term 'technical report' is usually applied to scientific or technical subjects, in spite of its wider possible applications. In this case, its main sections are likely to include all, or a selection from, the following:

1. *The title and contents pages* These are the same as for the other kinds of report previously discussed. The title is sometimes very long, for it must be comprehensive and very specific.

2. *Objective and sometimes an introduction* The objective will give the hypothesis which the report sets out to test; if there is no clear hypothesis, then an introduction will explain why an investigation needs to take place and will

give the aim in rather different terms. Some reports will include both if they are thought to be necessary.

3. *The theory* This gives an explanation of any equations or other theoretical work and their relationship to the problem in hand.

4. *Method or procedure* This may include any experiments, observations, calculations, tests or further theoretical work carried out in the process of analysing the problem under consideration. Again, the appropriate choice of methods is important. In these parts, too, a very careful and thorough approach to the methodology is essential. Diagrammatic material may need to be included within this section rather than in the appendix.

5. *Results* This section gives the results derived from all the methods undertaken in the previous section.

6. *Discussion or summary* If the results have been fairly straightforward, then only a summary is required before conclusions can be drawn, otherwise a discussion should take place which explores the results and implications further.

7. *Conclusions* These may be definitive (having solved a problem or proved the hypothesis satisfactorily), they may point to a need for further studies, or they may conclude that the results are so inconclusive as not to require any further attention at all. Whatever conclusion is drawn, the reader should be able to look at the objective and the conclusion only, and gain a complete overall picture of the report's aims and results.

8. *Appendices* Technical reports pose a particular problem to the writer in selecting what illustrative, diagrammatic or numerical material should appear within the main body of the report (usually in the 'Method' or 'Results' sections) and what should be put in an appendix. If the material is a vital part of the procedure, without which it cannot be understood, or immediate reference is needed to grasp the written explanation, it should appear in the report itself. If it is related and complementary, but not essential to a specific part of the report, then it should be contained in the appendix.

9. *References* This replaces the acknowledgments and bibliography sections of other reports and usually contains a list of sources, such as other research papers.

It is worth noting that each technical report is unique and may omit any of the above sections, if not relevant, or include others that are relevant, which are not listed above. (For example, in some high technology reports, the 'Theory' section will be omitted, but one on 'Background' will be included.) Some reports, too, may amalgamate sections, for example, the discussion and conclusions may be interactive and better included as one integrated section. The approach to the layout, therefore, will need to be flexible in response to the nature of both subject and reader.

Sections of projects – major subheading system and contents

Narrative projects, which are purely descriptive of a subject, are usually written at school, but the investigatory project is being used increasingly as a

Asteroid Electro Mechanical System PLC

Investigation report
into health and safety
hazards at the
Bamborough site

Date of submission: Compiled by: P D Hodges
                                                    Safety Officer

25 June 1984   For the attention of:

                                                    F L Slowfield
                                                    Managing Director

(i)

Fig. 15 An investigation report. (The appendix and bibliography have not been included for reasons of space.)

Contents page   Page no.

I.   Terms of reference   (iii)

II.   Methods of investigation   (iii)

         1. Legislation

         2. Observation

         3. Interviews

         4. Informal discussions

III.   Findings/analysis of information   (iii-iv)

         1. Legislation   (iii)

         2. Observation   (iii-iv)

         3. Interviews   (iv)

         4. Informal discussions   (iv)

IV.   Conclusions   (iv)

V.   Recommendations   (v)

VI.   Appendix 1 - guide to the Act   (vi)

VII.   Bibliography and Acknowledgements   (vii)

(ii)

Fig. 15   (Continued)

I.   Terms of reference

    The objective of this report is to investigate all the health
and safety hazards at the Bamborough site which may result in
contravention of the Health and Safety at Work Act.

    It was requested by the Managing Director in preparation for the
proposed visit by the Government Inspector at an unspecified date.
It was undertaken by the newly appointed Safety Officer and was
to be submitted before the end of June 1984. The report was to
give recommendations on any improvements which should be made.

II. Methods of investigation

    1. Legislation The Health and Safety at Work Act was carefully
    studied.

    2. Observation The Safety Officer inspected the Research and
    Development Annex, the Production Workshops and the office-based
    departments (Personnel, Finance and Marketing). Two hours
    were spent in each location, making observations and taking
    notes.

    3. Interview The line managers officially responsible for each
    location visited were interviewed to find out whether they
    had observed any problems. They were also asked how well they
    recognised their own responsibilities under the Act.

    4. Informal discussions These were carried out with some employees
    in the course of (2) above.

III. Findings/analysis of information

    1. Legislation The legislation makes very clear that all staff
    could become liable under the Act were an accident to occur.
    Responsibilities are clarified for senior management, supervisory
    staff and the employees themselves. A short guide to these
    appears in Appendix 1.

    2. Observation

        (a) The R & D Annex The environment here is a 'clean' one
        and conditions are generally good. However, during the
        visit to this location, one young graduate trainee was
        observed to be attempting to lift a very heavy CO_2 cylinder.
        When questioned, he said he had been told to do this
        by the project leader and that all personnel had to do
        this from time to time to maintain tests.

        (b) The workshops In most workshops, there appeared to be
        no problems, but in Workshop C the ventilation had broken
        down and men were working with open coats; it was a very
        hot day. These could easily catch in the machinery and
        cause accidents.

(iii)

Fig. 15 (Continued)

(c) <u>The offices</u> Generally, these had good working conditions. In the recently automated administration office, however, too many extension leads are being used; these are trailing on the floor. There is a general carelessness about trailing leads in all offices. Some employees are using the waste-paper baskets as ashtrays, and a small fire was actually started during a visit to the Marketing Department. The sand bucket was then found to be empty.

3. <u>Interviews</u>

(a) The Project Manager in R & D was asked about the CO_2 cylinders. He said that he himself had lifted them sometimes and that one trainee had suffered from a strained back. He had requested the R & D Manager for help in this matter, but, although trolleys for moving the cylinders had been supplied, it had not solved the lifting problem which had to be done in a very confined space. He did not appear to know that he could be liable under the Act.

(b) The Workshop C Supervisor was asked about the ventilation. He said that a memo to Maintenance, dated one week earlier, had requested action and the reply had said that they were short-staffed because of holidays and would do it 'as soon as possible'. He did realise his responsibilities, which had been covered in a training course.

(c) Two relevant office supervisors were interviewed; a memorandum had been issued about the waste-paper baskets, but the Administration Office Supervisor said that the extension leads were needed. Neither supervisor appeared to realise their own liability under the Act.

4. <u>Informal discussions with employees</u> None seemed to realise his own possible liability under the Act, although all employees had signed Contracts of Employment which stated that they were responsible for their own safety.

IV. <u>Conclusions</u>

1. There is an urgent need to provide some method of lifting CO_2 cylinders, or to explore different methods of cooling, or different methods of supply. If there is a back injury, the company will be liable.

2. More temporary staff must be taken on by the maintenance section so that they can deal with the fire buckets and the ventilation. Both of these have been neglected and render the company liable under the Act.

3. If (2) were carried out, more sockets could be fitted to avoid trailing leads.

4. There is an urgent need for training on safety at all levels.

(iv)

Fig. 15   (Continued)

V.   Recommendations

It is recommended that:

1. Industrial Lifting Gear PLC should be contacted immediately
    and that alternative methods of cooling and supply should
    be explored.

2. Four temporary maintenance staff should be engaged from the
    Jobcentre and an urgent memorandum should be sent from the
    Managing Director's office demanding instant attention to
    the ventilation in Workshop C, the maintenance of fire buckets
    and the supply of more power sockets in the Administration
    Office.

3. The Training Officer should be requested to design and run
    a series of short courses on safety for all personnel on an
    in-house basis. He should also be requested to make safety
    training an important part of the induction days.

Signed: ....

P D Hodges
Safety Officer

(v)

Fig. 15 (Continued)

method of training for management and of solving a problem which has arisen within a company or within a field of research. Examining bodies and institutes now demand narrative reports as proof of ability to order, to investigate logically, to organise time and material, to think a problem through and to present a professional report.

Narrative reports are really long investigation reports, their parameters and objectives usually being set by the immediate superior or institutional body concerned, and sometimes as a joint venture by both. The resulting document should be useful to the individual and to his organisation, in terms of development and problem solving. It is usually fairly lengthy, so no example has been included here. The most usual sections are as follows:

1. *Title and contents pages* These are the same as those for other reports.

2. *Terms of reference and objectives* These are the same as those for the shorter investigation report.

3. *Synopsis* As the project is usually a very long document, a summary appears on one of the initial pages which normally gives a brief resumé of the methodology and the major recommendations. Similar summaries can, in fact, be seen at the beginning of Royal Commission Reports or legal inquiries.

4. *Introduction* This section usually gives an outline of the problem to be investigated, an introduction to the organisation and/or section which it concerns, and any other background data which may be necessary for the understanding of the reader; for example, the reasons why the problem has arisen and is being currently investigated. If the project is to be prepared for an institute or other examining body, then a brief summary of the organisation's development and the nature of its operations, as well as an organisation chart, is useful to set the project in its context for the outside reader. Again, the writer must respond to the demands of the situation and to the intended readership. Such a full explanation will not be necessary if it is for internal submission only.

5. *Methodology* As in the shorter investigation report, this should list the methods chosen for the investigation and perhaps give reasons why these seemed suitable. If questionnaire methods have been used, then an example should be included in the appendix and referred to in this section.

6. *The existing situation* The current situation in which the problem has arisen should be described briefly.

7. *Analysis and identification of problems* The problems identified should be summarised clearly.

8. *Analysis of alternative solutions and costs* These should be discussed and compared; any cost factors should be analysed carefully.

9. *Conclusions* These should evaluate and select the alternatives possible, before making any recommendations.

10. *Recommendations* These should suggest what action should be taken, that is, what are the best alternatives *and* how they may best be implemented. It is often a good idea to reiterate how much each would cost here, as a superior reading the report may wish simply to refer to the recommendations at some future date, and not necessarily to the analysis sections.

11. *Appendices* The same problem arises here as with the technical report – what should you include in the main body of the project and what should you include in the appendices? If the illustration, diagram or calculation needs to be referred to immediately by the reader, in order that the written text can be understood, then it is better included opposite the relevant page. If, however, it is material which is of interest to the whole project, or is bulky, or can conveniently be referred to from time to time, then it should appear in the appendix. Examples of forms, pictures of products, and detailed statistics are usually included in appendices, for instance.

12. *Bibliography and acknowledgements* A list of published sources and acknowledgements to the work or help of others should appear at the end.

Before leaving the subject of the layout of reports and their presentation, two further points need to be made. One concerns methods of numbering and one concerns style.

Numbering systems

There are two kinds of numbering systems, either one is acceptable, provided consistency is maintained. The first is an alternating system of different forms of letters and numbers. A typical pattern would be as follows:

   I. Terms of reference
      1. Objective...
      2. Requesting authority...etc.
   II. Methods of investigation and sources of information
      1. Methods of investigation
         (a) Interviews...
         (b) Surveys...etc.
      2. Sources of information
         (a) Legislation...
         (b) Government statistics...etc.

The second is a system of arabic numerals that are added on with each subsection; in this case, the pattern would be as follows:

   1. Terms of reference
      1.1 Objectives
      1.2 Requesting authority
   2. Methods of investigation and sources of information
      2.1. Methods of investigation
         2.1.1. Interviews...
         2.1.2. Surveys...etc.
      2.2. Sources of information
         2.2.1. Legislation...
         2.2.2. Government statistics...etc.

The only argument against this is, as you can see, that the clusters of digits can be confusing. This is particularly the case where the report is likely to have a number of graded subsections and points. However, it is often employed in the services and in scientific/technical reports. Provided the writer and the reader can easily keep track, either layout can be chosen. It should also become clear from the above how important indentation and a use of white space on the paper is in adding to the impact of sectionalisation. It is much easier for the reader to run his eye down the page and select the section he wishes to refer to, as well as 'to see' the framework of the whole report clearly.

Language and style

As for language and style, the report is normally submitted to a superior; consequently, it is formal in tone and structure. The report should, therefore, be in the third person or in the passive. The word 'I' very rarely appears in report writing unless it is an eyewitness report of an accident or crime. For the purposes of most reports, the language should be impersonal and the writer unobtrusive.

The language, as has previously been emphasised, should also be chosen to suit the reader. A rule of thumb is that it should be simple and clear and should avoid technical jargon (particularly if this is undefined), patronising 'chattiness', colloquialisms and slang. The golden principle, as stated throughout this book, is to write for the receiver of the document, taking into account his level of expertise and vocabulary level.

Verbal reporting

This is normally based on a written report, but requires rather different techniques. These are discussed in Chapter 8 which deals with giving speeches.

Conclusion

It cannot be overemphasised that a good, clear report is one of the most valuable methods of communicating, whether to colleagues, superiors or other interested parties. If the information it contains is accurate and is clearly and logically presented, then it adds to the knowledge of all who read it, and can prove an enormous help to correct decision-making. As such it can help to ensure the future success of an enterprise. On the other hand, poor reports are worse than useless, as they are actively misleading and, sometimes, destructive. Anyone concerned in the management process, therefore, needs to foster the ability to write a thoroughly researched, factually precise report, which is logically and professionally presented in a clear, concise style. Competence in report writing can improve immensely the whole communication process within and between organisations.

* * *

Suggested activity for interest

Analyse the appraisal report form or any other routine report form within your company; carry out a critical evaluation of its design, and give suggestions for improvement.

Suggested activity for self-evaluation

Write a practice investigation report on the following subject:

The economics of communication have become very costly for most companies. You have been asked by the company secretary, in whose department you work, to investigate all the communication methods used by your company and to suggest ways of economising on these.

5 | Letter writing – an essential element in public relations

The letter as a PR exercise

Like forms, the letters sent by a company can affect its public image; they do, after all, represent the competence of its personnel and the professionalism of its operations to others. It is essential, therefore, that care should be taken to achieve exactly the right combination of approach, tone, good presentation and clarity of style. Unfortunately, many letters are still seen by their receivers in a very different light, and the sins of pomposity, outdated jargon and ungrammatical constructions still abound. The United States of America has influenced letter writing, introducing a more informal and pleasant tone and simpler, more concise English. Sir Ernest Gowers' book *Plain Words*[18] was written in an attempt to promote precisely this, and many people still have not taken in his message. There are three initial needs to be observed in any business letter if it is to achieve its objectives of representing its company in the best possible way and in gaining the required response from its receivers.

The need for the right approach

Each letter requires a different approach in the light of five different considerations. These are as follows:

1. *The objectives of the letter* Is it asking for information, giving information, filing a complaint, adjusting an error, asking for money, or attempting to persuade the reader to accept a product, or to consider the writer for employment? The approach for each will be distinctive and requires careful planning if the differing objectives are to be met, and the desired response acquired.
2. *The initiating action which precedes it* Often a letter is written in response to a situation – for example, a complaint is received, and someone has to plan how to deal with it, or a circular letter must be composed to persuade customers to buy a new product or take up a new service.
3. *The nature of the message* This is really connected with the objective of the letter. Some letters must give clear information about very complex material; letters from insurance companies or solicitors are a good example. Here the

need is for clarity of language and very careful paragraphing, so that a logical sequence promotes understanding. Some letters convey information which will not be welcome to the reader – news of a redundancy or an overdraft, for example – and thought must be given to their effects. This is linked, in turn, with the receiver's likely attitude.

4. *The receiver's likely attitude* Thinking about this in advance, in the light of the initiating action and the nature of the message, is an invaluable help in achieving the objective of the letter.

5. *The receiver's degree of familiarity with the situation or with the information that the letter contains* If we use legal letters as an example, there may be a need for a full explanation of technical points of law, which are familiar to the writer but not the reader. The same is true of letters about such matters as pensions or tax, and about many technical points. It is only too easy for the writer, familiar as he is with his own field, to forget this and to assume an understanding. He must be on his guard against this.

The need for good presentation, layout and clarity

The need for good presentation, in terms of both correct layout and language, is self-evident and, if a company is to be seen to be professionally competent, it is essential. There are now a number of possible layouts for business letters (see below), but it is vital that the writer should use the correct grammar, spelling and punctuation. Unfortunately, many people did not acquire these skills at primary school. For these people, as well as for foreign businessmen who find it difficult to cope with what is admittedly the most illogical and difficult language to learn, a brief guide to the use of English appears at the end of this book (see Part 5). Above all, letters should be clear – this means good paragraphing. Each topic should be dealt with separately and concisely, and in plain English, devoid of archaic or jargon expressions. Some of the main problems of language and style will be identified at the end of this chapter.

The need for the right tone

The aim here should be to be formal, without being stilted; the degree of formality will, of course, depend on the situation and on how well the receiver is known to the writer. For example, a letter from a bank to a client is usually fairly formal, but if it follows a recent interview with the bank manager, it may be more formal or more friendly (if the interview had been a pleasant one!) In the past, banks have suffered from a reputation of using 'officialese' and a somewhat headmaster-like tone, but the modern approach is much more 'client-orientated', creating a new image which is 'user friendly'. This enables the banks to market their services more efficiently.

Layout of letters

There are two quite distinctive letter layouts in use at present (with many hybrids of the two types). Whichever one you choose, the layout should be consistent and should look professional.

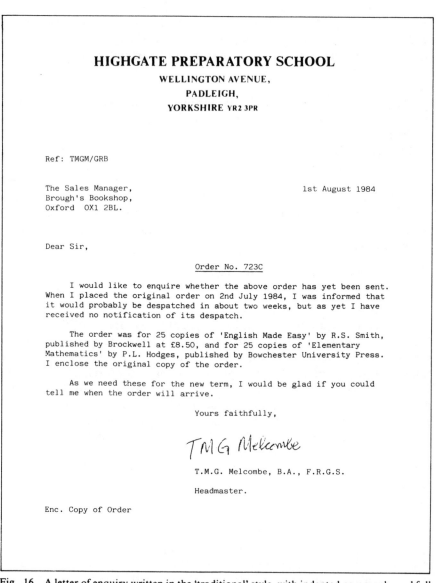

HIGHGATE PREPARATORY SCHOOL

WELLINGTON AVENUE,

PADLEIGH,

YORKSHIRE YR2 3PR

Ref: TMGM/GRB

The Sales Manager,   1st August 1984
Brough's Bookshop,
Oxford OX1 2BL.

Dear Sir,

                                Order No. 723C

   I would like to enquire whether the above order has yet been sent.
When I placed the original order on 2nd July 1984, I was informed that
it would probably be despatched in about two weeks, but as yet I have
received no notification of its despatch.

   The order was for 25 copies of 'English Made Easy' by R.S. Smith,
published by Brockwell at £8.50, and for 25 copies of 'Elementary
Mathematics' by P.L. Hodges, published by Bowchester University Press.
I enclose the original copy of the order.

   As we need these for the new term, I would be glad if you could
tell me when the order will arrive.

                        Yours faithfully,

                        T M G Melcombe

                        T.M.G. Melcombe, B.A., F.R.G.S.

                        Headmaster.

Enc. Copy of Order

Fig. 16   A letter of enquiry written in the 'traditional' style, with indented paragraphs and full
punctuation.

   The most familiar layout is the traditional or indented one, with full
punctuation (see Fig. 16). This layout has the address of the writer at the top
right-hand corner, if there is not a printed letter heading. This address will be
indented and punctuated. The date, written in full, will appear below it,
against the right-hand margin. The reference will be typed on the left-hand
side. If there isn't one, the first line of the addressee's name and address will
appear, punctuated and blocked against the left-hand margin. The superscription – Dear Sir – will appear below this, and below that, centred, will be

Brough's Bookshop
Oxford OX1 2BL

4 August 1984

REF LLS/CW

TMG Melcombe BA FRGS
Headmaster
Highgate Preparatory School
Wellington Avenue
Padleigh
Yorkshire YR2 3PR

Dear Sir

ORDER NO 723C

Thank you for your letter of 1 August 1984. I am sorry that there has
been some delay, which has been caused by staff holidays.

I am glad to be able to inform you that the above order was sent to
your school yesterday and should arrive within the next three days.

I apologise again for the delay and hope that the order is satisfactory.
If there are any queries, please contact me on Oxford 5601 Extension
73.

I enclose the invoice.

Yours faithfully

LL Sheldon

LL Sheldon
Sales Manager

Enc Invoice

Fig. 17   A letter of reply to an enquiry, with blocked paragraphs and open punctuation.

the subject heading. The main body of the letter will then follow, laid out in indented paragraphs. The subscription – Yours faithfully (or sincerely) – will be centred, two spaces below the last line of the letter. A space will be left for the signature, which will be followed by the writer's name and position. Any enclosures will be indicated by 'Enc' in the bottom left-hand corner.

The second type is the fully-blocked layout. This is extremely simple, which is why it has become very popular. It is quicker to type, which makes it cost saving. Everything is blocked against the left-hand margin (except, possibly, the printed heading). The paragraphs are indicated by a space between the lines rather than by an indentation and the addresses, superscription, letter-head and subscription are unpunctuated. Figure 17 is an example of a blocked letter with open punctuation. Normally, handwritten letters are written in the indented, 'traditional' style. Most firms have adopted the blocked style since it saves time and money. Most secretarial examining boards demand this style, so its dissemination throughout the commercial world seems inevitable.

Different types of letters and their composition

Each letter requires slightly different composition and paragraph planning. I will now give an outline for each category of letter.

Letters of application and curricula vitae

These are the most difficult letters to write because the candidate is effectively attempting to 'sell himself' and has to avoid the traps, either of being over-diffident (often interpreted as 'not very positive') or over-confident (inter-preted as 'conceit').

The factual information about the candidate is best listed in a typed curriculum vitae (CV) which can be attached to the letter. This prevents the letter from becoming long and unwieldy and is much easier to read than when included in the body of the letter. (If the writer is making more than one application he can easily duplicate the curriculum vitae and attach it to all his letters). The writer's main effort can then be concentrated on the main letter, which needs to be cogent, yet persuasive – a very difficult combination to achieve.

It is normally sufficient to write three principal paragraphs:

1. An introductory, brief paragraph which refers to the source of information about the post and states the writer's intention to apply for it.
2. A paragraph which gives reasons why the applicant believes he is suitable for the post and could make a contribution to the firm. This will refer to his attached curriculum vitae as giving further details of his particular qualifi-cations and experience. (It is sufficient to select, emphasise or include new information which is most appropriate to the advertisement, and/or details of the post received.) In some cases, it may be necessary to write more than one paragraph; however the writer should be concise – there may be over a hundred applicants and brevity will be attractive!
3. A final paragraph which states when the applicant would be available for interview were he to be short-listed. Although style is discussed later, it is worth noting here that the letter should *not* end with a 'dangling participle' – 'hoping to hear from you, etc.' This is ungrammatical as well as unnecessary. Concluding phrases are not needed.

Examples of a letter of application (Fig. 18) and curriculum vitae (Fig. 19) are given to show suitable layouts. Whatever the details of the curriculum vitae, the headings should be similar to those given, and it will be noticed that

```
                                            16, Kendal Avenue,
                                               Wokingham,
                                               Berkshire,
                                                RG11 6AR

General Manager,
Flexisystems P.L.C.,                  15th June 1984
Warnborough Road,
Reading, RG1 2AR


Dear Sir,

                    Post of Marketing Manager

        I would like to apply for the above post which was advertised in
    the 'Daily Telegraph' on 14th June 1984.

        Since gaining my degree, in which I specialised in Computer Studies
    and Marketing, I have had considerable experience in marketing both
    hardware and software for two major companies, as you will see from
    my enclosed curriculum vitae. This has involved me in working on my
    own initiative, visiting high level executives in a number of firms
    throughout the U.K. I have also travelled abroad to the United States,
    Europe and Japan in order to research markets and promote new business.
    The records of both the marketing departments of which I have been a
    member have been very successful, attracting many contracts from both
    home and foreign markets.

        I feel that the knowledge and experience which I have gained would
    enable me to contribute significantly to the future development of
    Flexisystems PLC and that I have now reached a stage in my career when
    the challenge of a managerial post would be highly motivating.

        Should you wish to interview me, I could attend at any time during
    normal office hours.

                            Yours faithfully



                            Neil J. Nokes, B.Sc.
```

Fig. 18   A letter of application.

they follow the same kind of layout as the normal application form referred to in Chapter 3.

Letters of enquiry and order; replies with enclosures

The first step in any business transaction is usually an enquiry about prices, range of goods (or services) and their availability. This kind of letter is, therefore, brief and concise. It consists of two or three short paragraphs, some of one sentence only. The letter of enquiry will normally conform to the following structure:

1. A reference to the source of information concerning the company, organisation or range of goods and services about which the enquiry is made.

```
                        CURRICULUM VITAE


Name:           Neil James Nokes

Address:        16, Kendal Avenue
                Wokingham
                Berkshire
                RG2 2AR
Tel. no.:       Wokingham (0739) 667857

Date of birth:  12.5.55

Nationality:    British

Marital status: Married

Number and ages of children: 1 child of 1 year

Education:  St Edward's Primary School, Kirtlington   1960-1961
            Fosters Grammar School, Kirkborough        1961-1971
            Portland Polytechnic                       1971-1974

Qualifications: GCE O level (University of Oxford Board)  June 1969
                English Language      Grade C            June 1969
                Mathematics               B              June 1969
                Physics                   C              June 1969
                Chemistry                 C              June 1969
                Geography                 B              June 1969
                History                   C              June 1969
                Economics                 B              June 1969
                GCE A level (University of Oxford Board)  June 1971
                Mathematics           Grade C            June 1971
                Geography                 B              June 1971
                Economics                 A              June 1971
                Degree: BSc in Business Studies
                        Specialist areas: Computer Studies and Marketing

Work experience:

1974 - 1975:  Management trainee:  Condor Business Systems
                                   Western Road, Bracknell.
1976 - 1978:  Marketing Assistant: Condor Business Systems
                                   Western Road, Bracknell.
1978 -        Marketing Executive: Silfax Software PLC
                                   Frimley Road
                                   Farnborough, Hampshire.

Interests:    Sailing, music, squash, motor sport.

Referees:     A.J.H. Porter, Marketing Manager, Condor Business Systems.
              F.L. Baker, BSc., General Manager, Silfax Software PLC.
```

Fig. 19   A sample curriculum vitae.

2. A request for specific information. It helps the receiver if adequate details are given here.

3. A concluding sentence or request.

The reply to this letter will be three paragraphs long. Its structure will be as follows:

1. A sentence which thanks the writer for his/her enquiry.

2. A paragraph which gives details of items requested and any relevant

information on non-availability of goods and services, delays or alternative suppliers. This will also include a reference to the enclosures, if any.

3. A paragraph which gives information as to who may be contacted, with a telephone and/or extension number should any further queries be forthcoming.

If there are enclosures, 'Enc.' will appear at the end of the letter, on the left-hand side, followed by a list of the items sent. This provides a useful check for the reader.

The third step is the placing of the order. Here, the writer must be careful to include all relevant information concerning his order. Once again, three paragraphs are sufficient. These will consist of the following:

1. An introductory sentence which thanks the sender for information received.

2. A paragraph which gives details of the order, including catalogue numbers, prices and precise descriptions quoted from the information received.

3. A paragraph which refers to method of payment and/or any further step required, such as placement of deposit, request for a discount, request for a receipt, etc.

Letters of complaint and adjustment

COMPLAINT

The important point to remember, when writing a letter of complaint, is to avoid rudeness or sarcasm, which create antagonism. A good firm will put the matter right if the facts are presented fairly. Rudeness makes the receiver defensive and uncooperative. A calm, reasoned letter is likely to receive favourable treatment. It should state the complaint, give details of the trouble, and request action.

ADJUSTMENT

The customer should be given the benefit of the doubt, but, if he is clearly wrong, a tactful letter of adjustment must be sent which details the relevant facts and points out the error. If a complaint is justified, some explanation and apology should be offered to the customer, and some action should be taken to restore his good opinion of the firm. The letter should refer to the customer's complaint, give details as to the cause of the problem, apologising if appropriate, and state what action will be taken to remedy the situation.

Letters aimed at the collection of outstanding debts

These letters must be carefully written, otherwise people will take offence. Statements are usually submitted several times before a collection letter is written – non-payment may be due to oversight or to unbusinesslike methods of dealing with accounts. The first letter should be cautious, allowing for the possibility of error, the second letter should be firmer in tone, but still polite, and a threat of legal action can be included in the third letter.

TELEX, WORD PROCESSING AND BUSINESS SERVICES

32 Broad Street
Wokingham, Berks RG11 1AB
Telephone: (0734) 791737, 792021
Telex: 848210 Infos G

Date as postmark

Dear ....

BUSINESS AND SECRETARIAL SERVICES

RUNNING A SMALL BUSINESS?

INFOSEND can provide the business and secretarial services which keep
your overheads down and keep your business going.

HOW WE CAN HELP YOU

SECRETARIAL SERVICES   We can:

Type or word process your letters, quotations, invoices, etc.
Answer the telephone and take messages for you.
Make 'phone calls on your behalf.
Provide you with a business address.
Arrange your business and/or personal insurance.
Photocopy your records.

TELEX SERVICE   We can:

Send and receive telex messages for you.

PROMOTION SERVICES   We can:

Word process your advertising mail shots.
Arrange your printing and advertising material.
Organise promotions.
Arrange conferences.

FREIGHT SERVICES   We can:

Arrange import and export of your goods.

INTERESTED?

If so, 'phone Trish or Margaret on 0734 791737.

Fig. 20   A circular letter.

Circular letters

A circular letter has various purposes. It may give information – for example, a change of address, an extension of premises or an introduction of a new line. The circular is often used to promote new products or to sell goods or services. The need here is to be persuasive and to be brief at the same time. A long letter is unlikely to be read. An effective layout, with questions or points aimed directly at the receiver, which is spacious and uses capital letters and underlining for emphasis of the major points, will hold the reader's attention. Often further contact is suggested at the end of the letter. (See Fig. 20 for an example of a circular letter.)

Other types of letter

This chapter has dealt with the main categories into which most business letters fall, and has given examples. However, I will now give brief notes on some other types of letter.

STATUS ENQUIRIES

These are normally made at the commencement of business transactions, in order to ascertain the good standing or reputation of a new customer. Information may be obtained from another firm or the customer's bankers. The sort of information required is the period of the firm's connection with the buyers, the frequency of orders received, the payment of accounts and the amount of discount and credit allowed.

THE REPLY TO A STATUS ENQUIRY

The reply to a status enquiry should answer the questions carefully, but avoid giving a definite guarantee of the integrity of the firm in question. (The name of the firm is often omitted from the reply, or enclosed on a slip of paper, in order to avoid complications should the letter pass into unauthorised hands.)

LETTER OF INTRODUCTION

This is a letter that introduces a firm's representative to a company that he visits for the first time. It should give the name of the representative, his connection with the firm and the reason for visiting. It should request the advice and help of the company visited.

LETTERS OF INVITATION AND REPLY

These are often printed on a card, and are usually written in the third person. They often have 'RSVP' on them – the request for a reply. The wording of the invitation, therefore, might be: 'The Chairman requests the pleasure of the company of Mr and Mrs... at his Retirement Dinner at 7.30 p.m. on 8th April 1984 at the Queen's Hotel, Farnborough. RSVP.' Occasionally, an indication of what to wear will be given – 'Dress formal'. The reply will also be in the third person: 'Mr and Mrs... accept with pleasure the Chairman's invitation to his retirement dinner at...'

Having discussed the layout, composition and tone of many types of letters, and having stressed the need to make them clear and understandable, I will conclude by discussing letter-writing language and style.

Language and style – a major problem in letter writing

The language and style adopted by many letter writers is often not brief, plain or understandable. Archaic expressions – such as 'We beg to remain your obedient servants' or 'We are in receipt of your esteemed favour' – are still used! Ungrammatical constructions are widespread and the 'dangling participle' is common. ('Awaiting your reply' and 'hoping to hear from you' are grammatically incorrect as the 'ing' form is only *part* of a verb.) Some rules for beginnings and endings, including those for superscriptions and subscriptions, together with some horrors to avoid, are given for reference purposes.

Beginnings and endings

The date Do not abbreviate, e.g. 7.4.84 or 7th April '84.
References If you are replying to a letter, or referring to a previous letter, quote any reference given, unless it refers only to the initials of the person writing and of his secretary.
Name If writing to someone by name always include their qualifications, e.g. A.B. Smith, OBE, FRGS. (Note, if Esq. is used, Mr is not, and vice versa.) Letters for a limited company (unless you are writing to a particular person at that company) will be addressed to 'The Secretary, The XYZ Company PLC' and will start 'Dear Sirs'. Letters for a firm will be addressed 'Messrs XYZ Company or Messrs XYZ Brothers' and will start 'Dear Sirs'.
Address This should be in full.
Dear Sir Letters addressed 'Dear Sir' or 'Dear Sirs' must always end 'Yours faithfully'. *Dear Mr Smith* Letters addressed 'Dear Mr Smith' or 'Dear Mrs Smith' must always end 'Yours sincerely'.
Heading You should decide whether to give your letter a heading. It is not possible to lay down exactly when to use a heading. The following is a list of cases where a heading would be beneficial:

1. If your correspondent has used one, you should use it.
2. If it helps to shorten your letter.
3. If you are beginning a correspondence which will probably lead to a sequence of letters on the subject.
4. To firms or companies, a heading is essential as it will make for more accurate filing, as well as saving time if reference has to be made to the letter at a later date.

Signature The name and title of the person signing the letter should be below his signature.
Enclosures If 'Enc.' or 'Encs.' is typed underneath the signature, this acts as a reminder to the person making up the post that something else has to be included in the envelope.

In order to make letters sound human and sincere, avoid hackneyed phrases, clichés and circumlocutions like the following:

Having our attention
Your letter is to hand
Use our good offices
We are in receipt of
I shall be obliged if you will kindly let me know

Never use the cliché 'Your convenience', e.g. 'A cheque book is enclosed for your convenience'. *Never* use 'Instant', 'Proxima' or 'Ultimo' when referring to the date of a letter received. Always quote the date. Finally, a list of clumsy or 'commercialese' expressions follows as a guide for all those faced with the difficult task of composing business letters. The main rule is to avoid pomposity, verbosity and abruptness.

Commercialese – expressions to be avoided

Commercialese is often vague and wordy and gives an impression of being pompous and offhand. The following are suggestions on how to avoid it:

Not this	*Perhaps*
We acknowledge receipt of	Thank you for (not we thank you for)
I have your letter of	Many thanks for
We have pleasure in	I'm glad to/We are happy to
Referring to your letter of	Your letter of...mentioned
The above/above mentioned	This/it
We note your comments regarding	You mention that
	We have received your report (they will assume you have read it)
Enclosed herewith	Here is
Enclosed please find	I am enclosing
Attached please find	
Further to	Following
Awaiting the favour of your reply	We hope to hear from you soon
Thanking you in advance	(Omit)
Assuring you of our best attention	(Omit)
Regretting our inability to be of service	(Omit)
Trusting we may be favoured by the receipt	(Omit)
Please do not hesitate to	Please

ARCHAIC OR LEGAL TAGS

Not this	*Perhaps*
Advise	Means to give advice; otherwise use: tell, say, let you know, mention
Beg	(Omit)

Favour	Letter/report/enquiry
As per	According to
Per	By
Per pro (PP)	For
Re	About (omit in headings)
Viz	Namely
It is/will be appreciated that	(Omit)
The undersigned/writer	I
Our Mr Jones	Mr Jones, our representative
May we take this opportunity of	
Allow me to say	(Take it or say it, don't sound apologetic!)
Permit me to say	
As stated above	As we have shown
As stated below	For these reasons
You claim/state/say	(Don't suggest he is a liar)
Your dissatisfaction/complaint	The trouble/difficulty you have had
Vague references to time	Specify the date if possible
In the not too distant future	Before long
In due course	Within a few days/weeks/months
At a later date	Later
At an earlier date	
In the near future	Soon
At the present time	Now
Up to this writing	Up to now, so far
Yours of recent date	Your letter/report of

WORDY PHRASES

Not this	*Perhaps*
Due to the fact that	Because/as
In the event that	If
On the occasion of	When/on
With regard to	
Regarding	About
Concerning, in respect of	
Prior to	Before
In the amount of	For
In the neighbourhood of	Near/about (unless town planning!)
With a view to	
For the purpose of	To
In order to	
In connection with	About, of, for
According to our records	We find/our records show
Answer in the affirmative/negative	Say yes/no

Ambiguity and the public

Ambiguity is another problem. These extracts have been taken from genuine letters to the Pensions Office, and illustrate the problem of ambiguity by showing their unintended results!

1. I cannot get sick pay. I have six children. Can you tell me why this is?
2. This is my eighth child. What are you going to do about it?
3. Mrs R. has no clothes and has not had any for a year. The clergy have been visiting her.
4. In reply to your letter, I have already co-habited with your office, so far without result.
5. I am forwarding my marriage certificate, and two children, one of which is a mistake, as you can see.
6. Sir, I am glad to say that my husband, reported missing, is now dead.
7. Unless I get my husband's money, I shall be forced to lead an immortal life.
8. I am sending you my marriage certificate and six children. I had seven and one died, which was baptised on a half sheet of paper by the Rev. Thomas.
9. In answer to your letter, I have given birth to a little boy weighing 10 lbs. Is this satisfactory?
10. You have changed my little girl into a little boy. Will this make any difference?

Conclusions

Letters are an important method of communication in the business world. They should aim to achieve the two objectives of good communication – to ensure clear understanding and to gain a favourable response from the recipient. As letters represent the organisations from which they are written, every attempt should be made to produce letters which convey a professional impression and thus an acceptable public image.

* * *

Suggested activity for interest

Compile an up-to-date curriculum vitae. Select an advertisement for a job you would like. Compose a letter of application which refers to, but does not overlap, your CV, concentrating on presenting yourself in the best light.

Suggested activity for self-evaluation

1. Your company has bought a vending machine which has developed several faults in the first six months after installation. It has been repaired free of charge as it is under guarantee, but its maintenance has been delayed, and it has gone wrong again. Write to the company who supplied the machine, Supersnax PLC, giving details of its unsatisfactory performance and stating that it has now developed a major fault once again and that you wish for immediate repair or replacement. Your letter should be addressed to the Sales Manager.

2. As Regional Maintenance Supervisor at Supersnax PLC, you have received a copy of the letter from the Sales Manager with a memo requesting repair. Write a reply (in letter form) to the Sales Manager, who is at Head Office, explaining that several of the original components were unsatisfactory, that you have changed your suppliers but that they are now suffering from an industrial dispute, so that you cannot offer any repair service at present.

3. As Sales Manager, write to the customer explaining the situation and suggesting appropriate action.

6 | The discussion paper – a problem of construction

Definition and functions of the discussion paper

A discussion paper is a preliminary exploration of a topic to form the basis for future discussion. It is prepared for a meeting, conference or seminar, where it will be considered by a number of colleagues or interested parties. It therefore fulfils several functions. It acts as a reference document for others, allowing them to prepare or add their own views; as a research document, presenting or adding knowledge on a topic which is currently considered by a number of people in the same field, as a basis for further exploration or study by others; and as a source of information which can be evaluated and may make a valuable contribution to future research or decision-making.

In professional and scientific fields, a discussion paper is an important method of communication; because of this, many institutes now include questions which require this format in their examinations. For these reasons, some brief guidance is given in this chapter as to its requirements, structure and presentation.

Analysing the requirements of a discussion paper

The first principle is to analyse the fundamental requirements for the specific discussion paper which has been requested. Like the report, this will mean looking carefully at the four major influential factors. These can be summarised as follows:

1. *The writer's objectives* The purpose of the paper being composed must be easily recognised – is it to give information, form a basis for further investigation, or persuade the readers to accept a particular set of proposals?
2. *The recipient's objectives and knowledge of the subject* These are what the receiver expects to gain from the paper. His knowledge of the subject will also affect the amount of explanation that must be given, and the terminology.
3. *The subject and scope* The type of subject – scientific, professional or general – as well as the mandate which the writer has been given, will give the parameters for content and language.
4. *The methodology or sources of information* Those that are available to the

writer will affect his research methods and the validity of his final paper. They will affect its acceptability to others and must be given a good deal of thought before the paper is undertaken.

The structure of the discussion paper

The discussion paper has many things in common with the report in that it contains subheadings, it may include numbered points and it must be presented in a logical sequence. Unlike the report, however, there are no permanently applicable major subheadings, although some are suggested which will *usually* be present in some form. The discussion paper often includes recommendations and in this, too, it resembles the report. In many other ways, however, it is closer to the traditional essay. The discussion in each section needs to be quite extensive, though concise, and it will normally be presented in paragraphs rather than adopt the brief numbered points to be found in reports. It is best seen as a hybrid between the two formats, and its structure will differ according to the demands of the topic. The following are some sections which are often included in a discussion paper:

1. *An introductory section* This possibly will be headed 'introduction' or 'background'. This will set out any or all of the following:
(a) Any necessary preliminary data, such as that found in the terms of reference of a report – for example, the initiating situation or request to which the discussion paper is a response, who is compiling it and for whom.
(b) The objectives and scope of the paper, including its parameters and limitations.
(c) Any preliminary background knowledge that is necessary to enable the readers or listeners to understand the subject to be discussed. This might include the present state of research on the subject, the reason why the topic is of current interest and any organisational or situational background material.
2. *Any sources consulted* These should be included if this is also relevant to the topic. Readers like to be informed as to where the facts come from. This might be headed, as in the report, 'Sources of information', or, if appropriate, 'Methods of investigation'. The sources and methods listed in the section on investigation reports might be equally appropriate here. Unlike other sections of the discussion paper, there is no reason why this section should not be presented as a numbered list.
3. *An analysis of information section* An analysis of some sort will normally come next. It usually takes the form of the following:
(a) An analysis of the existing state of affairs, or the existing research or knowledge.
(b) An identification of the problems which have become evident from this.
(c) A comparison of advantages and disadvantages of various courses of action to remedy the problems identified and to improve the existing situation. This may either include an exploration of the financial implications of each course suggested, or it may discuss possible effects on the organisation as a whole. This section will be the major one, and will contain the most

extensive part of the discussion. It is helpful if the writer can give further subheadings to guide the reader through the subject. These might be drawn from the sections mentioned above.

4. *A summary of the main facts or arguments* This is usually headed 'Summary' or 'Conclusion'. As the previous section is likely to be a complex one, a brief summary is very helpful – particularly if the paper is to be read out. For reference purposes, it is also a valuable aid if it is to be read later. This section, like the conclusion section of the report, also contains an evaluation of what is likely to be the best course of action in the future. It identifies priorities and indicates future trends, action or research.

5. *Recommended solutions, or courses of action* These will appear if they have been requested. (Sometimes these are not needed, and the discussion paper can end at section 4.) It should recommend briefly what should now occur, giving reasons.

The end result should be a coherent, well argued document, logically developed with some viable proposals in the last section.

Further points of presentation

1. *Subheadings and numbering* As in the report, care must be taken that subheadings give clear guidelines to the content. Any numbering system used should be carefully checked to make sure that it is logical and consistent.

2. *Language and style related to the roles and background of the receivers* The language and style adopted should relate to three things – the type of document (in terms of formality), the roles of the receivers and their background, and knowledge of the topic. As the discussion paper is a formal document, colloquialisms should be avoided in the text. The problem here is that it is easy to fall into the trap of becoming pompous or verbose; the best way of avoiding both pitfalls is to use clear concise English. The paper will have the most impact this way.

The receivers may be colleagues, superiors or interested parties. The important factor is their degree of knowledge of the topic. Care must be taken to give sufficient explanation without appearing patronising. If there is a range of knowledge among the receivers, it may be best to begin by stating this, then declare the writer's intention to explain terms or information which is not likely to be familiar to some. In this way, those who have a higher level of expertise are unlikely to become impatient! In particular, technical terms should be defined the first time they are used; if these are very complex and/or numerous, a glossary should be attached to the paper.

The paper, like the report, should be written in the third person although, if it is to be presented orally, this can be modified. For the reader, the writer should be unobtrusive. The document is an impersonal and professional presentation of information in which complex material is organised concisely and relevantly. It should give him what he hopes to gain in a lucid and logical form.

The visual element – illustrating discussion papers, with particular reference to oral presentation at conferences or seminars

Discussion papers are often presented orally at conferences and seminars; if they are, then visual aids may assist to make that presentation more interesting and to give the argument more impact. Visual aids have three distinct advantages as follows:

1. They vary *method* of presentation, considerably aiding concentration. (Listening to someone speak inevitably creates a tendency for the mind to wander, unless the speaker is particularly talented.)
2. They are *memorable*. We all tend to retain visual images for longer than the spoken word.
3. They can considerably add to the professionalism of the presentation if they are carefully and competently prepared – and this last point must be stressed! The worst visual aids I have seen actively *detracted* from this impression!

If a graph or diagram which is included in the written paper as an illustration can be presented on an overhead projector and discussed, it is usually given much more attention by the audience. If a model is appropriate then this, too, can arouse interest and focus the concentration of the listeners. If slides or film can be used, in conjunction with the explanation, the images conveyed are likely to stay in the receivers' minds long after the speaker has departed and they will remember them when they read the paper some time later.

To emphasise major headings, put the main themes, principles or summaries on a blackboard, flipchart, whiteboard or magnetic board. Video presentations will give maximum impact but should only be used where appropriate. The communication process can only be improved by effective visual presentation to illustrate a well structured paper; each will reinforce the other, and give a truly professional impression which will be retained by the audience.

* * *

Suggested activity for self-evaluation

You have been given the opportunity to put forward some proposals for the utilisation of computer technology in your particular area of work; the company is willing to expand its present provision to include your section or (if this is not the case) to spend funds on the introduction of new technology. You have been asked to produce a discussion paper for consideration by the senior management team, exploring the possibilities and outlining some proposals.

Some further points to bear in mind when attempting this activity are:
1. If you are in a purely administrative position in an office environment, then office automation will be the focus of your attention.
2. If you work in a financial section, computerisation has evident applications, and costs related to economies of scale will be important.

If you have very little first-hand knowledge of computer applications, you might find that Chapter 12, on information technology, will be useful.

7 | The essay – writing answers for examinations or assignments

Introduction

One form of written communication which is not found in the business world is the essay. Essays are possibly the most testing of all the exercises designed to assess an individual's ability to communicate with fluency, to organise complex material in a well structured form and to develop a clear line of argument. For these reasons, many of the professional bodies still ask for essay answers to their examination questions, and most colleges and universities include these as part of their course assessment – even if essays are now covered by the all embracing term 'assignment'. Assignments, of course, can be set in all kinds of ways, many of which have already been discussed in this book, but the traditional essay remains a requirement for most courses and for most examinations. It will be helpful, therefore, to give some guidelines as to its construction, composition and style.

Essays of exposition or discussion – a difference in approach and structure

These are the types of essay most often required at professional level. They require either *exposition*, that is the presentation of all the facts related to the topic given, which will require a descriptive approach; or *discussion*, that is the development of a balanced argument, based on evidence, because the given topic is one that requires some kind of debate.

Examples of these two types might be: 'Describe the present systems available for office automation', as opposed to the more provocative: 'Who needs the office of the future? Discuss the resistance to office automation and whether this is justified'. The exposition requires a simple factual presentation of what is available and, possibly, some discussion of the uses and limitations of the various equipment and systems described. The discussion is about the *value* of office automation, its advantages and disadvantages and the reasons why it is often resisted (or sabotaged!), and it evaluates whether this resistance is justified. Some consideration, too, will need to be given to methods of overcoming such resistance. The discussion, therefore, is far more complex than the exposition and makes more demands on the writer. It will give a very clear idea of whether the individual is able to analyse ideas and values as well as facts, whether he has the capacity to develop his thoughts lucidly and whether he can communicate them in an articulate way. The first step, however, to coping with either of these questions, is a careful analysis of the set question.

Initial analysis of the set question – the first stage in planning

Questions vary in their structure and in the direction that they give to the required answer. It is, therefore, essential to analyse them carefully if the correct response is to be given. Some questions contain an initial statement which may be controversial. Some ask the writer to 'examine and comment', or ask him to consider arguments for or against the statement, which will usually concern current policies or controversies in the field being studied or examined.

There is a trap here, in that too often the 'and' in the question tends to be ignored. This will produce an answer which may consist entirely of 'comment' with very little examination of the facts – or vice versa. This will inevitably destroy the balance of the question and marks will be lost. It is vital, therefore, to answer all parts of a question and that the right proportion of time is given to each part. A clause tacked on the end of the question often results in one 'after-thought' paragraph being written at the end of the essay. For example, if the question were to read: 'Give a brief account of the services offered by the major banks to domestic investors and evaluate them', the temptation is to spend a great deal of time on the first part at the expense of the second. In fact, it is probably best to describe each service and its value before continuing to the next service, providing a final summary as a conclusion to your essay which gives a brief resumé of the services, a short recapitulation as to their value, and indicates what developments are now desirable.

The initial analysis needs to take note of the key words; for example, words like 'examine', 'discuss' and 'comment' have distinctly different meanings which require different approaches. The initial statement may contain words which are technical, which are coloured by the speaker's views, or which are vague in some way. If this is the case, the essay must begin with some definitions to explain how these are being interpreted. This has the added advantage that, if the question actually contains some ambiguity, the writer has shown his recognition of this and chosen one meaning with which the assessor cannot take issue, unless the writer has misunderstood.

An example of an essay question which immediately requires a careful definition is: 'Educational standards have been sacrificed on the altar of equality'. Here the word 'standards' needs some initial explanation – what 'standards' have been measured and how? Does the word 'equality' mean equality of opportunity or equality of outcome? A further problem here is that this question stems from the opinion of the person quoted. It is necessary for the writer to examine what it is.

This initial analysis of a question is crucial if the writer is to plan and execute his answer in response to the demands of the task he has been set. The final part of this analysis is the planning stage itself but, before this takes place, the writer must ask himself one final question – what are the major areas of knowledge that are *relevant* to a question?

From examiners' reports, it is evident that, as one of them put it: 'Students insist on answering questions they themselves would like to answer, rather than the question asked'. This is due to the fact that they neither analyse the question carefully nor '*prepare* their answers; they merely write the first thing that comes into their heads'. Planning and preparation are things that require time, and the first stage is probably best undertaken by random notetaking. (An aid to keeping this *relevant* would be the 'star plan' discussed in Chapter 2.) The initial analysis should define key words and themes; if these are now written at the centre of the star, and notes grouped round it, it will soon become evident if some are irrelevant. However hard it may be to abandon cherished knowledge, irrelevant facts must be eliminated ruthlessly before you proceed to the next stage, which is planning the structure of the essay.

Structuring the essay, the planning stage: 'A beginning, a middle and an end'

Introducing the essay

The introduction should really derive from your initial analysis of the question. If the key words need definitions, these must appear here. If the essay is based on a quotation or statement, it needs some preliminary examination as to its meaning, possible context and the possible attitudes from which it is derived. The introduction might also contain any brief background knowledge that is necessary for understanding why the current topic is of interest and is under discussion. Finally, it should lead into the major part of the essay by expressing what the writer proposes to cover, in what order and in what way, preferably with some explanation as to why he has chosen these methods. If all these are included, the assessor is able to see that he has understood and appreciated the implications of the question, is aware of the issues which constitute its context, and has made some logical decisions as to what the discussion should involve and how it should be ordered. These are a useful guide to the writer himself, serving as a signpost to keep his subsequent exploration of the topic relevant to the original question.

The main body of the essay

The 'star' layout or the 'ladder' sequence should be used to plan an essay. No doubt we were all taught at school to write essays with a beginning, a middle and an end. Although this is sound advice, it is more difficult to recall any precise guidance we were given on *how* to start, what should constitute the 'middle' and how best to conclude. Suggestions have already been given as to the possible beginnings. It is the middle – or main part – which now needs a structured plan.

Although the traditional essay has no set headings or rules of layout, this does not mean that it should lack a structure. In fact *more* effort needs to be given to making this evident to the reader (often an assessor) if the essay is to be coherent and is to arrive at a justifiable conclusion. The random facts, which you have grouped around the main themes in your star, and from which you have already eliminated irrelevant material, must now be grouped into sub-topics. (The notes in Chapter 2 are useful here.) The related facts should appear under a topic heading, then the decision needs to be made as to what sequence might be most logical – which set of facts or ideas naturally follows from, or grows out of, another.

The essay may, of course, fall into obvious major subsections, such as the advantages or disadvantages of a certain course of action, or the points for and against a certain viewpoint. Within these there may be more subsections or groups of facts. If these appear in a note-form plan first, it is far easier to paragraph correctly and to produce a logical development.

If it is an essay which requires the development of a case or discussion, it is vital to marshall all the relevant facts and arguments under subheadings at this planning stage and to remember that it is necessary to produce a *reasoned* answer which includes *all* the evidence and factual information which is pertinent to *all* sides of the question to be debated. This demonstrates an awareness of all the issues involved and shows an ability to evaluate without bias. The resulting answer will be a fair, balanced and comprehensive one. Even if the writer has a specific viewpoint, he should be at pains to include and, if necessary, refute *logically* the opposite one, and to allocate sufficient points in his plan to accomplish this. Only in this way will his answer be an adequate response to the issues involved in the question.

If, on the other hand, the essay requires an exposition of facts, then planning in note form helps considerably in grouping those facts that are related into topic areas, which then form the basis of each paragraph. The subheading which you give each related group of facts will dictate the topic sentence of the paragraph – the indicator to what is to follow. This is usually the *first* sentence of each paragraph, giving direction to its development. Here, comparing alternative views of what these facts show may be relevant; if so, *all* views should be outlined, whatever the opinion of the writer.

Conclusions – summarising the salient facts and arguments

Essays need conclusions – an obvious rule often neglected. They should not stop abruptly or cease on the discussion of a minor point. The impact which the essay has, and the impression which remains with the reader, rest on the final paragraphs, which should summarise briefly the main issues and conclude the discussion. If this is missing, the major points are lost and the reader is left with a sense of bewilderment, feeling that the essay has led nowhere. A conclusion may include any or all of the following (the decision as to what exactly should be included will, of course, vary according to the topic or type of essay):

1. A summary of the main points, facts and/or arguments.
2. An assessment of these, evaluating them and sometimes giving a judgement

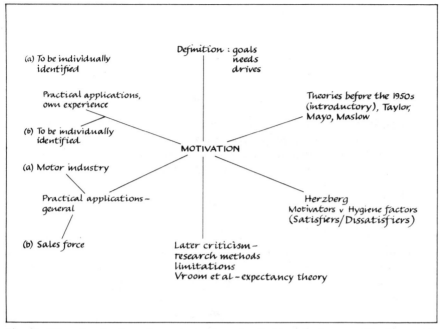

Fig. 21 Essay planning 1: random note-making, using the 'star' plan (see page 16), allows you to jot down your first thoughts on the subject of your essay.

in favour of one viewpoint. This is acceptable, *provided* that it is based on reasoned arguments and clear evidence in the main body of the essay.

3. An identification of possible future trends and developments or an identification of outstanding problems. Just as one way to introduce an essay is to give the background to the topic, one method of concluding is to look at the overall current situation or to speculate on the future.

If this advice is followed, the essay can be brought to a satisfactory and interesting conclusion, which leaves the reader with a sense that it is a complete entity, in which there has been a logical and clear development from start to finish, and which indicates issues for his further consideration.

Some examples (Figs. 21, 22 and 23) are given to illustrate the full planning process for an essay. The question taken for this purpose comes from a paper set by the Institute of Chartered Secretaries and Administators (ICSA) on Personnel: Principles and Policy.[19] It reads: 'Evaluate any major theory of motivation published since 1950 with special reference to the theory's practical applications (e.g. in your own organisation or in an organisation with which you are sufficiently familiar)'.

Before you look at the example plans given, it is worth noting that the word 'evaluate' is the key to this question (the writer is being asked to assess or judge the worth of a theory in the light of his/her own practical experience) and you need not have previous knowledge of motivation theory to appreciate the planning process.

85

I. Introduction

1. Definition of motivation – 'goal directed behavior' needs and drives.

2. First attempts to identify needs
(a) Taylor's bonuses.
(b) Mayo's accidental discovery on group and individual needs, independent of conditions.
(c) Maslow's theoretical hierarchy, showing one motivation succeeded by another after satisfaction.

Limitations of the last was lack of research, but all were important forerunners to the formulation of theories in the 1950s and 1960s.

II. Main sections of the essay

1. Herzberg's two-factor theory of motivation
(a) Question on which research was based – 'Think of a time when you felt exceptionally good or bad about your job' – reasons?
(b) Research – 200 accountants and engineers in Pittsburgh.
(c) Results – two sets of factors:
   i. Hygiene factors (those which prevented dissatisfaction):
   Company policy and administration
   Technical supervision
   Salary
   Interpersonal relations/supervision
   Working conditions
   ii. Motivators (those which produce positive motivation):
   Achievement
   Recognition
   Work itself
   Advance in responsibility
   Advancement
(d) Summary – management in the past has been perplexed when hygiene factors have not boosted productivity or morale; Herzberg provides an explanation that only a challenging job with the opportunities for all the motivators will achieve this.

2. Criticism of Herzberg's theory
Vroom and others criticised Herzberg in the 1960s for:
(a) Limited research.

Fig. 22 Essay planning 2: detailed structured notes, using the 'ladder' plan (see page 15).

(b) Limited interpretation. Vroom believed people's motivation was 'adjusted' by their expectations of a situation at any one time and that they would compromise on the factors involved.
(c) Type of research – critical incident method; when this was not used, different results emerged.

However, Herzberg extended his own research to hospitals, agricultural workers, etc. with similar results.

3. Evaluation related to practical experience
(a) General examples:
   i. Motor industry
      pro Herzberg – high pay but low morale – monotonous, uncreative work.
         but – co. policy can relieve this or better supervision can produce high morale (different methods of work – Sweden, or different policy – Japan).
   ii. Sales force
      pro Herzberg – high pay linked to high achievement.
         – good fringe benefits but high turnover of sales people.
         but – interpersonal relations with manager and colleagues can assist to remedy this.
(b) Own experience. This is likely to be different according to each writer but should follow the same pattern as 3(a).

III. Conclusion

1. Value of theory – made contribution to understanding motivation at work by stressing importance of job content factors previously neglected. Led to job design and enrichment.

2. The limitations – not a comprehensive theory; model describes only some of the content of work motivation, not the complex motivational process of individuals related to organisations.

3. Current and future developments – Vroom moved further towards a comprehensive theory; still work to be done in this area to increase managerial understanding in the essential area of motivation at work.

Fig. 22 (Continued)

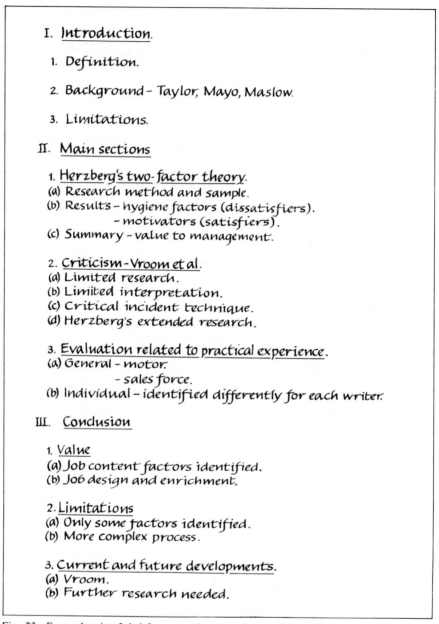

I. <u>Introduction</u>.

  1. Definition.

  2. Background – Taylor, Mayo, Maslow.

  3. Limitations.

II. <u>Main sections</u>

  1. <u>Herzberg's two-factor theory</u>.
  (a) Research method and sample.
  (b) Results – hygiene factors (dissatisfiers).
                – motivators (satisfiers).
  (c) Summary – value to management.

  2. <u>Criticism – Vroom et al</u>.
  (a) Limited research.
  (b) Limited interpretation.
  (c) Critical incident technique.
  (d) Herzberg's extended research.

  3. <u>Evaluation related to practical experience</u>.
  (a) General – motor.
            – sales force.
  (b) Individual – identified differently for each writer.

III. <u>Conclusion</u>

  1. <u>Value</u>
  (a) Job content factors identified.
  (b) Job design and enrichment.

  2. <u>Limitations</u>
  (a) Only some factors identified.
  (b) More complex process.

  3. <u>Current and future developments</u>.
  (a) Vroom.
  (b) Further research needed.

Fig. 23 Essay planning 3: brief structured notes, using the 'ladder' plan (see page 15).

Three examples are given which show the different stages or approaches to the planning process as follows:

1. *The random note-making plan (Fig. 21)* This forms the preliminary stage of either of the two plans which follow it; this is presented as a 'star' plan arrangement, with notes jotted around the central theme.

2. *A very full set of structured notes in a 'ladder' plan (Fig. 22)* This gives a comprehensive outline of what the essay might include in some detail. (This would be appropriate if the essay had been set as an assignment to be completed in the writer's own time; in this case, research and reading will form the basis of the notes.)

3. *A very brief outline 'ladder' plan (Fig. 23)* This helps to structure the essay, indicating briefly its content and sequence to the writer when he is doing an exam. Here, the facts should have been learnt and revised already. They can, therefore, be recalled quickly using a few 'cues'. Here the plan acts as a reminder and a checklist.

Style and language in essay writing

The assessor and the writer

Writing essays, when they are set as assignments by an assessor you know, is easier than writing for an unknown examiner, not only in terms of the ideas you may express, but also in choosing the language in which you express them. The examiner can be an unknown quantity – you do not know what his reactions will be to your own views or to your written style.

There are one or two principles which provide a useful guide to the writer which can be listed as follows:

1. The need is for a fairly formal approach. Plain, concise English should be used and colloquialisms or slang should be avoided, unless quoted.

2. The writer should be unobtrusive – the first person and personal reminiscence should be avoided, unless the experience to be recounted is directly pertinent, providing illuminating illustration. Sometimes this will be a requirement of the essay – as in the question shown as an example. Even here, the part it plays, although important, is limited and is only useful in relation to the whole subject. Long digressions, which are remotely connected to the topic, should be avoided.

3. Whatever the writer's own viewpoint, it must be stated only after a logical case (based on evidence and reasoning) has been presented, when it can be see as the outcome of this process. Statements beginning 'I think' or 'I believe' or 'In my opinion' are always suspect and usually precede a statement which cannot be seen to rest on any rational approach. The discussion must be impartial and the assessment at the end must be seen as emerging from a balanced debate. In this way, even if the examiner disagrees, he must reward the unbiased and comprehensive examination of the question.

Examination questions which are set as articles

Occasionally the wording of an examination question will ask for an article, not for a straightforward essay. It might also suggest at what readership it should be aimed, by indicating that the article would be for a business supplement of a national newspaper or for a professional journal. If this is so, then two points need to be borne in mind by the candidate.

The first point is that the language and style of the article should be carefully

Institute Education

Examination technique-4

In last month's article we covered certain types of question. This month, in the last of this series by the Institute's education officer, Gordon Owen, we move onto the presentation of answers — an area of considerable importance to Institute examiners.

A maximum of 10 per cent of the marks on any one question can be allocated for presentation. In practice the actual mark that can be attained is based upon the mark gained for technical content. Thus someone who gets approximately 45 per cent on technical content alone, could get the other 5 per cent needed to pass, purely on presentation. To gain this 5 per cent, the presentation would have to be exceptionally good. In other words the maximum mark for presentation is roughly 10 per cent of the mark achieved for the technical content. The presentation of answers covers a multitude of aspects from spelling, use of English and the logic of arguments included, to the general layout and approach to the answer. The mark awarded is arrived at by taking an overall impression so it is not really possible to single out specific aspects to indicate how they might affect the presentation mark. Poor spelling and English will give a poor impression, as will muddled arguments and logic. The introduction of new themes, factors or aspects of the answer will best be made by commencing new paragraphs and thus breaking what could otherwise be a long, seemingly unstructured answer which may jump from one point to another in a haphazard manner.

Where it is felt appropriate to illustrate answers by means of diagrams, these should not be freehand. The examiners will expect rulers, symbol templates and coloured pencils to be used as appropriate. All diagrams, as well as the axes of graphs, should be clearly labelled. Throughout the examination, candidates should keep in mind the possibility of including diagrams to illustrate and thus improve the quality of their answer.

Ambiguity

To wind up this series of articles on examination technique it seems appropriate to mention something about dealing with possible ambiguity in questions and the actual role of the Institute's examiners and assessors. On ambiguity, whilst every endeavour is made to ensure that questions are not ambiguous, it is a fact of life that ambiguous questions will not always be recognised at the moderation stage, with the unfortunate consequence that there will be the odd case where the ambiguity does not come to light until the question is used. Where a question is seen as ambiguous there is no need to be frightened off, by not answering it. Even if the ambiguous nature of a question is not recognised by an individual, what usually happens in practice is that the various approaches which can be taken, are made and thus the examiner quickly spots these alternatives in the early part of the marking process. Once it has been spotted he will then endeavour to ensure that each answer is marked in accordance with the way the student saw it, assuming that it was a valid interpretation, and thus no one will be disadvantaged.

If the ambiguity is recognised by a student and he does not know which way to proceed, then the recommended procedure is to make a statement at the start of the question to the effect that different interpretations can be placed on the meaning of the question, followed by the way one then intends to tackle the question.

If it seems appropriate then there is no reason why both ways may not be covered, for the examiner is not going to disadvantage any student because of such an unfortunate occurrence.

As part of the Institute's examining philosophy the following two entries taken out of the guideline notes to examiners may be of interest:

- the examinations are not seen as a battle of wits between the examiner and the examinee, but a vehicle for the examinee to display his knowledge and understanding of a given topic.

- examiners are instructed that if an answer 'is a reasonable and feasible answer to the question posed' it must be marked in accordance with the line taken by the candidate, and not in accordance with any preconceived ideas.

Examiners and Assessors

The examination procedure itself has two stages. Firstly, an ordinary examiner makes the initial marking and then all of the scripts are passed, together with the detailed markings, directly to a senior examiner, who is known as an assessor. He is a person of longer standing in the Institute's examining system than most other examiners, who over the years has proved himself most capable and competent to take an impartial view and maintain a consistency of standard over a range of subjects. It should be said that the Institute does not use examiners who are so specialist in a particular subject, that they have a desire to push up standards year by year to the point where no one is able to pass. Thus, in the main, all assessors have a wide range of expertise, and through their experience will endeavour to maintain a consistency of standard from not just examination to examination, but from year to year. An increase in standards would only be made where specifically announced in advance, and usually through the introduction of a new programme of study.

Note for internal examinations, it would be the lecturer who taught the subject who would first mark, and then the scripts would be considered by the external examiner attached to the college.

Apart from the role of maintaining consistency of standards, the assessor needs to ensure that where

Fig. 24   An article on examination techniques from Management Services, May 1983 (courtesy of the Institute of Management Services).

chosen to respond to the type of reader suggested. This will, of course, affect how many technical terms can be used without definition, and how much explanation needs to be given. The second point is that an article has a slightly several examiners are reporting to him on the same subject, they are applying consistent standards and have taken the same approach to problem questions so that no one is disadvantaged by virtue of an individual examiner's approach. When the examiners do their marking, they are not required to make any adjustments where they feel someone might be marginal. This is the assessor's job, and he will make such adjustments when he is fully satisfied about the general standards applied by the examiner(s) reporting to him. If by any chance he is unhappy with the markings of an examiner, it may be necessary for him to completely re-mark all answers. He will then look at border-lines, passes as well as fails, and adjust the result accordingly after due reflection. An approach taken by some assessors when looking at borderline cases is to read the whole script through as a totality, irrespective of how individual answers match up to individual question requirements.

Then after reading the whole script, ask themselves whether if that person presented himself before them for a job, they would be prepared to employ him or not. If the impression gained is that the person does match up to that condition, then they would increase the total mark to a pass level.

Some do's and don'ts

DON'T
● make gratuitous statements.
● include chunks of pre-prepared work learnt by heart.
● give BSI definitions unless specifically called for.
● keep making the same point, but in different ways.
● allow your answers to wander away from the point.

REMEMBER TO
● analyse the question before putting pen to paper in order to determine the component parts.

● make rough notes, or at least jot down headings and factors etc so that you keep to the point of the question.
● read through your answer afterwards in order to correct obvious errors and where necessary add in additional material that comes to mind at that point.

Finally, candidates working in a nationalised undertaking or multi-national company with its own data banks, procedures and practices etc, should not approach every question from the point of view of his or her own company, which is sometimes evidenced in scripts. The examiners will interpret this as a very blinkered and limited view of the outside world. The use of examples drawn from one's own employment is good, but candidates should recognise that their own employers' procedures and practices might not necessarily constitute an acceptable answer. ∎

Fig. 24 (Continued)

different format from an essay. It will need a headline, for example, to attract the attention of the reader. Sometimes subheadings will be needed, too, for, if the article is long or complex, these help to guide the reader and make the subject matter more digestible. Above all, an article must aim to attract initially and then retain the interest of its readers.

Figure 24 shows an example of an article.

Conclusion

The essay remains the most comprehensive and demanding of exercises in written communication. Because of this it has been retained as a test, by professional and academic bodies, of a candidate's ability. Considerable attention must be given to the techniques of planning and composition if high standards are to be achieved.

* * *

Suggested activities for interest

1. Analyse and evaluate the example plans given (Figs. 21, 22 and 23). Is there anything you would add and/or omit? Would you have planned them differently – if so, how? What illustrations would you have given from your individual experience under II 3(b) of Fig. 23?

2. As a piece of further reading and analysis, study an essay by a modern writer on a topic which interests you and try to break down the construction. Some suggestions for possible reading in this direction are given on page 225.

Suggested activity for self-evaluation

Give a full essay plan (as in the example given in Fig. 23) for the following subject which was taken from an ICSA paper entitled 'Management: Principles and Policy': 'Discuss the advantages and disadvantages of large scale organisations.'[20]

Part 3 | Oral communication - the need for effective techniques in a variety of business situations

8 Oral presentations – instructing, reporting and giving talks

Introduction

In any business career today, a number of situations arise in which an individual is required to prepare and deliver a clear oral presentation. Sometimes this will be for a small group or for one person (usually for one's immediate superior). Occasionally, however, it might be for a very large audience. Many find this an ordeal, perhaps because the English educational system (as opposed to the American one) does little to develop our oral skills or our confidence in public. When we are called upon to address a large group of people we experience 'stage-fright' – extreme nervousness, lack of voice control and, sometimes, 'drying-up'. This reaction is not unusual; many famous actors, politicians and monarchs have suffered in this way. Some, like Aneurin Bevan and George VI, have had speech impediments and still have had to face the heavy demands of public life. They were able to overcome the worst of their difficulties by hard work and constant application. The key to the improvement seems to have been constant and conscientious preparation.

In any act of oral communication, including the daily interchange of conversation and discussion at work, it helps if the fundemental objectives – to obtain understanding and the desired response – are kept in mind constantly. Thorough planning is an essential prerequisite of effective oral communication and is neglected often. Oral communication has every chance of being *more* effective than its written counterpart, since we can draw on a number of different media to assist us. All the advantages of what has been called 'body language' – expression, gesture and stance – can be employed to clarify our meaning and to persuade others to accept our ideas. We can vary the pitch, tone and volume of our voices to express differences in emphasis. We have a number of sophisticated audio-visual aids at our command to illustrate what we have to say and to add to the comprehension and interest of our audience.

A great deal of oral communication is unsatisfactory and fails to achieve its basic objectives. At the same time, people have come to expect a high degree of oral and visual communication. Consequently, expectations in the business world have changed, too, therefore, managerial staff have to have highly developed oral skills and demonstrable confidence. It is on their oral ability

95

that these people's daily effectiveness as communicators will depend, and it is on this that their potential for appointment or promotion will be assessed. This chapter will begin by giving some guidance on the most usual oral presentations at work, the written techniques for which have been examined in Part 2. Subsequent chapters will explore the planning and control of situations where effective oral *interaction* is essential.

Situations in which a formal oral presentation is required in business

Apart from daily conversation, there are certain situations that require the individual to prepare and deliver an oral presentation in a formal and structured manner. These are as follows:

1. Training or instructing newcomers in their induction period, or existing employees in a new task.
2. Reporting to a superior, a group of colleagues, or at a seminar.
3. Giving a talk on an area in which the individual's expertise, knowledge or experience is of interest to a wide audience. (This can sometimes include giving a speech at a social function connected with work.)

All these have much in common, in terms of preparation and planning, although the final outline or structure will differ slightly for each type of presentation. These common aspects will be discussed first, before some guidelines are given on the different structures required in each case. Later in the chapter, the choices of audio and visual aids as illustrative material, together with their most suitable application, will be examined. Finally, an indication of the characteristics and qualities needed for effective public speaking will be given.

Common factors in the preparation and planning of oral instructions, reports and talks

The initial questions

In every type of oral presentation, there are some essential questions that must be asked initially. These are as follows:

1. What is the main aim or objective of this particular presentation? Is it merely to inform (as in instruction) or is it to persuade the listener to accept recommendations, ideas or arguments (as in a report or talk)?
2. Who is the audience? How many are there? What is their position or job? What is their level of knowledge and technical familiarity with the subject? How old are they? What is the level of their interest and motivation likely to be? Are there likely to be any hostile reactions? (This can sometimes occur in instructing new procedures that people are reluctant to accept; in reporting, where one or more of the listeners may profoundly disagree with the recommendations made; or in talks, where the topic is controversial and opinion sharply divided among the audience.)

3. How much time is available for planning and preparation? How much time is available for actual presentation?

4. Where is the presentation to take place? Are the layout and conditions of the environment suitable? If training or instruction is to be given, can everyone see any demonstration which needs to be carried out? If visual and/or audio aids are to be used that require a power supply, where are the relevant plug points? If giving a talk, is the seating comfortable and arranged as the speaker would wish? If you are intending to use diagrams or slides, is it possible to do this in the intended location? What about heating, lighting, noise factors, etc?

5. What illustration or amplification does your presentation require (in terms of material which needs to be circulated), audio and/or visual aids and equipment, or objects for demonstration? Are these readily available, or will they take time to obtain or assemble? Can they be used in the intended environment, or will the methods planned for presentation need to be changed?

It is only when these questions have been answered fully that it becomes possible to plan the oral presentation in an appropriate manner to meet the specific requirements, which will have been systematically identified in this way.

The 'research' stage – gathering the material

The second stage in planning is to gather all the material you will need; this is likely to come from a variety of sources. An indication of the kinds of sources used in report writing was given in Chapter 4 and these are also relevant to preparing a talk. In giving instruction or training, however, the sources are likely to be rather different. They may be one of the following:

1. Personal observation, knowledge and experience of the job which is the subject of instruction.
2. Discussions with others who have similar knowledge and experience.
3. Manuals describing the operations or procedures concerned.
4. A job analysis or job description already in existence.

Whatever the sources, the relevant material should be selected carefully, according to the answers concerning aims, audience and timing. The note-taking techniques described in Chapter 2 will be of considerable assistance here, for full notes should be taken from all appropriate sources at this stage.

Planning the content and sequence

A careful note-form outline of the instruction, report or talk to be given can now be prepared. Again, the amount and type of content you include, and the sequence in which you arrange it, will rest on the time available. The presentation must begin with the audience's present level of knowledge and lead carefully from there through a logical sequence that can be followed clearly. In addition, there is the problem of deciding not *where* but *how* to begin, and this will depend on the level of interest and the amount of agreement on or hostility towards the subject of your presentation.

The content of your talk must be *selective* so that there is not too much for the audience to digest in the time available. The two most valuable aids in this part of the planning stage are as follows:

1. *Good, clear note-making* If you make notes with subheadings and numbered points, which are large enough and easy enough to refer to, you will not lose 'eye contact' with the audience. These will also prompt you with a sufficient number of cues to aid your memory and fluency. (Comprehensive guidance on this is given in Chapter 2.)

2. *Practice* If you practise with a tape recorder, or rehearse in full, including any demonstrations necessary, you will ensure that your timing is correct. If you can find a surrogate audience to listen to your talk and give constructive criticism, this can help enormously. Listeners may also assist you in deciding on the best introduction.

Choosing an introduction

In oral reporting and instructing, this does not really constitute a problem. A statement of the objectives and of the plan you intend to follow is the most helpful way to begin. Your audience will then have a clear understanding of what is to follow, and see the point of the exercise – an aid not only to comprehension but also to motivation.

The first step is to capture the attention of the audience and to stimulate a *favourable* attitude, if possible, to what is to be said. There are several ways in which to do this, as follows:

1. *Shock tactics* Anticipate the audience's likely reaction and preconcieved notions on the topic, paraphrase these and then lead into the arguments which might change them. This is particularly useful where hostility is likely to be present, e.g. 'Some of you in this training group/audience may well be saying "Not another computerised system which is bound to create more trouble than it's worth", but...'

2. *A question* Begin with a question which they might have asked themselves, e.g. 'Why are the communications in this organisation always so appalling?'

3. *Contrasted facts or statistics* Begin with contrasted statistics which provide a shock to the audience. It is best if these are brief and in round figures, for they must be grasped quickly, e.g. 'We spend a average of ten years at school; yet 60 per cent of school leavers have no O levels'.

4. *A joke, anecdote or story* This is usually more suitable for social occasions, but it can be used in talks on aspects of business, and in training groups, and it *can* be effective. It must, however, be strictly relevant and extremely short, preferably containing an *unexpected* 'twist' at the end which will lead into the topic. A willingness to tell jokes against yourself will normally bring most audiences on to your 'side'!

5. *A quotation* This must be pithy, short, *relevant* and by someone well known to your audience. Preferably it should be humorous.

6. *A local reference* A reference to someone well known, or to the local area, can prove interesting.

Care must be taken, of course, that the selected opening is appropriate to the situation and clearly leads into the main topic. The objectives and planned structure can then follow briefly, in order to guide the audience.

Choosing the appropriate language

The answers to the set of questions concerning the audience will determine this. (If the listener is a superior, for example, the language will be formal. It is possible, however, that he will have little familiarity with some aspects of, say, a specialist report. Technical or professional terms will need explanation therefore.) The degree of explanation needed and the vocabulary chosen can be decided only after a careful analysis of the audience. The principle of choosing the language of the receiving group (discussed in Chapter 1) is very relevant here. Two pitfalls must be avoided – assuming knowledge where there is none (if in doubt, explain the term used) or 'talking down' to the audience, which is liable to produce impatience and resentment.

Choosing a conclusion

The oral report should end with its recommendations and the instruction should end with a summary of what has been said, perhaps reinforced by a précis hand-out. It may indicate also what the next phase is to be in the learning process if it is part of a continuing training course. Concluding a talk may pose a problem to the speaker. Some kind of summary, of course, must be given. A brief review of the main points made clarifies the major issues and revises them. If the talk has been such that a number of alternative solutions or conclusions are possible concerning the problem under discussion, then a choice of these can be offered for their further consideration. If the speaker favours one particular alternative, then weight can be given to this in his closing remarks.

In addition to summarising and offering alternatives, however, the speaker may wish to leave the audience with points for further consideration, food for thought, or even an appeal for action. If an action is required of the audience, then aiming at their conscience, or offering some kind of incentive (even if this is only to point out the benefit which they may gain from taking action), is likely to increase their response.

Whichever method seems most appropriate, it is important to remember that a conclusion should be precisely that, not another talk! Once having said 'Finally' or 'In conclusion', it is not a good idea to carry on speaking for very long. The audience will expect a quick close, and the talk will be more effective if this is done.

The note-form plan, when complete, will take into consideration all the initial questions. In addition, it should provide a draft introduction and conclusion, for it is at these points in any presentation that a speaker should be particularly sure of his 'lines', if the listeners are to perceive him as confident and professional, and to be aware of the main objectives, facts and arguments. The plan forms an outline, which should help the speaker to convey a clear structure to the audience so that it may easily follow and understand what is said. Although this structure will differ slightly with the subject matter, there are some standard divisions which are found in the well planned oral instruction or report, or talk, and it will be useful to mention these now.

Standard structures for oral instructions, oral reports and talks

Oral instructions

The typical major divisions will be as follows:

1. *Introduction* This gives the *objectives* of the instruction, stating what the trainee should be able to accomplish by the time it is complete and what part this particular task plays in the work he will be expected to undertake. It states *aims* and gives *reasons* to motivate the trainee(s).

2. *Explanation of the task* This is an oral explanation of the task in stages, beginning with the trainee's previous knowledge and building on this gradually. At this stage, the trainee is required to *listen* (and to *watch* if diagrams or models are to be used). Questions may be asked at this stage, and time should be allocated for these.

3. *Demonstration of the task* Any task is easier to learn if the trainee can *see* how it is done. This part of the instruction may require the use of equipment, machinery or paper examples of procedures (how to fill in forms, reports etc.). The demonstration should be accompanied by an oral commentary following the same stages as the original explanation. It will thus reinforce and extend the trainee's initial understanding. Again, time should be allowed for questions.

4. *Participating in the task* The best way to check whether any trainee has understood is to ask him to undertake the task, watched by the instructor, and preferably to 'talk it through' too. If there is a large group of trainees, only one or two may be able to do this but, ideally, each trainee should participate. The instructor needs to *correct* mistakes as they occur, preventing the formation of a permanent error – we all learn bad work habits quickly. Here, all the trainee's senses are actively involved, reinforcing and extending the previous two learning stages; participatory involvement also acts as a motivator. In the cases of some training, participation may be in a group activity, e.g. managerial training for problem solving.

5. *Checking, questioning and review* A final check, on whether the main points or principles have been understood by all, now has to be carried out. Beware of the open question – 'Have you all understood?' – unlikely to produce a negative reply! Specific questions on the main points need to be put to specific members of the group. These will clarify for everyone present the main points over which difficulties may arise, or the main principles which are fundamental to the objectives of that training session.

6. *Concluding the instruction* The conclusion needs to summarise the main points and principles learned (and relate them to the next session to be held, if

this is part of a training course). A written hand-out may be given, summarising the main points made, or reference may be made to the appropriate manual to be consulted if trainees are in any doubt. Occasionally, especially during induction training, an experienced employee, who is willing and able to answer any queries which trainees may have, may be named.

Oral reports

The typical divisions will be as follows:

1. *Introduction* This contains the *objectives* of the report, describing the situation which gave rise to its instigation, the reasons for which it was undertaken, its main purpose and its *terms of reference*. These state its *aims*, *mandate* and *background*.

2. *Methodology* The main sources of information consulted or the major methods of investigation chosen should be *briefly* described; reasons for the choices of sources and/or methods, and any limitations or difficulties experienced should also be mentioned here (e.g. if a questionnaire method was used, only 20 per cent may have been returned; some information may have been unavailable for security reasons, etc.)

3. *Analysis and findings* This will be the main part of the presentation; it may be illustrated in various ways with diagrams, charts, statistics or even pictorial displays. These might be circulated as hand-outs or appear as appendices, but it is probably best to include some visual aids to help the speaker, too. Those available and appropriate are discussed later in this chapter. As this is likely to be the longest part of the presentation, it is very important that a good note-form outline, with clear subheadings and points, should have been prepared by the speaker if the listeners are to follow his analysis.

4. *Conclusions and recommendations* These should be deduced from the analysis and it should be clear to the audience that they are derived logically from the previous section. No new material should be introduced at this stage. The conclusion should summarise the major points, facts and priorities for action and the recommendations should give a number of viable solutions. These should be put persuasively if they are to further the speaker's purpose effectively and meet the original objectives stated. A clear argument should be used throughout, and a copy of the report and relevant data should be circulated for further reference. A question and answer session may follow, for which the speaker should be prepared.

Talks

A talk is likely to vary in its structure rather more than the previous two types of presentation. Nevertheless, there are some major divisions that will normally appear. These are as follows:

1. *The introduction* This should always state the *objectives* and *intended structure* of the talk, but the initial sentence must gain the attention and interest of all the members of the audience, who may have varied interests and

opinions. Methods of achieving this have already been suggested earlier (see pages 98–99).

2. *The main body of the talk* This is likely to have the following pattern:

(a) Presentation of the main point to be made.

(b) Reasons/evidence in support of this.

(c) Illustrations and examples.

(d) Possible objections, with evidence.

(e) Summary of position on this point. The speaker's reasons must be logically deduced from the composed points in favour versus objections previously discussed.

(f) Presentation of the second main point to be made; this should be followed by a repetition of the pattern above.

The main body of the talk should be prepared carefully in a note-form outline, where each main point is given a clear subhead and the points for and against noted below this, with examples to be given. (Guidance on this appears in Chapter 2.) Audio and/or visual aids may be used as illustration, as may hand-outs of statistics or data which are otherwise difficult to remember. (The choice of aids and their applications appears later in this chapter.) They should be carefully selected to be relevant and simple if they are to be effective.

3. *The conclusion* This must contain a summary of the main facts and arguments, a review of these and an assessment. It may, however, ask the audience to consider the topic further or to undertake some action in reponse to the talk. It should be brief and may be accompanied by a written précis hand-out, if appropriate. (Various types of conclusion are discussed in more detail on pages 99–100.) The talk may be followed by a 'question-time' session and the speaker should have allocated time for this and be prepared for the likely questions.

The last part of the planning process involves the choice of appropriate audio and visual aids, and we shall now examine what is available.

Choosing appropriate audio and visual aids for oral presentations – planning for their effective use and management

There are an increasing number of visual, and audio visual, aids to oral presentation. In addition, other illustrative material can be given in hand-out form, and equipment can be used to demonstrate tasks in training sessions. All these have the advantage that they involve the audience's visual sense, which assists the memory by giving the words a visual application. It is always easier to remember what we have seen than what we have heard, and it is easier still to recall information that has been reinforced in both ways. If the aids available are to be effective, they need to be chosen carefully as their applications vary and some are particularly suited to the communication of specific types of material. Aids can be expensive. Used badly, they can distort and confuse; used well they can be interesting, entertaining and memorable, thus justifying their cost.

Let us examine the ways in which each aid might best be applied. The following check list might prove helpful:

Black and white boards

These are most useful for the following:

1. Building up information or ideas in training groups.
2. Illustrating something quickly to clarify a misunderstanding which has become evident.
3. Displaying permanent themes to which reference will be made throughout the oral presentation.
4. Clarifying alternatives.
5. Erasing and changing ideas in 'brain-storming' groups.

Their main advantages are that you can change the information on them easily and they are not prone to breakdown! The main disadvantages are that the chalk or felt tip pen are rather messy and cannot be kept on permanently.

Magnetic boards, slot-, pin-, felt-boards, etc.

These are most useful for the following:

1. Building up visual presentations.
2. Building up flexible displays where pieces can be moved.

Their main advantages are that they create dramatic effect and more interest than the traditional boards. For this reason they are used for television displays – movable maps for the weather report, etc. They are permanent and can be used again and again. Their main disadvantages are that, unless they are kept simple, they can confuse. They are also expensive to make and are heavy to transport.

Flip charts

These are useful for the following:

1. Providing background information during a presentation.
2. Providing major themes in sequence which can be flipped over.
3. Building up group presentations – recording facts or data from syndicate work, using one or more sheets for each group's findings.
4. Building up information in successive stages on separately headed sheets.

Their main advantage is that they allow a sequence of information to be built up, each part of which can be revealed successively. Their main disadvantages are that they can be unwieldy and difficult to manage – as each sheet can tear when being folded back or can come apart. They can be untidy and the information presented too small.

Objects, models and equipment

These are most useful for the following:

1. Providing examples that the audience may never have seen, e.g. of a product, piece of equipment or component.

2. Demonstrating a process, concept, procedure or task.
You must practise in advance, so that the demonstration or display is professional and is carried out smoothly.

Their main advantages are that they are 'real', adding interest, vitality and involvement and they are invaluable in training in that the trainee can practise the task for himself. In reporting, they elucidate the written word, and, in talks, they add an important dimension of reality. Their disadvantages are that not everyone can see them and that even the most carefully constructed model, or reliable piece of apparatus, will fail to work sometimes.

Overhead projectors

These are devices for projecting prepared transparencies, or spontaneous writing or drawing, on to a screen, above and behind the speaker. They are useful for the following:

1. Showing complex visual displays, which can be achieved by overlaying and masking.
2. Emphasing the main themes to be discussed, which can be displayed separately.
3. Displaying neatly prepared images, diagrams or charts.

It is important to check that the image is straight. If pointing, use a pencil. (fingers tend to shake!) on the projector plate *not* on the screen. Remember to switch off after each viewfoil, when the need to see it has passed.

Their main advantages are that the viewfoils or transparencies can be prepared neatly, kept permanently and used again, and that the speaker need not turn his back on the audience to write, or point at, anything, thus maintaining 'eye contact'. Colour and light are both added advantages in keeping an audience's attention, and acting as visual stimuli. Their main disadvantages are that some are noisy, having a fan component, and that they can be fatiguing for the audience if kept on for long periods, or annoying if kept on after the image displayed has ceased to be under discussion.

Slide projector

This is useful for the following:

1. Showing real photographs of people, works of art, places or objects.
2. Showing microscope slides as photographs.
3. Showing diagrams, plans or charts that are very complex.
4. Giving a synchronised tape and slide display.
5. Magnification.

It is best to preload slides in a magazine, in order that they appear in the proper sequence and in the right position, and to prepare a smooth-linking commentary or tape recording.

Films, videos, closed-circuit television (cctv)

Most useful for the following:

1. Showing something you could not otherwise bring into the room at all – an expensive piece of equipment, an unusual process, another geographical location, for example.
2. Giving a dramatised example to illustrate a specific situation (e.g. health and safety hazards) in a particulary memorable way.
3. Demonstrating examples of interaction, e.g. negotiations or interviews for the purposes of critical appraisal.
4. Simulations, e.g. to teach driving or flying in an 'off-the-job' safe environment.

You must ensure that the person who is doing the operating is competent to do so and that the film is selected carefully. The main advantage is that this method combines instruction with entertainment, making it a more memorable medium. It also allows access to those things which it is impossible to show by any other means. The main disadvantages are expense, the need for a special location and the possibility of breakdown.

Hand-outs

These are most useful for the following:

1. Giving extra diagrammatic or written material for the reference of the audience.
2. Giving extra charts, data or diagrams to illustrate reports or to distribute during instruction.
3. Giving a summary at the end of a training session and giving a subheaded outline of a talk or lecture.

Their main advantages are that they provide something accuratè and permanent for the audience, and that they amplify or summarise what is being said. Their main disadvantage is that, unless they are produced at the right time, or referred to and explained well, they may distract or confuse the audience. They can be ignored altogether.

Tape recorders

These are mainly useful for the following:

1. Critical appraisal of communication skills, i.e. preparing talks, monitoring interaction in interviews, meetings, etc.
2. Teaching language skills of all kinds.
3. Illustrating training sessions on communication skills.
4. Illustrating other sounds in instruction.

Their main advantages are that they are simple to operate, they provide a very useful self-monitoring device for learning, and the tapes are inexpensive. Their main disadvantage is that some people become very self-conscious when on tape, or have their confidence shaken by hearing their own voice.

When planning to use aids for a presentation, you must remember not to use too many in one presentation, as this tends to confuse, and to organise the layout of the location in advance. Aids to oral presentation should always be simple, clear, relevant and integrated into that presentation. The presenter should be well rehearsed in their use, and have a contingency plan for an alternative method of presentation in case of breakdown.

Having prepared a note-form plan to meet all the initial requirements identified, which is suited to the type of oral presentation to be undertaken, and having chosen the appropriate audio and/or visual aids carefully, the next step is the delivery itself.

Characteristics and qualities essential to effective public speaking

There are two elements which are important in successful public speaking. The first concerns the physical persona, the appearance and characteristics of the speaker, for our perception is affected by the speaker's voice, eyes, expression, gesture, mannerisms and stance. The second element which creates an impression on an audience concerns the qualities demonstrated by the speaker in his expertise, his attitude towards his subject, and the way in which he approaches his audience and presents his material. These will affect his credibility and arouse or destroy interest and understanding in those who listen.

Characteristics of the speaker

1. *The voice* The speaker should try to speak audibly and with variety. Audibility will be considerably improved if the speaker has good clear notes to which he refers briefly. If he writes them in large letters on a card, he can keep his head up, projecting his voice to the back of the room. Reading close-written notes means that the speaker's voice is projected downwards and that the audience is presented with a very boring view of the top of his head!

Variety in tone, pace and volume helps to give emphasis where it is needed or to indicate an anecdote or digression. It also prevents the monotone that either sends the listeners to sleep or makes them daydream! Another point to watch out for is whether the ends of sentences get lost, for, in the normal pattern of English speech, the voice drops at this point. It is a good idea to practise on tape and to listen for the intonation.

Ideally, the voice should be flexible, acting rather like a musical instrument accompanying and enhancing the main theme. It *must* be heard.

2. *The eyes* 'Eye contact' with the audience is extremely important in creating rapport and interaction between the speaker and his listeners. It conveys the speaker's interest in them, and allows him to monitor their level of understanding and motivation. Eye contact is vital in training or giving instructions; it is extremely useful in any oral presentation for it allows the speaker to respond to the needs of his audience and, if necessary, to adjust his approach to a more appropriate one. Any actor knows how important this kind of flexibility is, if the attention of the audience is to be held, and if its sympathy with the speaker and his subject matter is to be maintained. Having prepared notes, which can be quickly referred to rather than read, assists this process. The speaker should also avoid staring out of the window, at a spot on

the wall or at the clock, all of which tend to reflect the fact that the audience is not there! It is not, however, a good idea to stare at one member of the audience – a very uncomfortable situation for him!

3. *Expression* The audience, listener or group will be looking at the speaker's face. For this reason the speaker's expression should indicate the right kind of response to the audience and to the subject matter. The eyes are very expressive, as is the mouth – whether we smile or not, for example.

Initially the speaker needs to look cheerful, confident and glad to see his audience – there is nothing more off-putting than someone who appears miserable or bored. As the presentation continues, he needs to show *enthusiasm* for his subject and give *quick responses* to the questions and comments of his listeners. Expressions which change according to what is said give an impression of intelligence and vivacity – much more likely to arouse interest than inscrutability, however desirable that might be in a game of poker!

4. *Gesture* Gestures can be used very effectively in oral presentation to emphasise, explain and demonstrate. Politicians and actors use them to make an impact. The English seem to fear gesture as somehow overdramatic or foreign – of course no one would recommend presenting an oral report, accompanied by arms flailing about. Nevertheless, controlled gestures can be used to great effect.

5. *Mannerisms* Mannerisms of speech, and moving about whilst speaking, should be avoided as they are extremely distracting. The speaker who interjects 'er – er', 'you know', or 'um – well', every few seconds, is likely to have his audience counting the number of times he uses these expressions, rather than listening to him. The speaker who paces up and down, jingles money or keys, drums fingers, or taps with pen or pencil, is likely to create more distraction than interest. This is really a question of control and confidence and brings us to the problem of stance.

6. *Stance and posture* The speaker should stand upright, should neither lean on the desk with both hands, which tends to project the voice in the wrong direction, nor stoop to look at notes, since this destroys eye contact. Weight should be evenly balanced, so that the speaker does not shift disconcertingly from one foot to the other, creating a swaying effect. Pacing about should be avoided, too, as should facing the board or diagram display, and, therefore, having your back to the audience. Again this breaks eye contact. The final problem is what to do with your hands. If cards, for reference, or a pointer, for visual aids, is used, this tends to take care of any awkwardness.

The rules to observe are to maintain a confident upright posture, which is generally still and calm, and to look at and to speak to the audience. This creates an impression of assurance which will be imparted to the audience and tend to increase their own confidence in the speaker – a fidgety or nervous speaker has the opposite effect.

As well as the physical charactersitics exhibited by the speaker, the qualities and attitudes which he demonstrates will condition the degree to which he is acceptable – and credible – to the audience. Let us, therefore, examine the qualities that seem to promote effective oral communication.

Effective qualities in a speaker

There are a number of distinct qualities which are fundamental to success in public speaking. These can be indentified as follows:

1. *Expertise and enthusiasm* The greater the expertise the speaker has in his subject, and the more thorough his preparation, the more credible he will be. This is why the research and planning stages are so crucial to the success of any oral presentation. In addition to a sound knowledge, however, the speaker needs to have a keen interest in his topic, for enthusiasm, like confidence, communicates itself to the audience – it is infectious. Similarly, a bored speaker will create nothing but boredom. To listen to someone who is both well informed and stimulating can be a satisfying and, at best, an inspiring experience. These two qualities are probably the most important in rendering an oral presentation effectively.

2. *Honesty and sincerity* Even though a speaker may be well qualified and have researched his subject well, there may be some questions raised by the audience that he cannot answer. This can happen in any situation – in instruction, reporting or at the end of a talk. It is essential that he should not try to 'bluff'; it is always obvious, and will lose him both credibility and respect. The most honest reply has to be: 'I'm sorry, I don't know; but I will find out and make sure you will receive the correct information'. With training, this safeguards two people's competence – the speaker's and the trainee's – improving the quality of work as a whole. In reporting, it proves that the speaker is concerned for the truth above all, thus establishing that his research for the rest of the report is likely to have been painstaking and objective. In a talk, it demonstrates a genuine desire to respond to the audience's needs.

If the speaker is sincere – believing in the message he is attempting to convey – then he will inspire trust in his words. Even if a member of the audience is in disagreement, he is likely to respect his opinions if he feels that they are sincerely held and are based on sound arguments. No speaker, however, is likely to command a credulous audience if it thinks that he is presenting a case because he has been told to do so, or because it is in his interests to do so.

3. *Respect for the audience and lack of bigotry* It is important, however, not to mistake sincerity for bigotry, and to respect opinions and arguments that may be expressed by members of the audience. Any speaker needs to keep an open mind and to be willing to modify his own views, if a sound point or good evidence is presented to the contrary. Even with training, this can happen – sometimes the trainee, fresh to a task, may see an easier, safer or quicker way to do something. It would be obstinate stupidity not to accept it and incorporate it into later training. Accepting constructive criticism is an important demonstration of the speaker's respect for his audience. To be patronising or defensive creates resentment which will render the speaker and

his message unacceptable, making his presentation ineffective as a result.

4. *Humour* Oral presentations can be nerve-racking ordeals; they also have the potential for conflict. One of the best ways of defusing these situations is by the demonstration of a healthy sense of humour. It helps in responding to an audience, in gaining its sympathy and interest, and in making any topic more entertaining – and therefore, more memorable. (People often remember what has amused them and then, by association, remember the serious points that it illustrated.) It can help combat hostility, provided the humour used is gentle, not barked ridicule or sarcasm. Above all, an ability to take or even make a joke at our own expense when something has gone catastrophically wrong (audio visual aids are a typical source of disaster) usually induces laughter and help, rather than mockery.

Finally, one useful tip, when doing any public speaking – do not speak too quickly. This is an easy trap to fall into when you are nervous; the result is that your talk is delivered in a garbled manner. It is vital that you speak slowly and carefully, therefore, and, as already mentioned, it helps, too, if you vary the tone and volume of your voice.

Conclusion

This chapter has been concerned with oral communication in situations that are one sided. The techniques and principles of preparation, planning, presentation and delivery discussed have all been related to the presentations of monologues by a single speaker to one listener or more. (Although some questioning may take place at times, there is really only one person attempting a sustained communication process.) Consequently, if the guidelines are followed, and sufficient practice and review undertaken, it should be a relatively straightforward process to improve the standards of oral present-ation continually. Potential for promotion may be recognised as a result of an effective oral presentation.

As an individual's career develops, the demands on his ability in public speaking are liable to increase. This is not only in circumstances where he, alone, is privileged to speak on a previously planned basis, however, but also in the many business situations where he is faced with the more complex problems of initiating and controlling dialogue and group interaction. It is with these more demanding situations that the remaining chapters on oral communication are concerned.

* * *

Suggested activities for interest and self-evaluation

1. Look back at suggested activity 2 at the end of Chapter 2. List the audio and/or visual aids you would use in this situation and give a reason for each.

2. Analyse a talk/lecture you have attended recently, or one broadcast on the radio or television, by answering the following questions:

(a) What was used to open the programme? Was it successful in attracting the attention of the audience?

(b) Were there any characteristics or qualities demonstrated by the presenter(s) which you found successful or unsuccessful? Why?

(c) How well was the talk or lecture structured? Could you see a clear outline? Try to note down the main points it made.

(d What illustrative material did it use? How successful was it?

(e) What was used to close the programme? What advantages and/or disadvantages did it have?

(f) Would you have used a different opening and/or closing gambit? If so, what would you have done and why?

The programmes prepared for the Open University are particularly useful here, but any talk or lecture that interests you could be used.

9 | Meetings – using valuable time

Meetings and the manager – a cost effective approach

Rosemary Stewart[21] and others found, in surveys of managerial work, that between 35 per cent and 50 per cent of any manager's time is spent in meetings of one kind or another; many managers would put it even higher than that. Yet the conduct and the outcome of meetings are often criticised severely; we have all heard the wry comments which meetings have attracted: 'A camel is a horse designed by a committee'; 'A committee is a body of people who keep minutes and waste time'; and 'A meeting is a process by which a body of people decide when to have the next meeting'.

There is little doubt that there is some truth in these allegations and that valuable manpower hours can be wasted by ineffectual meetings, both formal and informal.

Too often, this is because the person officially in command of the meeting is ill-prepared, lacks the expertise to lead and control a group, or is unaware of the communication problems which may arise. It may also be because those who attend the meeting have been briefed inadequately as to its intended content, in which case they, too, will lack preparation, or arrive with 'hidden agendas' – objectives of their own which have little to do with the original aims of the meeting. These will often dominate the discussion. All these problems and more have been explored amusingly in one of John Cleese's excellent management training films, which goes by the title of *Meetings, Bloody Meetings*[22]. The title itself is an indication of the reactions of many who have had the misfortune to suffer the frustration of lengthy and apparently pointless discussions where the outcome is vague and time is wasted.

In this chapter, the differences and similarities between informal meetings (by far the most frequent) and formal meetings will be explored, and the essential requirements in terms of preparation, procedures, control and record-keeping will be discussed. As with every other method of communication, a systematic approach must be adopted if it is to be effective, and *only* if it is effective can a meeting be worth its cost.

Types of meetings: differences and similarities

The definition of a meeting is a legal one, based on case law precedent – 'the coming together of at least two persons for any legal purpose'. This, however, is more relevant to formal meetings (such as statutory meetings of companies and public institutions – 'an assembly of persons meeting in accordance with legally-defined rules and procedures to discharge business as required by law') than informal ones.

Differences between informal and formal meetings

1. Informal meetings do not have a constitution, a set procedure or specific needs for documentation; they are usually called and controlled by the most senior member present, in order to meet the requirements of routine planning or the exigencies of problem-solving. They can be advisory in nature – the senior member retaining the right to make the final decision. The majority of meetings held at work are of this type, yet far too little consideration is given to the methods by which they are conducted, and to their results. They may degenerate easily into unstructured discussion, yet the person controlling the meeting has to achieve two basic objectives – to accomplish a task and to maintain the group as a team working towards this.

2. Formal meetings, on the other hand, always have a set constitution and procedure, as well as basic terms of reference. These may be defined by Memoranda, Articles of Association, Acts of Parliament, Standing Orders, or other forms of written constitution, according to the type of institution, public body or organisation in which they take place, and the requirements of company law.

Formal meetings have officers to conduct their business and record their proceedings and are controlled by a Chairman or President who is elected or appointed and has well-defined duties. Meetings can be executive in nature and decisions are taken by voting. Written documentation is an essential requirement. As the procedure is laid down, such meetings are perhaps a little easier to control, but the main objectives, as already stated for informal meetings, are just as relevant. Having contrasted the two types of meetings, it is now useful to see what they have in common.

Similarities between informal and formal meetings

The similarities between these two broad divisions lie in *the general objectives and aims* and in *the problems of leadership and control* which are common to both. They may attempt to promote good communication in the following ways:

1. To give instructions, to test opinion and to provide opportunities for feedback from all concerned.
2. To plan work or activity for the future.
3. To solve problems arising from work.
4. To provide an opportunity for discussion about any of 1 to 3, either between members of an organisation having similar responsibilities and

status, or between members of that organisation at different levels.

5. To provide an opportunity to 'pool' expertise and ideas, particularly in planning or problem-solving.

6. Resulting from either from 3, 4 or 5, to achieve *effective* action, backed by *joint consultation*, with all those people concerned with the action to be taken.

7. To record and communicate the policies, aims or required action for all those concerned.

In terms of leadership and control, there are two sets of specific objectives for either the person conducting the informal meeting or for the Chairman of a formal one. The first set relate to the achievement of the task itself; the second set relate to the control of the group working on that task. In each case, there are various functions which the leader should perform. These can be listed as follows:

1. *Task functions* These keep the group working on the task or project and include the following:

(a) Initiating – proposing tasks and goals, defining the group problem and suggesting procedures or ideas.

(b) Information/opinion seeking – requesting facts, seeking relevant information and asking for suggestions or ideas.

(c) Information/opinion giving – stating a belief and providing relevant information.

(d) Summarising – pulling together related ideas, restating suggestions after the group discussion and offering a decision or conclusion for the group.

(e) Clarifying – elaborating, interpreting or reflecting ideas and suggestions, clearing up confusion, indicating alternatives and issues, and giving examples.

(f) Consensus testing – checking to see how much agreement has been reached.

(g) Action planning – delegating the tasks, now agreed, to those appropriate, and confirming them in writing.

2. *Human relations or group maintenance functions* These ensure that the group works as a team to achieve the objective and they include the following:

(a) Encouragement – being friendly and responsive to the group, accepting contributions, and giving opportunities for recognition.

(b) Expressing group feelings – sensing feelings, moods and relationships within the group, and sharing one's feelings with others.

(c) Harmonising – attempting to reconcile arguments and to reduce tensions, and getting people to explore their differences (not always an easy task).

(d) Modifying – when the leader's own ideas or status is causing conflict he needs to modify his position, be able to admit error and maintain self-discipline for group cohesion (particularly difficult for some).

(e) Keeping the channels of communication open – ensuring participation by providing procedures for discussion.

(f) Evaluating – expressing standards for the group to achieve, evaluating the achievement and the degree of commitment to action.

Further common problems related to the control of groups

Perhaps the most difficult problem of leadership and control is one that concerns human relations – the individuals in any group have different personalities and objectives which condition how they behave. Although there is no space here to discuss the psychology of individuals and group dynamics at length, it may be worth enumerating some general principles.

1. Every group contains those who wish to talk and those who, for a variety of reasons, are silent. It is a mistake to suppose that the extrovert 'talkers' have necessarily the greatest contribution to make. Those who listen may have learnt more and may have considerable expertise!

2. In order to involve those who are silent, one or two strategies can be suggested. A procedure should be developed by which each person is asked for a contribution in turn, or the speaking time of those who normally have a great deal to say should be limited by inviting someone else to comment. Those members who are either shy (or withdrawn for some other reason) should be asked questions concerning their particular area of expertise; this combines the advantage of asking them something which they find easy to answer, thus developing their self-confidence, and giving them special recognition, to which they are likely to respond.

3. If conflict develops between two members of a group, the rest of the group should be asked to comment on the two sides. This avoids driving the conflict underground, where it is likely to smoulder, leading to withdrawal and frustration; it also avoids the leader taking sides. This is sometimes known as 'the conference method'.

4. If aggression is shown towards the leader, paraphrase the aggressive statement in a milder form, and ask the group to comment. If it becomes evident that there is truth in what is said, the leader must be prepared to modify – this is not 'backing down' but allows progress towards a new position.

5. If it becomes evident that some members of the group are repeating themselves and holding on tenaciously to one view only, the discussion should be stopped and the alternative views expressed should be summarised. Often it is helpful to do this in writing if a visual aid is available (a flip chart or board in the room is very useful). This prevents those members from retaining a mental image dominated by their own view, and can be used to move the discussion forward.

6. When agreement *seems* to be present, a true consensus must be reached *before* defining what action should be taken and allocating tasks, otherwise people will depart from the meeting still in disagreement and proceed to sabotage the recommended action by expressing doubts to others – often their own subordinates!

7. Ensure that everyone knows what *action* is expected, and that the meeting is not closed finally until this is decided. Too many meetings appear ineffective to those who have attended them because they leave, unsure what has been achieved and what results are expected. There is more motivation and

satisfaction if they are clear on these points, and a written reminder always helps.

These are some basic guidelines which have been found helpful in the difficult task of managing groups, whether in a formal or an informal meeting. It is now necessary to look in more detail at the different categories of informal and formal meetings and at the procedures which should be adopted for their conduct.

Informal meetings

Categories of informal meetings

'Informal meetings' is a very broad term covering a number of categories and these can be defined as follows:

1. *The briefing meeting* As its name suggests, this is normally called by a manager in order to give instructions to his work group, to train them in new tasks or to plan work. It is an extremely useful method of communication, giving people an opportunity to interpret policy, to test opinion and to give personal explanations. It allows people to ask questions and clarify for themselves what is required. It may even result in points and problems being given, which the manager (and possibly his superiors) may not have considered, thus avoiding difficulties in advance.

2. *The progress meeting* This reviews the progress of work, in discussing the problems which have arisen, measuring achievement and planning further action. The advantages, in terms of communication, are similar to those described for the briefing meeting. In addition, it allows problems to be detected and discussed at regular intervals so that they can be remedied quickly.

3. *The planning meeting* Similar to the previous two categories, this type of meeting may initiate a project, plan its strategy and allocate work to the appropriate divisions and personnel. Its main purpose is to achieve a rational approach to a task, in consultation with all those who can offer expertise or who will take part in its completion, thus taking advantage of their advice and achieving their support.

4. *The problem-solving meeting* This is called usually to attend to a particular emergency or solve a major problem which has arisen. All those who can offer advice, evidence, help or expertise should be consulted if adequate information is to be available to reach a solution, and if their support is to be forthcoming in putting it into action.

5. *The brain-storming meeting (also called a 'buzz group')* Connected with categories 3 and 4, this is a particular approach which can be taken when planning (for example, the marketing strategy of a new product) or problem-solving, when the causes of the problem may be particularly diverse, complex or impenetrable. It is the most unstructured of the meetings, as anyone present has a right to call out any ideas which may give a 'lead'. These are usually recorded on a flip chart or board; the elimination of the impossible or unlikely

ones is then followed by an open discussion of the others, until a few possible alternatives are chosen for further consideration or development.

6. *The 'T group'* This is one method sometimes used in management training circles ('T' stands for training) when self-criticism is promoted by allowing a group to comment freely on each others' characters, personalities, faults and virtues. Undoubtedly useful for senior managers whose subordinates are too job-dependent to offer any criticism, it can shock nevertheless – and needs to be handled very carefully!

Procedure of informal meetings

All the informal meetings categorised above, except for the 'T group', can be broadly described as 'command' or discussion meetings – command because they are normally called by a senior manager and controlled by him, and discussion because they allow subordinates to contribute, advise or question. In this sense they are also 'advisory' or 'consultative' meetings. Whether the manager acts finally on that advice, however, is at his discretion, so these meetings are rarely executive. They do, however, provide an extremely useful basis for managerial decision-making if conducted well and if the manager concerned takes their consultative function seriously.

Although they do not have a set procedure or rules in the sense that formal meetings do, there are nevertheless some basic principles which should be observed by anyone conducting such a meeting. These are as follows:

1. *Preparation* Any manager calling an informal meeting should try to give sufficient notice, by memorandum, of what he wishes to discuss. This should give *sufficient* explanation – not simply a topic heading if this is ambiguous. To quote *Meetings, Bloody Meetings*[23] once more, the incompetent manager (played, of course, by the inimitable John Cleese) asks for one item to be considered, which appears on his agenda as 'Communication'. One member interpreted this as telephones, one as a new layout for the house magazine, etc! Considerable impatience results and, of course, another meeting has to be planned. Later, he is accused of 'failing to signal his intention' and 'blatant time-wasting' – quite rightly.

In addition, the manager should request relevant information from those people he has asked to attend, and should circulate, with his memorandum, any information he has for their prior consideration. In this way, his staff are likely to arrive at the meeting already having given some thought to the problem.

The manager also needs to prepare a 'speaking procedure', related to the time available to spend on a particular problem, and to prepare an introduction which will clarify the objectives of the meeting and give any necessary background. Finally, he needs to prepare the environment – to ensure that interruptions are avoided and that coffee/tea will be available if necessary (both tend to promote concentration).

If the meeting is very urgent, and has been called quickly, then a brief explanation of the reason should be given on the telephone to focus the attention of those attending on the problem, and relevant information should be explained and circulated at the beginning of the meeting.

2. *Initiating* In the first few minutes of the meeting, the manager should clarify its objectives, give any further information he has on the subject and begin the 'speaking procedure' by calling on each person for their ideas and contributions.

3. *Observing the task and group maintenance functions* As the discussion develops, the manager should keep the group moving towards its objective, ensuring that it remains cohesive and that everyone participates by observing the task and group maintenance functions previously listed.

4. *Recording* The manager should take notes for his own reference and make notes on major alternatives for the reference of others.

5. *Check consensus and allocate work* The manager should ensure agreement and allocate work appropriately to achieve the action agreed.

6. *Confirmation* The manager should confirm to each attending member the decisions reached and the action required of that member in order to clarify, give an *aide-mémoire*, and confirm for both parties the expected results.

7. *Check and review* The manager should review the consequences and results and, if any problems have arisen, check *why* these have occurred. In addition he should modify instructions as a result of this check – it may even be necessary to hold a further meeting if the problems are serious. The check and review process is extremely valuable in assessing the effectiveness of the meeting and of the manager's own communication ability. This process helps him to evaluate, improve and progress and should thus be carried out conscientiously after each informal meeting. At its most sophisticated level, this check and review process has been introduced formally thoughout some companies as part of what is now called 'Organisation Development' and it is believed that it does promote company efffectiveness as a whole.

Formal meetings – categories and procedure

Categories of formal meetings and types of committee

There are two main categories into which all formal meetings may be divided initially before they are classified further; these are the *public meeting* and the *private meeting*. In *public meetings*, matters of public concern are discussed and obviously the public is allowed to attend them. Special provisions are made for the constitution and procedure of such meetings. In council meetings, for example, the rules by which they are conducted and their terms of reference are usually governed by Act of Parliament and approved Standing Orders. The British Parliament is exceptional – it operates on rules of procedure or what has been accepted by custom and practice throughout its history.

More usual, and more relevant to communication in business, is the *private meeting*. In this type of meeting, matters of interest to the specific organisation, institution, sector or division are discussed. The attendance is limited to a prescribed membership and the rules by which such meetings are conducted are written down. In the case of the statutory meetings of companies, they are governed by the Memoranda and Articles of Association required by company law. These define their aims, activities and procedures, and are lodged with the Registrar of Companies. In this category, too, there are the voluntary clubs, associations and societies which adhere to rules set out in a constitution drawn up by the founder members. These rules define their terms of reference and govern the composition of the committees concerned, as well as their procedure.

Formal meetings are usually conducted by some type of *committee* and these can be further classified into another five basic categories. These are as follows:

1. *The standing committee or meeting* This is a permanent committee meeting held, at regular intervals, to discuss matters in a continuous area. It keeps permanent records of work/decisions/progress in a minute book. Examples are board meetings, sports committees, vouluntary bodies and committees of local councils.

2. *The ad hoc committee* This meets for one purpose, once or twice, to make decisions in one area in response to a current need or problem. Examples are a shop stewards' meeting, a problem-solving meeting, and a committee for action (e.g. petitions). If there is more than one meeting, the ad hoc committee will keep minutes.

3. *The joint committee* This is formed of two or more committees when they need to pool their expertise in order to solve a problem.

4. *The joint consultative committee* This is a committee which exists for the consultation of different levels or parties. It is often an important industrial relations exercise, e.g. works councils and staff associations. It may include a number of personnel from different divisions or departments, e.g. a management committee.

5. *The subcommittee* This is appointed by the main committee to take care of matters in one area. Members are appointed because of their expertise in that area and will advise the members of the main committee by submitting reports to them for their consideration, e.g. library or other subcommittees of academic institutions or councils.

In addition, it is worth noting that every standing committee has an Annual General Meeting when the re-election of officers takes place, the annual balance sheet is presented by the Treasurer and any yearly reports by officers or subcommittees are given.

The procedure of formal meetings or committees

The procedure and regulations of formal meetings and committees are given in their constitution and terms of reference. As stated earlier, the sources from which these derive vary according to the category or type of meeting for which they are intended. Whatever form these take, they always give rules for procedure which cover the following areas:

1. *The terms of reference* Sometimes known as 'the mandate' given to the

meeting or committee, this means that the areas and matters which it is empowered to discuss are clearly defined, as well as whether it is to be advisory or executive. To stray outside the limits imposed is known as *ultra vires* and the Chairman must direct the committee to return to its terms of reference.

2. *Membership regulations* These will include regulations and procedure for the election or appointment of members, for their numbers, and for their qualifications. It will also give rules for the 'co-option' of outside people as members. ('To co-opt' means to invite someone, who is not a regular member, to attend one or more meetings because he can offer expertise or advice on the matter in hand. Whether he will to be allowed to vote or not will be clarified also.)

3. *The quorum* This means the number of members required to be present before a valid decision can be made. It is usually, though not always, two-thirds of the members. It is important that it should be laid down, otherwise all members would be required to be present – usually impossible in practical terms!

4. *Motions, amendments and voting procedure* The rules governing the submission of proposals, motions, amendments and voting procedure will also be given, e.g. whether they are required in advance, how they should be proposed, seconded, etc.

5. *Duties and length of service of officers of the committee* These will be clearly defined together with rules for their election or appointment.

6. *Regulations concerning documentation* Two such regulations are how much notice should be given of a meeting and the normal sequence of the agenda. The formal keeping of minutes will also be laid down.

Some of these areas, notably the regulations governing documentation, conduct and the duties of officers, are quite complex and do have some legal implications. They therefore require some further explanation and discussion.

The documentation required for formal meetings and committees

Apart from the constitution and regulations which initiate the existence of a meeting or committee, there are several documents through which its business will be conducted and recorded. In order that this may be systematically carried out, and all requirements met, a Secretary is appointed or elected who prepares the essential documents in consultation with the Chairman. These documents are the main vehicle of communication concerning the business of any meeting and thus are crucial to its competent and professional conduct. They provide, whether for existing members, for those whom they represent, or for new members attending for the first time, a permanent record of the policies, aims and history of the work of that meeting or committee with which they are concerned.

The notice of meeting

The requirements of any constitution demand that a notice of meeting should be circulated in advance to every member; the legal situation is that if this is

---

PAN WORLD INTERNATIONAL BANK

BOARD OF DIRECTORS'

NOTICE OF ANNUAL GENERAL MEETING

The Annual General Meeting will take place on

Wednesday, 6 June at 11.00 a.m. in the Board Room

at the London Head Office, Grosvenor Square.

An agenda is attached.

Signed: *P L G Lawford*

P.L.G. Lawford, Company Secretary

Fig. 25   A special 'notice of meeting' for an AGM.

not carried out, then the decisions of the consequent meeting are not valid. The amount of notice required is usually at least 21 days, but this can vary and will be written in to the relevant regulations.

The notice of meeting is sometimes known as a 'summons'. It gives the date, time and place (the 'venue') of the next meeting, and occasionally a request is added that members should attend or bring relevant information. Often, the agenda is attached, since this gives adequate time for members to prepare their comments. If not, items for the agenda may be requested.

A notice of meeting may appear on a pre-designed post card (for brevity), on a memorandum (often used for internal meetings, e.g. departmental meetings, as it can be circulated conveniently by internal post), by personalised letter (often used if the meeting is a particularly formal one or is concerned with public business, e.g. Council meetings, when the word 'summons', rather than 'notice' is used) or by special notice of meeting (see Fig. 25). This latter is often used for official meetings but can also be used for any formal meeting. Sometimes it refers to an agenda, which is attached, or requests items for an agenda. Whatever way it is presented, the notice of meeting must be sent to everyone concerned. It is normally signed by the Secretary and, sometimes, by the Chairman.

The members' agenda

The agenda is a numbered list of items which gives the order in which they are to be discussed. It should be circulated to all members well in advance, preferably with the notice of meeting, so that they can consult anyone whom they represent and clarify what points they wish to raise before attending the meeting. It is thus a very important piece of communication, acting both as a guide and as a briefing.

Some committees have a permanent agenda in a set order, from which they never deviate – many union meetings are like this. Others vary the agenda slightly according to the business to be considered that day, but usually will included certain permanent items. Items such as apologies for absence, minutes and any other business will always be included, though, in some ad hoc meetings, even they may not be relevant. The sequence in which agendas are arranged also tends to be common to all meetings, certainly of the standing committee type, and will differ only according to the inclusion or exclusion of some items which may or may not be relevant at the time.

The normal sequence for a standing committee is given below, with indications of what may be included or excluded on occasions, and of what items are permanent.

Normal sequence of agenda items – standing committees

1. Apologies for absence.
2. Minutes (to be read by the Secretary or circulated and signed by the Chairman).
3. Matters arising from the minutes.

⎫ Permanent items, always included.

4. Correspondence (to be read by the Secretary).
5. Reports (e.g. financial report from the Treasurer and subcommittees' reports).

⎫ Items which appear if documents have to be read.

6. Any following numbers will be the topics to be discussed on that day. These may appear as the topic headings to be discussed (e.g. 'The contract for the DB5') or as a motion already formulated, with the names of a proposer and seconder (e.g. 'It is proposed that the contract for the DB5 should be rigorously revised. Proposed by D.G. Douglas, seconded by F.W. Payne.')

⎫ Items varying in number and format, according to the topics to be discussed.

7. Any other business (often appearing as AOB).
8. Date of the next meeting.

⎫ Permanent items, always included.

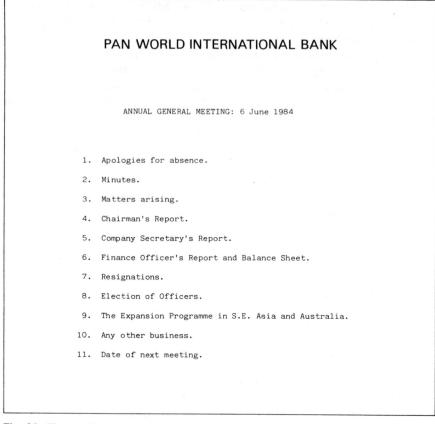

Fig. 26   The members' agenda for an AGM.

Sometimes, if it is an *Annual General Meeting*, or if one or more of the officers have resigned, an item known as *Election of Officers* is included (see Fig. 26). This may appear directly after matters arising out of minutes, or after the reports have been given by the previous officers. In an *ad hoc meeting*, however, particularly those called as a result of an emergency, or the need for immediate action, the meeting will have to *begin* with the election of officers before it can be conducted. If this is so, then the permanent items 1 to 3 will be omitted.

The Chairman's agenda

The Chairman should have an expanded and annotated version of the members' agenda which will assist him in conducting and controlling the meeting. The Secretary normally prepares this in consultation with him. It will include the following items:

1. A space for added notes which he may need, in order to give any relevant information or to comment on a particular item to the rest of the committee.

To give a simple example: under the apologies for absence received will be a note of the name of the absent person, with the reason for his non-attendance.
2. A column where an appropriate time allocation is given for each item. This helps to ensure that matters which may be urgent but not important (a distinction too infrequently made), such as the car parking allocation to be changed for the next day, are dealt with rapidly. In its turn, this will give adequate discussion time for items which are essential to the company's business, such as a new contract.
3. A space for further notes which the Chairman may wish to take during the meeting to remind him of actions to be taken or matters requiring his attention.

The Chairman's agenda (see Fig. 27) is an invaluable aid in giving him a useful, brief guide and *aide-mémoire*, as well as the opportunity to prepare for the committee's further business. Considerable attention, therefore, needs to be given to its preparation if he is to control and conduct the meeting in a professional and effective way.

Minutes

Minutes are perhaps the most difficult of the committee documents to prepare well, for they pose many problems for the Secretary. They are vital to the proper conduct of the committee's business, for they should provide an accurate record of its proceedings for the reference of everyone who has attended. Unfortunately, most of us forget exactly what we have heard or what has been said. Consequently, it is essential that we have a precise written account of the important decisions that were made, so that it is possible to check exactly what occurred.

It is for this reason that the first major item on any agenda is the reading and/or circulation of the minutes, so that all the members can verify that the record kept by the Secretary is accurate and that they agree with what has been written. Only when all the members confirm this, can the Chairman sign the minutes as correct. Those minutes then become a legal document and no one may alter them subsequently. The only way in which minutes may be altered at a later date is by putting a full formal proposal of the changes before the whole committee, which should then be seconded. A vote must then be taken in the normal way and only if the proposal is passed may any detail of the minutes be altered.

The minutes are then filed by the Secretary in the Minute Book and are numbered accordingly. The layout of the minutes follows the original guidelines of the agenda. Each minute will be subheaded by the original item which was listed there. All proposals or motions, with their proposers and seconders, all amendments, the exact votes on each, and the final decisions *must* be recorded. Apart from these, however, any other information which may be recorded will either be dictated by the kind of minutes which the committee or its constitution expects, or it will be governed by the discretion and ability of the Secretary.

PAN WORLD INTERNATIONAL BANK

ANNUAL GENERAL MEETING

CHAIRMAN'S AGENDA

Time allocation (Minutes)	Item and Information	Chairman's notes
2	**Apologies for absence** Mr T. J. Hanks is in the United States and unable to attend. Mr P.L. Purset is still in hospital.	
5	**Minutes** These have been circulated, so can be taken as read.	
10	**Matters arising** **Minutes 606/A** The Singapore East Branch has been opened as arranged. There will be a full report on its first six months' trading at the Board Meeting in December.	
20	**Chairman's Report** Copies are available for circulation at the meeting: with Secretary.	
20	**Company Secretary's Report** Copies available for circulation at the meeting: with Secretary.	
20	**Finance Officer's Report** Balance Sheet and Report available for circulation at meeting: with Secretary.	

(i)

Fig. 27 The Chairman's agenda for an AGM.

5   Resignations

         Vice Chairman: Mr P.L. Purset
         (ill health).
         Finance Officer: Mr L.P. White
         (joining South Pacific Bank).

20   Election of Officers

         Nominations for Vice Chairman:
         R.W. Grainger, P.A. Montgomery,
         E.J. Yokouchi.
         Nominations for Finance Officer:
         C.F. Stuart, K.L. Tan, J.G. Morand.
         Any further nominations can be
         taken at the meeting: election by
         ballot.

30   The Expansion Programme: SE Asia,
         Australia

         Mr L.P. Bruce to give an address
         on progress in Australia;
         Mr E.J. Yokouchi to give an address
         on progress in Japan.

15   Any other business

         Date of next meeting

         5 September 1984.

(ii)

Fig. 27 (Continued)

Minutes of the Committee Meeting of Westleigh School

Parent Teacher Association held on Thursday, 14 June 1984.

Present: Mr T.E. Grange, Chairman
           Mr L.G. Thorn, Secretary
           Mr S.W. Payne, Treasurer

Teachers: Mr S.L. Jackson, Headmaster
           Mrs P.R. James, Senior Mistress
           Mr L.W. Mackintosh
           Mrs P.L. Swann
           Mr K. R. Vines

Parents: Mr M.J. Allen
           Mrs S.L. Burford
           Mrs K.M. Chitty
           Mr C.G. Coriali
           Mr L.B. Harold
           Mrs L.C. Mercer
           Mrs K.W. Norris

1. Apologies for absence

    These were received from Mr L. Whitehead, who was on holiday, and
    Mrs P.J. Hartley, who was conducting an evening choir practice.

2. Minutes

    The Minutes of the meeting held on 24 April 1984 had been circulated,
    and were taken as read. The Committee agreed that they were a correct
    record and the Chairman signed them as correct.

3. Matters arising

    The Headmaster referred to Minute 5 of the last meeting, concerning
    the proposed field trip to the Welsh Mountains and stated that this
    had now been arranged with the help of PTA funds.

4. Correspondence

    The Secretary read a letter received from the Rotary Club which
    had been approached to provide speakers for the Careers Conference
    on 5 July 1984. It had offered three speakers who were available
    on that date: Mr L.P. Watson, a Chartered Accountant; Mrs T.L. Hazel,
    a Systems Analyst; and Mr S.R. Bright, a Building Society Manager.
    The Committee agreed unanimously that the offer should be accepted;
    and the Secretary agreed to send individual invitations to the three
    speakers.

(i)

Fig. 28   An example of narrative minutes.

5. Treasurer's Report on the Bring-and-Buy Sale

The Treasurer stated that this had raised £150.34 and that the funds of the PTA now stood at £563.56. He also stated that most of the PTA expenditure on the Swimming Pool Project was now at an end.

6. Motion

The motion that a bursary for travel abroad should be awarded annually to one pupil who showed an outstanding talent for languages, proposed by Mr C.G. Coriali and seconded by Mrs L.C. Mercer, was then discussed. The Treasurer agreed that there was normally sufficient funds at the end of the summer term for £100 to be awarded. Mr K.R. Vines said that although this was a worthwhile idea, any travel proposal should be scrutinised by the language staff to ensure that sufficient study and practice opportunities would be present; he felt that otherwise advantage might be taken of the scheme. Mrs P.L. Swann, speaking on behalf of the language staff, stated that they would certainly do this. The motion was then carried nem con; Mr L.B. Harold abstained.

8. Any other business

There was no other business.

9. The date of the next meeting

This was arranged for 28 September 1984.

Signed: T. E. Grange

Chairman.

(ii)

Fig. 28 (Continued)

127

There are two types of minutes; the first is known as the *resolution minutes* which only record the proposals forwarded and the decisions taken. The other type is known as the *narrative minutes* (see Fig. 28) and do include some record of the discussion which took place. It is more usual for full narrative minutes to be given with voluntary bodies, for the reference of members who could not attend, and to add to the motivation of those did not participate. It is with the second form of minutes (the most usual) that the problems arise as to how much or how little to include.

The Secretary needs to avoid recording every word and to summarise the gist of the discussion, particularly the factual points, as the meeting progresses. (The guidance given on listening and note-taking in Chapter 2 should prove of some assistance here.) Obviously any digressions, reminiscences, quarrels and libellous statements should be omitted! Relevant facts and decisions, as well as requests for action from various members, must be recorded.

It is best to keep the minutes brief, yet as accurate as possible. It is helpful to record in advance the information already known, such as those absent, or to take a list of those present in the 'settling down' which precedes any meeting. A sheet of paper giving the agenda headings, with blank spaces for notes, is also helpful in pinning down progress and keeping up with the discussion. Very brief notes will suffice – it is better to listen than to record too much. Afterwards, the notes must be reviewed and the minutes written up in the layout required, if the events are to be remembered and recorded accurately for the benefit of all. The required layout may vary slightly from committee to committee, but can easily be checked by reference to the Minute Book or to the Chairman. Some brief general points can be given as guidelines, however. These summarise the main points in the preceding discussion and give further assistance on layout.

GUIDELINES ON THE LAYOUT AND COMPOSITION OF MINUTES

1. The names of those present should be recorded first (after the main heading). The names of the officers should be given precedence, and their office should be designated after the name. The names of all other members present should then be given in alphabetical order.

2. Each minute should have a clear subheading, derived from the items listed on the agenda; the minutes should also follow the order of the original agenda.

3. In resolution minutes, some brief indication of the main points discussed should appear below the subheading, before recording the vote on any proposals.

4. In narrative minutes, care should be taken to record the names of proposers, seconders and other speakers correctly; if they were officers, they should be designated by office. Care should be taken, too, to record the exact wording of motions and amendments, and to record the vote accurately. You should also record any requests for action from either officers or members; check dates, figures, prices, times; include vital facts and major points of discussion, and omit unnecessary material (e.g. digressions, repetitions, etc.).

5. The numbering of minutes may begin at number one, but may follow on, particularly in standing committees, from the last number in the Minutes Book; this should be checked.

6. A space should be left at the end for the Chairman's signature (which will be added at the next meeting), below which his name, office, and date of the next meeting should be given.

7. Minutes should be written up immediately following the meeting.

8. If possible, they should be circulated to members before the next meeting.

9. Once signed at the next meeting, they should be filed in the Minute Book in correct sequence.

The duties of officers of a committee or meeting

The most important of the officers of any committee, as we have seen, are the Chairman and Secretary; there may also be a Treasurer if the type of business conducted by that committee warrants one. They are usually elected, but on some occasions they may be appointed by the authority which brought the committee into being, usually because they have some special expertise in the area required; for example, the Chairman of a Staff Association or Works Council is often the Personnel Manager or the Industrial Relations Officer. If this is the case, it is said that the Chairman was appointed *ex officio*, meaning 'by virtue of his or her office'.

The Chairman

The overall duties of the Chairman, and the qualities which he requires to carry them out effectively, have already been indicated in discussing the task and group functions of the leader of an informal meeting. In addition, however, it is possible to list his specific formal duties further as follows:

1. *Knowledge of the regulations* A Chairman must study the constitution and regulations governing his committee, and be able to answer fully any points of order or procedure which may arise in the committee. He must also be aware of the precise terms of reference and therefore the limits of the committee's authority. Otherwise he could be accused of being *ultra vires* or of being *outside* his terms of reference. He must be aware of his *own* powers, particularly whether or not he is allowed a casting vote, in the case of an exactly split vote.

2. *Preparation* Before any committee meeting, the Chairman needs to consult with the Secretary to ensure that all the necessary documentation has been sent in good time to the members, according to the regulations, and that any extra data which they may need has also been circulated. He needs to prepare carefully his own agenda with his Secretary, ensuring that it contains all the information and appropriate timing to assist him. He needs to ensure that any further factual information which the committee might need has been obtained, so that he may answer any points of information which may arise.

3. *Conduct of the meeting* The meeting is called or 'convened' by the Chairman. He should check first whether there is a quorum. If there is, he

should begin by reading the apologies. He will then sign the minutes, once read or circulated and agreed. It is then his duty to move the meeting on to each item of business, keeping as far as possible to the timetable he has prepared. In addition he must answer any points of procedure or information raised. He must summarise the issues, help with the wording of motions and amendments when these arise from discussion, and ensure that there is a proposer and seconder.

He should also take and count the vote, ensuring that the Secretary records this accurately. If the vote is even, he may choose to use his casting vote if one is postulated in the constitution. On the other hand, he may decide *not* to use it if he believes the issue needs further thought or that no action is required. In the first case, he may adjourn the matter until the next meeting and, in the second, 'let the motion lie on the table', or not proceed further with it. He may adjourn the meeting if he believes it to be best for the concentration of the members and he will decide on the date of the next meeting before closing the existing one.

He must keep the group working together. How difficult this can be is shown by the fact that sometimes, a Chairman can be empowered by his constitution to eject members who come to blows – not, of course, a usual situation!

4. *After the meeting* The Chairman should refer to any notes, taken on his Chairman's agenda, which require action and should make sure that members receive a written reminder, if necessary. Any action required by him should be taken before the next meeting and reported back in time. He may also help the Secretary to check the accuracy of the minutes.

The Vice-Chairman

The Vice-Chairman carries out all the Chairman's duties in his absence. If one has not been elected or appointed, the members may elect one for any occasion when the Chairman is unable to attend. If the Chairman then arrives, it is the Vice-Chairman's decision whether or not to retain the chair.

The Secretary

Many of the duties of the Secretary have already been mentioned, for it is he or she who takes care of all the documents concerned with the committee's business. Briefly, the duties of the Secretary may be summarised as follows:

1. To retain copies of the constitution and regulations for the reference of new and existing members, ensuring that all new members are given a copy.

2. To prepare the notice of meeting and agenda in consultation with the Chairman and circulate these in advance, according to the regulations.

3. To prepare the Chairman's agenda in consultation with him.

4. To receive, and read at the meeting, any relevant correspondence, filing these where necessary.

5. To receive any subcommittees' reports, or reports from other officers, keeping file copies and circulating copies to members where necessary.

6. To prepare the circulation of any further data which members may require.

7. To deal with any queries from members or outside bodies concerning the business of the committee as necessary.

8. To take minutes in note form during the meeting (some guidelines on this difficult task have already been given).

9. To prepare the fair copy of the minutes directly after the meeting, ready for the Chairman's signature at the next one.

10. To circulate copies of the minutes to members and/or read the minutes at the next meeting for their approval.

11. To keep the Minute Book updated and in correct sequence.

The Secretary is really the administrative and communications officer of any committee and must employ a systematic approach. In addition, the post of Secretary demands considerable organisational ability and highly developed skills of listening and summarising in order to carry out the required duties effectively, In voluntary organisations, sports committees, etc., this demanding role, which is titled 'Honorary Secretary', is unpaid.

The Treasurer

Some committees have a Treasurer or finance officer to keep the accounts and manage the monetary matters, though not all committees need one. Committees with funds, however, need to allocate this crucial role carefully. The Treasurer keeps a careful account of income and expenditure; he also monitors the outcome and implications of projects decided upon by the committee, to ensure that the financial resources are not overcommitted. His duties can be summarised as follows:

1. To keep records of all financial transactions carried out by the committee.

2. To present the Treasurer's report and the balance sheet at the Annual General Meeting.

3. To keep all records, such as receipts, bank statements, etc., relevant to the balance sheet.

4. To pass accounts and records to an independent auditor for checking before presenting them for the scrutiny of members at the AGM.

5. To act as financial adviser to the committee, in order that they do not overspend in one direction through over-enthusiasm for particular schemes.

Above all it is the Treasurer's duty to maintain the solvency and integrity of the committee's financial affairs.

Final points of procedure – motions, amendments and voting

The term 'point of procedure' has been used before. It is sometimes called a 'point of order' and it can be raised by any member when he or she believes that a meeting is not being conducted according to the regulations. The Chairman must then answer and remedy it where necessary. The final procedural points in this chapter concern proposals and voting, the methods by which committees make the decisions. They can be listed, giving the necessary definitions and explanations, as follows.

Motions

1. A motion is a proposal; it must be proposed and seconded. It usually begins with the words: 'It is proposed that...'
2. In committee meetings, motions are usually submitted in advance and are signed by the proposer and seconder.
3. More usually, matters are discussed *before* the motion is formulated, usually at the committee meeting, assisted by the Chairman.

Amendments

1. An amendment is an alteration made to some detail of the motion. (In formal meetings, it must be proposed and seconded.)
2. If the amendment *adds to* the wording of the original motion, it is sometimes known as a 'rider' or 'addendum'.
3. The amendment is voted on *before* the motion; if it is not passed, voting takes place on the original motion. If it is carried, voting takes place on the 'substantive' motion.

Voting

This is usually by show of hands; a 'poll' or 'secret ballot' is unusual, though it is sometimes used where vested interest or elections are involved. The terms used for the various kinds of vote which can be recorded are as follows:

1. A *unanimous* vote – meaning *every* member votes *in favour* of the motion.
2. A vote *nem con* or *nem dis* meaning 'no one dissenting'. Therefore if no member votes against the motion but some *abstain* (i.e. do not vote at all) the vote is not exactly unanimous; it is therefore recorded as *nem con/nem dis*.
3. An *even* or *split* vote. This is used to describe a vote when the same number of members vote for and against the motion. The Chairman may resolve this by using his casting vote if he has one and he chooses to do so.

In all other situations, the number of votes are recorded for and against the motion. No special terminology is required. In formal committees and meetings, however, terms are often used which are unfamiliar elsewhere; some (the most common) have been used and explained in this chapter. For further reference of the reader, however, these and others have been listed alphabetically in the glossary at the end of this chapter.

The formal meeting as a method of communication – the duties of the representative member of a committee

Many members who attend committees represent other people or groups. They have a special responsibility for promoting good communication by consulting their group and reporting back to it. Too often this is neglected and the point of their attending the committee, in terms of a consultative exercise, is lost. This happens especially when new facts and ideas are given at a meeting so that, although it is known that the views of the group which a member represents are in favour of a certain line of action, the representative must in all conscience, or in his new knowledge, choose another. In this case, it is particularly important that he explains the reasons for his change of mind to the group, otherwise suspicion and distrust are bound to result. The duties of a representative member on a committee can be summarised as follows:

Preparing for the meeting

The representative member should do the following:

1. Read the agenda and make sure it is understood.
2. Discuss the problem or situation with his group and carry out any relevant research on facts and attitudes.
3. Note what actions are recommended and what their effects on members of the group might be.
4. Spend time clarifying and summarising the issues.

Participation at the meeting

The representative member should do the following:

1. State the issue clearly.
2. Examine the courses and results.
3. Propose possible solutions and discuss advantages and disadvantages.
4. Select a solution which can lead to action.

Reporting back to the group

Finally, the representative member should show the members of the group the following:

1. How their view differed from others expressed.
2. What added facts were given.
3. What solutions were suggested and the advantages and disadvantages of each.
4. What the final solution was and the reasons for it.

This approach is disciplined and systematic and only in this way can joint consultation result in action and become really effective.

Conclusion – realising the potential of meetings for communication

Meetings, both formal and informal, can help to promote effective communication; they can also help to destroy it if they are mismanaged. Both those who attempt to run meetings, therefore, and those who attend them should define their objectives clearly and seek to realise them through proper conduct and control. Sufficient attention must be given to preparation on everyone's part – care should be taken over procedure and timing and an adequate system for recording and review of results must be maintained. Only in this way can the valuable potential of meetings as a communication method be fully realised and the managerial time spent on them become truly cost effective.

* * *

Suggested activities for interest and self-evaluation

Make an analysis of a 'live' case study. Visit a local Council meeting which the public is allowed to attend and do the following:

1. Take notes of the proceedings and then try to produce some brief narrative minutes.
2. Try to answer the following analytical questions:
(a) How well did the Chairman manage his task and human relations functions?
(b) What were the major problems which arose, and how were they solved? Were the solutions satisfactory? If not, what would *you* have done?
(c) How well was the time allocation managed?
You might like to carry out a similar activity the next time you attend a meeting within your company or within any other association to which you belong.

Glossary of committee meeting terms

Ad hoc committee Sometimes called a special, or special purpose, committee. This is a group of people appointed to deal with one particular piece of work.
Addendum An amendment which adds words to a motion.
Addressing the Chair A member wishing to speak on a point must rise and address the Chair in the following way: 'Mr Chairman' (for a man), 'Madam Chairman' (for a woman). All remarks must be addressed to the Chairman and members must not discuss matters between themselves at a meeting.
Agenda A list of items to be discussed at a meeting.
Adjournment Subject to the articles, rules or constitution of an organisation, the Chairman, with the consent of the members of the meeting, may adjourn it in order to postpone further discussion or because of shortage of time; adequate notice of an adjourned meeting must be given.
Adjourned by consent This means that the unfinished business of the meeting will discussed at another meeting by agreement of those present.
Adjourned sine die The unfinished business of a meeting will be discussed at a further meeting, for which a date is to be fixed later.
Amendment A proposal to alter a motion by adding or deleting words. It must be proposed, seconded and put to the meeting in the customary way.
Annual General Meeting A meeting of all members of an organisation, or shareholders of a company, that must be held each year.
Attendance record The book in which each member present at a meeting signs his name.
Ballot A written vote which preserves the secrecy of each individual's vote.
Casting vote An additional vote, usually held by the Chairman, to enable a

decision to be taken in the case of an equal number of votes being given for and against the motion.

Chairman The person who controls the business of a meeting.

Chairman's agenda The agenda prepared for use by the Chairman. It contains notes about individual items and has space for him to make his own notes.

Closure A motion submitted with the object of ending the discussion on a matter before a meeting.

Co-option The power given to a committee to allow others to serve on the committee. It must be the result of a majority vote of the existing members of the organisation.

Disturbance An obstructor who causes a disturbance at a meeting may be ejected with or without the aid of the police, provided that the meeting has not been announced as 'public'.

Dropped motion A motion that has to be dropped either because there is no seconder or because the meeting wishes it to be abandoned.

En bloc The voting of, say, a committee *en bloc*, i.e. the electing or re-electing of all members of a committee by the passing of one resolution.

Ex officio A person may be a member of a committee *ex officio*, 'by virtue of his office'. In other words, the holding of one office may qualify a person automatically to hold another.

Extraordinary General Meeting A meeting of all members of an organisation, or shareholders of a company, to discuss some matter of importance for which the consent of all or the majority of members is necessary.

Going into committee A motion 'that the meeting go into committee' is moved if less restricted discussion is thought necessary. When this happens, the members of the meeting are divided into groups and each one undertakes discussion on specified subjects. A motion 'that the meeting be resumed' gives the meeting authority to proceed from the point where it left off.

Going into division The physical division of members for voting purposes.

Intra vires When something is *intra vires* it means that it is within the power of the person or body concerned.

Kangaroo closure The Chairman of a committee is empowered to jump from one amendment to another, omitting those which he considers to be less important or repetitive.

Lie on the table A matter is said to 'lie on the table' when no action can be taken on it.

Majority The greatest number of members either for or against a motion. The articles and rules of the organisation will define the majority of votes required to carry a motion.

Memorandum A document setting out information to enable the committee to make a policy decision.

Memorandum and Articles of Association These are regulations drawn up by a company setting out the objects for which the company is formed, and defining the manner in which its business should be conducted.

Minute Book A book containing a signed copy of every issue of minutes from the date of the first meeting of the committee.

Minutes of narration A summary of all points raised in discussion before a decision is taken on a particular item of business.

Minutes of resolution A summary of all the resolutions passed. The resolutions, motions and amendments must be recorded verbatim; the names of the proposer and of the seconder are usually given as well.

Minutes A summary of the proceedings of a meeting.

Motion A proposal that certain action be taken. A motion must be written and handed to the Chairman or Secretary before a meeting. The mover of the motion speaks on it and has the right of reply at the close of the discussion; the seconder may speak on the motion only once. If there is no seconder, the motion is dropped and cannot be introduced again. When put to the meeting, the motion becomes 'the question' and when it is passed it becomes 'the resolution'. A motion on a matter which has not been included on the agenda can be moved only if 'leave of urgency' has been agreed by the meeting or it has been included under the customary item 'any other business'.

Nem con (*Nemine contradicente*) The passing of a resolution without opposing votes, but with some members abstaining.

Nem dis (*Nemine dissentiente*) Sometimes used instead of *nem con*.

Next business A motion 'that the meeting proceed with next business' is a method of delaying the decision on any matter brought before the meeting.

No confidence When the members of a meeting disagree with the Chairman they may pass a vote of 'no confidence' in the Chair. When this happens the Chairman must vacate the Chair in favour of his deputy or some other person nominated by the meeting. There must be a substantial majority of members in favour of this decision.

Notice A notification to members of the time, date and place of a meeting (often included with the agenda).

Point of order A question regarding the procedure at a meeting or a query relating to the Standing Orders or constitution, raised by a member during the course of the meeting (e.g. absence of a quorum).

Poll This is the term given for the method of voting at an election. In a meeting this usually takes the form of a secret vote by ballot paper. The way in which a poll is to be conducted is generally laid down in the Standing Orders or constitution of the organisation.

Postponement The action taken to defer a meeting to a later date.

Proceedings The business discussed, the main points of discussion and the decisions and agreements taken at a meeting.

Proposer The person who recommends a particular decision to be taken by stating a motion formally.

Proxy A person authorised by a member to vote on his behalf or a document authorising a person to attend a meeting and vote on behalf of another person.

Putting the question To conclude the discussion on a motion it is customary for the Chairman to 'put the question' by announcing: 'The question before the meeting is...'.

Quorum The minimum number of members necessary for a meeting to be held. The quorum is laid down in the constitution or rules of the organisation.

Reference back This is an amendment referring a report or other item of business back for further consideration to the body or person submitting it. If the motion 'reference back' is defeated, the discussion is continued.

Resolution A formal decision carried by a meeting. It must be proposed, seconded and put to the meeting in the customary way. A resolution cannot be rescinded (cancelled) at the meeting at which it is adopted.

Rider An additional clause or sentence added to a resolution after it has been passed. It differs from an amendment in that it adds to a resolution instead of altering it. (It has to be proposed, seconded and put to the meeting in the same way as a motion.)

Right of reply The proposer of a motion has the right of reply when the resolution has been fully discussed. He is allowed to reply only once and afterwards the motion is put to the meeting.

Scrutineer The person who counts and examines closely the votes at an election.

Seating arrangements It is customary for the Chairman to be seated at the head of the table with the Secretary on his right and the Treasurer on his left.

Seconder A person who supports the proposer of a motion.

Standing Orders These are the rules compiled by the organisation that regulate the manner in which its business is to be conducted. They may be called the 'constitution'.

Secretary The person responsible for all the arrangements connected with a meeting and for advising the Chairman on procedure, etc. (Do not confuse this with private secretary.)

Subcommittee A few people appointed by a main committee to undertake certain specified work on its behalf. The subcommittee must report to the committee periodically.

Substantive motion A motion altered by a previously agreed amendment.

Take the Chair This means that someone does the work of Chairman during a meeting.

Teller The person appointed to count the votes at a meeting.

Terms of reference A statement of the work to be done by a committee.

Ultra vires When something is *ultra vires* it means that it is beyond the legal power or authority of a company or organisation.

Unanimous When all members of a meeting have voted in favour of a resolution it is said to be carried unanimously.

Vote To express, either verbally or in writing, whether one is 'for' or 'against' a motion.

10 Interviews – assessment techniques

The definition, aims and functions of interviews

An interview can be defined briefly as any planned and controlled conversation during which two parties speak and listen. To be effective, therefore, an interview must be a two-way communication; it must be planned systematically and it must have clearly defined objectives and controlled interaction. It will require, too, some method of collecting the relevant information prior to the interview, and of recording what occurred during the interview for future reference.

The aim of interviews, therefore, is to exchange information. Their function is usually to assess a situation or a person's behaviour; often, it is to assess both, as well as their inter-relationship. In order to achieve this, it is essential that all the relevant evidence and facts are available to the interviewee and to the interviewer. Some of this evidence will be available at the interview itself; for this reason, the observation of the non-verbal clues and the development of skilled questioning techniques are crucial if all the relevant information is to be elicited and a full assessment made.

For these reasons, some guidance will be given on these important aspects. This will be related to the different types of interviews discussed here. Although only those kinds of interviews related to employment will be examined (and not specialised interviews, such as those conducted for market research), many of these guidelines could be applied to any interview situation. These guidelines will be of particular use to a manager as he or she will be the person who will control the interview. It is hoped that this chapter will be useful to interviewees, too, as it outlines what managers are looking for and may help interviewees to be successful at interviews.

There are four main types of interview related to any individual's employment over a period of time; all of them share the general aims and functions discussed above. Each, however, has slightly differing objectives, and will therefore take a slightly different approach. These four categories are: interviews for employment selection; interviews to assess (or appraise) work performance; interviews to counsel or discipline an employee; and finally, interviews to detect the reasons for an individual leaving a job. The objectives, planning and conduct of these will need to be discussed separately, as will the techniques of questioning and the problems of interaction peculiar to each.

The objectives, planning and conduct of employment selection interviews

Objectives

The objective of the selection interview is to match the right person to the right job. It must be noted, however, that the right person does not necessarily mean the most highly qualified. It is only too easy to choose a candidate who is over qualified and this may result in problems of high turnover of staff and demotivation. It is vital, therefore, that the choice should be made rationally, and that systematic planning should take place. This must begin with the requirements of the job itself, which must be examined carefully before any conclusions can be reached as to the person best fitted to undertake it.

The first stage of planning for employment selection – the job description

The job must be analysed first in consultation with the present job-holder and the immediate superior concerned. Methods of analysis include the observation of employees performing the job, discussions with them and their superiors, the examination of questionnaires and operating manuals, and the review of the factors that are critical or are of key importance to the job. A record is then made, which is known as the job description. It is a subheaded systematic document which usually includes the following:

1. General: job title, location, and broad limitations, (e.g. age, etc.).
2. Broad type of work: office, executive, operative, etc.
3. Job content: list of duties and responsibilities, limits of authority, and special demands.
4. Recruitment, selection, training: normal source of recruitment, existence of training and/or trial period, and the main difficulties.
5. Job conditions: physical conditions of work, special demands, (travel, etc.), and social and psychological conditions of work (team work, etc.).
6. Economic conditions of work: remuneration, benefits, etc.
7. Prospects: opportunites for transfer, promotion, etc.

Once the job description is complete, the second stage of planning can be carried out; this consists of listing the things which would be required of anyone who might apply for the job.

The second stage of planning for employment selection – the personnel specification

The task of drawing up a list of characteristics needed for the job could be very complex. In order to use it for selection effectively, however, it must be brief and systematic. The National Institute of Industrial Psychology has given a useful rule of thumb with its subheaded 'Seven Point Plan'. Others are in existence, but this one gives some indication of what needs to be considered when choosing the right person for the job. The plan includes the following divisions:

1. *Physique* Physical demands of the job, e.g. strength, size, nervous state, general health. The standard of personal appearance, bearing and speech, eyesight, colour vision and hearing.

2. *Attainments* Type and standard of education, of occupational training and experience and of occupational success.

3. *General intelligence* The level of intelligence that is required to do the job satisfactorily or well. It needs to be clearly and specifically defined – 'average intelligence' means very little.

4. *Special aptitudes* These include verbal, mechanical, manipulative, literary, mathematical, artistic, musical or other special aptitudes.

5. *Interests* The special interests considered desirable for the performance of the job include constructing mechanical things, making social contacts, solving problems that require a logical approach, artistic expression, etc. Special interests, for which the job might provide an outlet, include social contact, outdoor activities and sports.

6. *Disposition* This means acceptability to others, leadership, steadiness and reliability, self-reliance and responsibility, perseverance, loyalty and co-operativeness.

7. *Circumstances* This means things like a willingness to travel and to accept a transfer.

The priority areas in such a plan are also indicated, for some headings may contain certain information which is far more relevant than others, and therefore will need to be given due weight by the interviewer when preparing questions.

The third stage of planning for employment selection – the application form and the advertisement

The application form and the advertisement should be based firmly on the job description and personnel specification. Bearing the requirements of both in mind, they should be as brief, yet as comprehensive as is required to gain relevant information and the appropriate applicants. The priorities identified must be prominent. This sort of form and advert need, too, to fulfil their function as a public relations exercise and to attract the right candidates, rather than put them off (as was pointed out in Chapter 3, which dealt with application forms). It is helpful to send a job description with the application form as this will prevent unsuitable candidates from applying and, therefore, from wasting time.

As for advertising, there are one or two further points that must be borne in mind:

1. *Choice of medium* This includes national papers, employment exchanges, local papers, etc. This must be appropriate to the level of the job.

2. *Wording the advertisement* Priority requirements must be stressed, but the

advertisement should be brief. It does not need to contain all the information in the personnel specification.

The fourth stage of planning for employment selection – the short list, references and certificates

If the application form, job description and advertisement have been well prepared, with the major requirements in mind, and have succeeded in communicating these to would-be applicants, the job short-listing should be simple, especially if the personnel specification, too, allows the selector to match the application forms quickly and in a helpful way. This is the first 'screening' process. After this, unsuitable candidates will be eliminated (and informed of this politely and quickly) and a short list will be prepared of those applicants who seem to match the personnel specification. Short lists should not exceed six people, for interviewing is a very costly business, in terms of man hours, especially if more than one interviewer is involved, as is often the case.

Once the short list has been prepared, references may be taken up, although sometimes this is not done until after the interview. The days of a 'testimonial' – a long written reference obtained in advance by the candidate – are over, for no one ever submitted a bad one! They were, therefore, of little use. Confidential references are of more value. In addition, in the letter which informs the candidate of his interview time and date, he may be asked to bring along his examination certificates, diploma certificates, etc.

Planning the interview – degree of structure and formality

With the evidence available – the application form and other relevant information, such as the job description and the personnel specification – it is now possible to plan the interview itself. Several things must be decided by the interviewer or interviewers. If there is to be more than one, then obviously the planning must be carried out in consultation.

The first decision concerns to what degree the interview is to be a structured one, for example, are all the questions to be rigidly scheduled in sequence, or are some open-ended, which will give the candidate an opportunity to expand on his answer? In market research interviews, a very structured approach is taken often so that responses can be specifically and statistically compared; at the other end of the scale, in counselling interviews, questions are often very open, in order to allow the interviewee to talk freely. In selection, a moderately structured approach is probably the best, with a mixture of closed factual questions and the more open-ended kind which might help to give an overall picture of the candidate.

The second decision concerns the type of interview, in terms of number of interviewers and interviewees.

1. *A one-to-one interview* This is usually with a direct superior as the interviewer, but is sometimes with the personnel manager. The main advantage is that this type of interview is the least nerve-racking for the

candidate; the major disadvantages are that one person's opinion can be very biased and the direct superior may not have any training in interviewing.

2. *A two-to-one interview* This is usually with a direct superior as one interviewer and a member of the personnel department as the other. This has the advantage that each can cover different aspects and that two assessments are made. The member of the personnel department is likely to be a trained interviewer, too. The disadvantage is that there may be repetition or a major disagreement.

3. *A board interview* This is the most difficult to conduct successfully and is the most nerve-racking for the interviewee. It is used usually for very senior posts where a very formal approach is required and where some degree of stress would be part of the job. Unfortunately, it is sometimes used when it is unecessary and inappropriate, in which case it adds to the cost, with no guarantee of an increase in the quality of the decisions made.

4. *A group interview* This is where there is more than one interviewee. This is only used when a high degree of oral ability or competitiveness is required in the job, or when leadership/initiative qualities are important. Case study questions are given often, and the groups are observed, in order to examine the qualities of each individual.

In addition, the degree of formality must be decided; sometimes a series of interviews is used, the informal being utilised as a preliminary so that both candidate and interviewer can assess whether it is worthwhile to continue to the final, formal interview. This can save time and cost and can aid selection. In fact, in this way, selection becomes a two-way process, as it should be if it is to be truly effective.

Preparing the questions and rating sheet

Once these decisions have been taken, a list of questions can be prepared; the questions can then be allocated if there is more than one interviewer. Accompanying these, some kind of quick rating sheet should be prepared, for making brief notes. The two major disadvantages of this are that it can be disturbing to the candidate and is liable to prevent him from talking in a relaxed (and therefore revealing) manner and it prevents the interviewer from listening with sufficient attention to what is said and from observing the very important non-verbal responses. A rating sheet with grades (which can be ticked quickly), related to the most important qualities required, and to the candidate's ability to answer the questions, is most useful, therefore.

Immediately prior to an interview, every interviewer should 'do his homework' and study the application form, in relation to the job description and personnel specification. If it becomes evident that there is something inconsistent or missing, or something which is difficult to understand on the application form, then, in addition to the other questions, some probing ones must be prepared to clarify the situation. If there is a three-month gap in employment, it could mean an unfortunate redundancy, a trip round the world or a spell in prison. Good preparation for the interview assists the 'detective work' involved in assessing whether this is the candidate who will prove most effective.

Finally, there are certain kinds of questions which should be avoided in a selection interview. These are as follows:

1. Questions which repeat information that is on the application form or that can be seen from the certificates and qualifications of the candidate.
2. Questions, known as leading questions, which suggest certain answers to the candidate, e.g. 'You do like working with other people, don't you?' The answer will always be 'Yes'!
3. Questions which attempt to evaluate qualities best measured by other means, e.g. 'What is your speed as a typist?' (This is best measured by tests or by qualifications.)
4. Questions which repeat what has already been asked or are irrelevant.

Equally, there are certain kinds of questions which are useful. These are as follows:

1. Open questions which allow the candidate to expand, e.g. biographical questions of the 'tell us about yourself' variety.
2. Situational questions concerning the work the candidate will be expected to undertake, e.g. 'In the following situation, what would you do..?'
3. Questions which probe any discrepancies, or anything which is unclear, on the application form.
4. Questions which explore the candidate's own view of his likely future progression and prospects.

If an adequate rating sheet, which is quick to mark, can be devised for these questions, then the assessment will be well recorded without much effort.

Conducting the selection interview – techniques and problems

Several factors need to be borne in mind during a selection interview that relate to the techniques which should be used and the problems which can arise. These are as follows:

1. *The environment* The interviewer should ensure that adequate reception and waiting facilities have been arranged and that the physical conditions of the interview room are comfortable. This will enable the candidate to relax initially. Some interviewers prefer not to have a desk between themselves and the interviewee, believing that it creates an unnecessary barrier, and favour the 'easy chair and coffee-table' approach. However, this will depend on the required degree of formality.

2. *Introductions and establishing rapport* The candidate should be introduced to the interviewer(s) present and their position in the firm should be identified, as this will help the candidate to answer and frame his questions related to each person. An invitation to be seated, and a polite enquiry concerning the journey, establishes a friendly approach, and the beginning of the rapport which is essential if the candidate is to overcome any nervousness and be able to talk freely.

3. *Initial impressions – the problems of perception and bias* It has been said that the result of any selection interview is decided in the first five minutes. This is not so incredible as it sounds, for we all respond rapidly to the initial physical impression given by anyone we meet – to their appearance, expression, mannerisms, dress, bearing, etc. We respond irrationally, too, and often will make judgements about an individual's character, based on our like or dislike of these things – a young man or young woman with a certain kind of hairstyle often can arouse quite strong feelings in the interviewer, for example! The interviewer needs to be aware of this bias in himself and be wary of his own attitudes, if these are indeed unfounded. This kind of prejudice – that we tend to see everyone as immediately likeable or disagreeable – has been called the 'halo' and 'horned' effect. The interviewer needs to compensate for this consciously if each candidate is to be assessed objectively on his merits.

4. *Information giving* It is often a good idea to begin by giving information about the position offered, and about the company, allowing the interviewee to question first. Often this can be allocated between appropriate interviewers.

5. *Questioning* It is usually a good idea to begin this with an open-ended question which will allow the candidate to talk on a subject which is relatively easy – what he or she enjoyed most at college, or in previous employment situations, and why, for example. This question can be initiated from the application form and expands on what the candidate knows, before leading on to more demanding, 'probing' questions. Interviewers should take care, when asking questions, that they do not interrupt each other!

6. *Listening* Interviewers often mishear, miss a point or interrupt. Occasionally, they enter into monologues that give the candidate the opportunity to assess them. If this does happen, an interviewee can discover far more about an interviewer than he does of the candidate. The candidate may then be able to manipulate the interviewer and this must be avoided. Also, if the interviewer argues with the candidate, this will indicate his temperament. Interrupting the candidate damages the interaction between him and the interviewer and care should be taken not to do this. The objective, after all, is to assess the candidate, and this is done by listening, with concentration, to what he has to say.

7. *Encouraging the candidate to talk* Two techniques that avoid argument or interruption, and encourage the candidate's flow of conversation, are the reflective statement and paralinguistic sounds (sometimes known as 'phatic communication'). The reflective statement helps the candidate to clarify his views without the interviewer having to comment on them. For example, if a candidate has just been discussing an aspect of his past work, which he seems to have found unacceptable in some way, a statement, such as: 'You found this unacceptable', will help him to clarify whether he did or not, and *why*. This elicits more information without the interviewer having to pass judgement, by reflecting what *seems* to be the candidate's feeling, and it demands clarification. The paralinguistic sounds – the approving 'mm' sound, in particular – help to encourage the flow of conversation, but do not interrupt the candidate. Discouraging sounds or exclamations should be avoided!

8. *Responding to non-verbal clues* There are all kinds of non-verbal clues which we use to assess people. Facial expressions, gestures, posture and eye movements all provide important indications of what a person is actually thinking or feeling – which may not be the same as what he is saying. They show also whether an individual is confident or whether he is uncertain and, in extreme cases, whether he is trying to bluff an answer. The interviewee can betray himself here by the non-verbal signs – the slight frown, the avoidance of the interviewer's eye, etc. – and the observation of these elements can assist the interviewer to assess the degree of his real expertise, or to see what impression he might make on others, both of which might be essential to the job. (There is now an interview technique devoted to this that relies on recording the non-verbal behaviour of a candidate and drawing a personality profile as a result – the ultimate in selection by man-watching!)

9. *Giving time for questions* The candidate should be given time to ask questions himself, particularly after the information-giving session at the beginning of the interview, and at the end. Sometimes, valuable conclusions as to how much homework the candidate has done (and therefore how keen, as well as conscientious, he is liable to be), or to his future ambitions (if he is concerned about prospects, this could be a sign that he is willing to make a career in the organisation) can be drawn from his own questions, which may be relevant to the personnel specification required.

10. *Note-taking and recording* Only brief notes (or marks) on the previously prepared rating sheet should be made during the interview. However, notes should be made immediately after the interview, concerning the priority areas on the personnel specification. These will act as an important record and will allow comparisons with other candidates.

11. *Closing and following up the interview* After any final questions from the candidate, the interview should be closed in a friendly manner with a parting handshake, a word of thanks for attending and the exact information as to when the candidate will hear the result and by what method.

If the candidate is rejected, then a polite letter should be sent as soon as possible; it helps if this is encouraging in tone. If the candidate is to be accepted, then a congratulatory letter should be sent which should give the date of appointment, the details of salary and the arrangements for induction.

Supplementary tests

Occasionally, supplementary tests may be appropriate. The kinds of test most often employed are as follows:

1. *Medical tests* These are required by many companies, once a candidate is appointed. (In some posts, there are specific requirements for physical fitness.)

2. *Performance or trade tests* For specific skills or trade tasks (craft skills, typing, etc.) a short test may be set.

3. *Aptitude tests* If a particular aptitude is required – numerical, verbal, or artistic, for example – an appropriate test may be set.

4. *Personality tests* There are a number of these and care should be taken that any applied are relevant, well proven and administered by trained personnel. There have been a number of very inconclusive tests (including the famous 'ink blot' test) which proved to be of little value. Indeed, Professor Eysenck, after showing, on film, a number of psychological tests designed to assess personality, demonstrated that an astrologer could be just as accurate![24] Good, validated tests do have their place in appointments that require some particular personality traits, but they should be used with caution and care.

If selection interviews are carried out observing the principles, planning and techniques discussed here, then it is likely that appointments will be made rationally. In terms of cost, this is vital to any company, since personnel resources are expensive. In addition, its efficiency and ultimate success will depend on the quality of the people it employs. Choosing systematically and carefully is, therefore, an essential managerial function.

The objectives, planning and conduct of performance appraisal interviews

Objectives

The main aim of an appraisal interview is to assess the performance of an employee over a given period of time, usually a year, but sometimes shorter than this, in order to achieve the following objectives:

1. To identify his main strengths and weaknesses.
2. To decide from this how best to develop his strengths and overcome his weaknesses.
3. To set goals for the coming period.
4. To review how far he has achieved the goals set during the previous period.

From this it should also be possible to do the following:

1. To identify his training needs.
2. To allocate suitable work for the coming year, in order to develop his potential.
3. To identify what that potential might be for the future.

Appraisal, therefore, is an extremely important aid to using costly personnel resources in the best way possible and to reconciling the goals of the individual with those of his company. It is an instrument which can be used to promote Management by Objectives (MBO) and to develop successful manpower planning. In addition, it can be highly motivating if conducted well, and quite the opposite if it is only paid lip service, or regarded as an unpleasant chore by the manager who must implement it. Therefore, a committed attitude and a carefully considered approach to the appraisal interview are essential if appraisal is to be effective in achieving its objectives.

Planning appraisal interviews

Like the selection interview, the success of the appraisal interview rests on adequate preparation and the gathering of evidence. In this case, the necessary information should be gathered from the following sources:

1. *The observation of the employee's work performance throughout the year (or other appraisal period)* No employee assessment can be carried out adequately on the basis of what his superior remembers. This is bound to be conditioned by the outstanding incidents in the superior's mind – not always to the employee's advantage! – or the most recent. Notes must be kept on each employee throughout the year. These should record briefly successes, problems, strengths and weaknesses.

2. *The employee's records, including his last appraisal* These should be compared with the observations noted most recently. The following questions should be asked: have the strengths identified been developed – if so, in what direction? Have the weaknesses identified been overcome – if so, how and with what degree of success? Finally, how far have the set goals been achieved? (This last question is the most important one.)

The appraisal form

Careful attention needs to be given to the design of the appraisal form if it is to provide a valuable assessment and achieve the objective of recording adequate information to make employee development possible. (In Chapter 3, were discussed of the forms which attempted to give fair and full assessment, and those which gave misleading or inadequate information. It might be useful to refer to these now.)

Ideally, the appraisal form should be in two parts (one for the manager and one for his subordinate), with spaces on each part for the same kind of information. They should be filled in separately by the manager and the employee, in order that a comparison can be made. The views held by each of the year's performance can then be discussed, keeping the objectives previously listed clearly in mind. Any action, such as entry to a training course, or allocation of a particular type of work, and any goals set for the succeeding year, can be decided on in the interview, on the basis of the forms previously filled in. For this reason, both the manager and the subordinate need to spend time and attention on the form before attending the interview.

Degree of formality and structuring of the appraisal interview

The appraisal interview is crucial to the interviewee as it has implications for his career development and future salary. The appraisal interview needs to be given a formal place in the timetable at work and to be conducted in a formal environment that is free from interruptions. Sufficient time must be allocated to it in order that the employee feels that he is receiving an adequate assessment, and sufficient preparation needs to be carried out by the superior in order to show that he, too, regards it as an important event.

The questioning at the interview is structured, to some degree, by the form itself. However, there is no reason why the interview itself cannot be conducted along fairly informal lines, as this may well assist the rather difficult communication process involved. The two participants are not strangers, but are in direct contact, and the objective is to reconcile what may be different views of the same event. An informal approach may help to establish the necessary rapport and atmosphere in which this may be achieved in a friendly manner.

Conducting the appraisal interview

1. *Opening the interview* A friendly greeting and an innocuous enquiry after something unconnected with work may help to put the interviewee at ease and establish a relaxed atmosphere. The offer of a seat, not necessarily opposite the barrier of the desk, but perhaps at the side, since forms are to be compared, also stresses the need for a united approach and a harmonious interaction. The courtesy of offering a cup of coffee or tea can also help here.

2. *The objectives* These need to be spelt out at the beginning of the interview; both parties need to have a common view of what these are if they are to be achieved, and be aware of the mutual benefits in terms of personal and departmental development which can result. These objectives have been listed already, and need to be stated by the manager conducting the interview.

3. *Information giving by the employee* The employee needs to be invited to give his view of his performance first. Often, even though he has prepared, he will be hesitant, or omit information; possibly, he may give a view with which the manager may not agree. At this stage, however, the interviewer must not pass judgement or interrupt.

4. *Encouraging the employee to talk* Nevertheless, during the information-giving session, reflective questions may be used to encourage the employee to clarify a situation. If he is hesitant, open questions, posed in a friendly manner (e.g. 'What do you think are the main problems in this area of work?'), may help to elicit information, although the approach must be sympathetic, not judgemental. Encouraging, paralinguistic noises can help to increase the freedom with which he talks. All these techniques have been discussed under the heading of employment selection interviews and may be applied here equally.

5. *Information giving by the employer* An analysis of the employee's work now needs to be given. If, when listening to the employee's own analysis, it has become evident that there are explanations or views which have not occurred to the manager, he may wish to change or modify his prepared approach, which he will by now have had time to do.

6. *Reconciling the views* There are rarely any extreme views which have to be reconciled – it is usually a question of degree. Nevertheless, this is the most difficult part of the interview. Some probing may be necessary to find out about incidents which the manager may view differently from the employee. Reflective techniques can help to clarify what he really feels about one area of his work.

It is important that the benefits to be gained from a reconciliation of views, in terms of making rational decisions about the employee's best course for the future, should be stressed.

7. *Reaching decisions – action and goal-setting* Once views as to the major problems and the major strengths of the employee have been discussed, the manager should come to a decision as to how the problems might best be remedied and the strengths developed. He should outline the choices open to him, describing the advantages and disadvantages or limitations of each course of action. Through doing so, he may guide, but not direct, his choice. In this way, the actions are taken by consultation, and are much more likely to be implemented well and supported by the employee. This is particularly important if training is to be given, or development tasks be delegated – the employee will take full advantage of these only if the rationale, in terms of his own development, is clear.

Finally, goal setting should be decided by the same process, if the objectives of the manager for his department and of the individual employee are to be seen as mutually beneficial and achieve full support. It is on this note that the interview should be closed, with an assurance that the employee's performance will continue to be given attention, and assessment, on a continuous basis.

8. *Following up the interview* Copies of the appraisal form, with decisions on the action to be taken and goals set, should be kept by both the manager and the employee, and should be sent to the personnel department. Any action for which they are responsible, e.g. training, should be discussed with the interviewer before its implementation. The decisions arising from these discussions will need to be communicated to the employee in writing and, possibly, in a further interview. He should receive also written confirmation of any other actions and goals on which decisions were taken.

The records will then be filed for reference. They will be needed after the next appraisal period has been completed, in order to measure progress. If appraisal is carried out in this way, its benefits will become evident to all concerned. Conducted well, it is the most valuable aid to the motivation of employees and efficient manpower planning. Only through these two factors can the productivity and success of an enterprise, which rest ultimately on the proper use of its personnel, be assured.

The objectives, planning and conduct of counselling interviews

Objectives

The counselling interview is sometimes called the problem-solving interview, and this is perhaps more accurate for, although counsel or advice is sought from the interviewer, it should be implied rather than directly given. The objectives of a counselling interview are as follows:

1. To help someone to identify the cause of a problem which has arisen.
2. To assist them to reach a solution.

The interviewer in this kind of interview acts as a kind of therapist, attempting to remain neutral, listening, but offering no judgement. Although he may suggest possible remedial actions, these need to be offered as alternatives. It is the interviewee who must choose the solution; otherwise, if the action chosen does not have the desired effect, or worsens the situation, the interviewer will be in an invidious position and likely to attract blame and condemnation. Ultimately, the individual is alone – he or she must deal with the situation which has arisen, and live with the results.

Planning the counselling interview

Sometimes, such interviews are, and have to be, unplanned; if an employee is evidently distressed or upset, he or she will have to be interviewed at once. The only preparation possible is to delegate other work quickly or plan to do some tasks later, and arrange for no interruptions. A quiet and private place for the interview will have to be found, and a cup of tea can help.

If, however, the problem is one which has been apparent for some time – someone's work deteriorating, two employees constantly quarrelling, someone who is usually reliable becoming unpunctual or absent frequently – then more preparation is possible, and should be carried out before the interview takes place. The evidence and information required in this case will be as follows:

1. The employee's previous records.
2. Personal observation and recording of the recent behaviour that has given rise to the need for the interview.
3. Any witnesses of relevant incidents.
4. Consultation with the employee's previous immediate superior, if there is such a person available.

Degree of formality and structuring of a counselling interview

This is the least formal type of interview, for the first objective is to find the root cause of the problem. In some cases, the individual may not recognise it himself; in others, he may be reluctant to talk about it. The more informal the approach and sympathetic the response, the more likely it is that the employee will begin to talk about the problem and to explore it. It may be better, therefore, to adopt informal surroundings and an informal seating arrangement.

Structured questions cannot be asked either, since the cause of the problem is not known. If the employee is to examine the situation freely, it will be necessary to begin with some open questions and continue by responding to what these may reveal in a sensitive way, choosing the techniques which might help to achieve the objective.

Conducting the counselling interview

1. *Opening the interview* This will depend on whether the interview has had to be arranged hurriedly to meet a crisis in which the employee is evidently distraught, or whether the need for it has arisen from a number of previous incidents which are inexplicable, but have been observed and recorded over a period of time. In the first case, the interviewee needs to be relaxed. An initial

open question, put as sympathetically as possible, must begin the interview: 'If you are feeling a little better, perhaps you'd like to try to tell me what has upset you?', rather than, 'Come along now, what is it all about?' Stringency has its place, but is not appropriate at this point. In the second case, however, the interviewer needs to give the reasons why he has asked to see the interviewee. Again, the evidence should not be presented accusingly, but stated with obvious concern – both for the effect on the job itself, for which the interviewer is ultimately responsible, and for the individual.

It is these two aspects that should be stressed. The employee's previously blameless record should be emphasised also, at which point the interviewer can ask that, since there is evidently a problem which has occurred recently, it would be best if it could be discussed. In both cases, an assurance of confidentiality and a statement of the intention not to interfere, but to help the individual to decide what is best for himself, will need to be given. This is the approach most likely to establish rapport and to give the individual sufficient security and confidence to speak freely on what may be a difficult, even a personal, problem.

2. *Questioning* This should be kept to a minimum, if the interview is not to be perceived as an interrogation. If this happens, the interviewee will react either with fear or resentment – in either case, silence or lies are likely to result. The initial open question, such as those suggested for the opening of the interview, may need to be followed by a secondary one as a prompt. After this, however, it is best to listen.

3. *Listening and encouraging the interviewee to talk* This is particularly important in a counselling interview, and it is here that the reflective statement can really assist, particularly in clarifying the cause of the problem. If the interviewee appears to be talking about poor relationships with colleagues, then a statement such as: 'You feel you can't work with them', may help the employee to examine whether it is all or some of them to whom he objects, or whether the cause is quite different – that he is a faster worker, for example, and might be better employed elsewhere. Sometimes, too, a need for probing further becomes evident: 'I'm too old for promotion' *might* mean 'I don't understand the new technology', in which case some training and development might be required if total withdrawal is not to result. Here, some probe questions about the nature of what he envisages as being the work involved in the next step up the ladder might help; from his reply, his *real* problem may well become evident.

Encouraging sounds and small phrases – 'Mm, I see' – help to keep the interviewee reassured that the listener is sympathetic, but they do not interrupt. The most important rule here is to listen with full attention to everything which is said and to make no judgement.

4. *Observing the non-verbal clues* The importance of these clues has been discussed already in the section on selection interviewing. They are also an aid to discovering the real problem and measuring the reactions of the interviewee being counselled, and the interviewer should watch, as well as listen, in order to detect the truth and to gauge response as the interview continues.

5. *Offering alternatives* Once the cause or causes of the problem have been identified, the interviewer, still without making any judgement of the situation, might suggest a number of alternative lines of action. Some of these may involve reference to other people who might help – a doctor, the personnel department, or another colleague – or may involve a transfer to another department. These will obviously involve later arrangements, but for the moment these should not be discussed, nor should one solution appear to be favoured by the interviewer. The crucial question must now be put to the interviewee: 'Which of these seems the best solution to you – for yourself and for your work here?' It is thus he who must make the choice, undirected by the interviewer, and who must stand by the results.

6. *Closing the interview, agreeing a solution and making arrangements to implement it* Once a solution has been chosen by the employee, two things need to be done. Firstly, practical arrangements have to be made to implement it and here the interviewer may give advice or active help. Secondly, a period of time needs to be set during which an improvement should occur. Sometimes it is appropriate to make a time for a further interview at the end of this time, in order to check that all is going well. This shows continued concern on behalf of the manager, to which the interviewee may respond well.

7. *Noting, recording and confirmation* It would be inappropriate to take notes during this kind of interview. However, notes on the problem, its solution and the time set for improvement, as well as the date for any further interview, should be recorded directly afterwards by the interviewer and then filed for future reference. A written reminder of the decisions made, any practical arrangements completed, and relevant dates, should also be sent to the interviewee confidentially.

If the counselling interview has been concluded well, the outcome can be an acceptable solution for all and a marked improvement in the employee's performance – a very satisfactory result for all concerned. The approach and techniques outlined here help to achieve this. Occasionally, of course, the problem persists, in which case further action may need to be taken, perhaps of a more disciplinary nature, or the employee may leave of his own volition. This brings us to the final two kinds of interview – the disciplinary interview, and the exit interview.

The objectives, planning and conduct of disciplinary interviews

Objectives

The objective of this kind of interview seems to be clear from its title; however, the full objective of a disciplinary interview is not only to administer a reprimand, as many seem to believe, but also to restore respect for whatever rules have been broken. Otherwise, this problem is likely to recur, and all sorts of side-effects may exacerbate the situation, including a deterioration of industrial relations. The objectives of a disciplinary interview are as follows:

1. To verify the facts and to hear anything the employee has to say.

2. To explain what rule has been broken to the employee.

3. To ensure that the employee will accept the rule and conform to it in future.

4. To demonstrate 1 and 2 to other employees in order that they should be aware of the rule and the reasons for it.

5. To prevent any further deterioration in industrial relations.

Planning the disciplinary interview

Particularly careful preparation must be made for this type of interview; all the evidence and facts must be collected beforehand. The relevant information in this case will be as follows:

1. The exact wording of the rule or order broken.

2. Where this rule appears, and whether the contract of employment signed by the employee implies that he has accepted this and the other rules of the company.

3. The interpretation of the rule and its possible modification by custom and practice.

4. The exact nature of the offence committed by the employee and the circumstances surrounding it.

5. Any eye witness accounts, if relevant.

6. The employee's record.

7. Whether there have been any other offences by the employee and therefore whether the proper outcome of the interview should be a verbal or written warning, according to the disciplinary and grievance procedure of the firm.

In addition, the employee should be informed that it is his right to have either a colleague, or a union representative, present at the interview.

Degree of formality and structuring of a disciplinary interview

This is perhaps one of the most formal and structured interviews. Unlike the counselling interview, this should be conducted in formal surroundings, with a witness present, and the outcome must be recorded formally. The content is very structured and factual, consisting mainly of information already known and a few possible outcomes which will be laid down by the formal disciplinary and grievance procedure.

Conducting the disciplinary interview

1. *Opening the interview* Although the tone is formal, everyone should receive an invitation to be seated and the general approach should be 'firm, fair, and reasonably friendly' if adverse effects on the rest of the work group are to be avoided. The objectives listed on pages 152–53 should be communicated to all present, in order that everyone is acquainted with the aims of the interview.

2. *Information giving – a review of the facts* From notes prepared in advance, the interviewer should state to all present the exact wording of the regulation broken, its relation to the contract of employment, and the reason for its inclusion in the company rules. If it is there because of a legal requirement, e.g. to meet the requirements of Health and Safety at Work Act, this should be

stressed. The exact nature of the offence, and the evidence that it occurred, should be stated. The employee's record should be reviewed briefly, with special reference to whether any previous offences have been recorded.

3. *Questioning, listening, observing and noting* An open question should be put to the employee, asking him to state his side of the case, together with any extenuating circumstances. Supplementary probing questions can be asked if anything appears to be inconsistent.

Generally, however, it is sufficient to listen attentively to the employee and to observe any relevant non-verbal clues. If the employee is young and nervous, for example, it may mean that he has made a genuine mistake resulting from inexperience, and this will become evident from listening to the case and observing his reactions. Brief notes may be made at this time, but the main attention should be given to the interviewee.

4. *Making a judgement* The judgement at the end of the interview will depend on three things – the employee's previous record, whether there were any genuine reasons for the breaking of the regulation, and what is required within the disciplinary and grievance procedure of the specific organisation. If appropriate, a verbal or a written warning may be given, depending on the severity of the case and these three factors.

5. *Closing the interview and following up – implementing the decision and recording* Once the decision has been made as to what is the appropriate action, a time should be given, during which improvement should be made if this is appropriate. The decision must be recorded and copies sent to the personnel department, the employee and his representative. Review notes should be made immediately afterwards and kept by the interviewer in case they are needed for future reference.

The objectives, planning and conduct of exit interviews

Objectives

The objectives of an exit interview are firstly, to discover why an individual is leaving a company and, secondly, to use the information gained in order to remedy any faults in the company; occasionally it may have a third objective – to change the employee's mind. The recruitment and training of personnel is expensive; if labour turnover is high, then those costs increase, and, with every employee who leaves, money is lost. It is, therefore, worth while to identify the reasons for which any employee leaves, to analyse whether there are common reasons given by many employees and, if so, to try to improve the situation. Unfortunately, many companies neglect the simple process of giving exit interviews. They are a method of making personnel policies more cost effective by obtaining much needed feedback and should perhaps receive more attention than many firms give them.

Planning the exit interview

It is sometimes difficult for people to discuss their reasons for leaving – it may be that they have personal reasons for doing so, for example, an overwhelming dislike for a more senior member of staff! For this reason, the interview can be supplemented with, or even replaced by, a written questionnaire, called an exit questionnaire (see Fig. 29). This gives an opportunity for the employee to state an honest opinion, if he so wishes.

Once a letter of resignation has been received, an exit interview should be arranged as soon as possible, especially if the employee leaving is valued. In this case, it may be possible, having identified the reason for his resignation, to persuade him to change his mind. The information needed in advance for an exit interview is as follows:

1. The employee's records, including his length of service with the firm, his appraisal records, etc.
2. The situation affecting his pension, as he will need this explained to him.
3. Any facts about the post to which he is moving, if available.

Ideally, the exit interview should be conducted by a member of the personnel department, as it may be that the employee will talk more freely to him, and the information which he needs is usually kept in this department. However, there may be an argument for his line manager to talk to him, too. If the interview is conducted by a member of the personnel department, consultation should take place with the line manager both before and after the interview. In the consultation beforehand, it may be possible to do the following:

1. To frame some questions concerning the reasons why he is leaving, based on the line manager's knowledge of any recent causes for dissastifaction.
2. To enquire as to how valuable the line manager believes him to be to be to the firm. (This may affect the direction and objectives of the interview.)

Degree of formality and structuring of an exit interview

Although the exit interview needs to be accorded a formal place in the company's procedure, it is a good idea if it is conducted informally. In this way, the interviewee may be able to talk more freely about his real reasons for leaving – which may not be the official reason he has given in his letter of resignation. Although the first part of the interview may be structured, e.g. giving information on pension rights, the second part will be a fact-finding exercise where an unstructured approach will be more appropriate.

Conduct of an exit interview

1. *Opening the interview* After greeting the interviewee, and asking him to be seated, the first two objectives of the interview should be communicated to him, (see page 154) and the point made that the company makes every effort to use the information gained to improve its personnel policies. This has the value of leaving the employee with the impression that the company cares – a good public relations exercise, even if he is joining another firm.
2. *Information giving* The employee should be given any information which is necessary for the termination of employment, such as details about transferring pension rights.

EXIT QUESTIONNAIRE

IN CONFIDENCE

A. Will you please tick the appropriate <u>main</u> reason for leaving your job at Racole Ltd. If there were additional reasons for leaving, please mark these with a cross.

Reasons for leaving

Better prospects offered elsewhere .... ☐

Difficulties with management .... ☐

Difficulties with supervision .... ☐

Difficulties with workmates .... ☐

Not enough training .... ☐

Not made to feel at home .... ☐

Work is too heavy .... ☐

Work is too boring .... ☐

Working conditions are not good enough .... ☐

Poor amenities (e.g. cloakroom, canteen, toilets, etc.) ..... ☐

Hours of work are unsuitable .... ☐

Earnings are not high enough .... ☐

Earnings are less than other workers .... ☐

Travelling difficulties .... ☐

Illness or accident .... ☐

If you have left for a reason not shown above, please say what

it was ....

What was your job at Racole Ltd?

....

(i)

Fig. 29   An example of an exit questionnaire.

B. Please say what you liked <u>best</u> about your job?

Please say what you liked <u>least</u> about your job?

Would you recommend a friend to work at Racole Ltd?
Please say why.

If you wish to say anything else that you think will help, please
write it here.

THANK YOU FOR COMPLETING THIS FORM
YOU NEED NOT SIGN IT UNLESS YOU WANT TO

(ii)

Fig. 29 (Continued)

3. *Questioning, listening, observing and noting* It is probably best to begin with an open question, e.g. 'What was it that attracted you to this post?' This is a more positive approach than: 'Why are you leaving?' With some 'probing' questions – 'What will you be doing that will be new to you?' – and some reflective statements – 'You feel you haven't really been stretched here?' – the actual reasons why the employee is leaving may well be discovered.

Again, observations of non-verbal clues will be useful to detect feelings – especially concerning colleagues or managerial style! Only the briefest notes should be taken at the interview, otherwise an inquisitorial air will be given to the proceedings which will not be conducive to the employee revealing anything.

4. *Closing the interview* The employee may be left with a questionnaire to be filled in and handed back on his last day. This has two advantages: he may wish to expand on his reasons for leaving, and he may feel more able to be honest as he shakes the dust off his feet for the last time! He should also be told if the company is sorry to lose him, and congratulated on attaining a new post.

Exceptionally, if it seems possible that the causes given can be remedied, and the company highly values the employee, a further interview should be arranged with the line manager to see if the employee can be persuaded to stay (e.g. if he is leaving because he is not happy with his salary, he might be given an increase).

5. *Recording and following up* The reasons which emerge from the interview and from the questionnaire, if there is one, should be recorded carefully immediately afterwards. Comparisons can then be made, with the results of other exit interviews/questionnaires, in order to identify common factors. The resulting information should be fed back to the upper management levels in the personnel department who can then pass this on to the people concerned and to those who have the authority to make the relevant changes and decisions.

If exit interviews are conducted conscientiously and are recorded well, and if the information they provide is communicated to the appropriate people, then action can be taken to modify the personnel policies of the company. This will lead to improvement and increased cost effectiveness.

Conclusion

Interviewing is an extremely important method of communication; it provides an interchange of information, on the basis of which vital decisions are made. It has an important role to play in the control and effective use of human resources. It is, therefore, essential that managers should be skilful in the interviewing process, since all are managers of personnel. It is hoped that the guidelines given in this chapter clarify the objectives of each kind of interview with which managers are likely to be faced in their work, and help to improve the techniques with which they undertake this crucial managerial task.

* * *

Suggested activities for interest and self-evaluation

1. (a) Write a job description for your own job under the headings given in this chapter. Compare this with your official job description if you have one. How do they differ? What are the reasons for this?

(b) Write a personnel specification, not necessarily basing this on your own qualities.

(c) List at least three situational questions which you feel are very relevant to your work, and which you would like to ask anyone who applied for your job in the future.

2. At the next appraisal interview you either attend or give, try to analyse the following:

(a) What kinds of questioning technique were used.

(b) How fair the assessment was.

(c) What non-verbal communication took place.

3. You have an employee who is late every Monday morning. You have mentioned this to him three times and he has promised to improve, but, on the next Monday, he is late again. How would you tackle the problem?

11 | Telephone and reception techniques – a public relations function

Introduction

Telecommunications have become an indispensable method of conducting business and public affairs. The telephone, in particular, is widely used for communicating the spoken word in business, for it has two major advantages – it is fast and it obtains immediate answers. It is now possible to communicate, in a few seconds, with people in other locations within one's own company, or internationally, by means of satellite, radio, undersea cables and land-lines. The range of methods by which such communication can take place is expanding rapidly; telex, computer and video conference links are already available to modern businesses and there seems to be no doubt that, in the near future, video telephone services will be developed.

At the moment, however, the traditional telephone remains the most common method of establishing immediate contact between two or more people who would not normally be able to converse because they are not in the same place. A mastery of telephone techniques is essential, therefore, to those in business and professional careers, for two major reasons. The first is that time wasted on the telephone is very expensive. The second is that it can also be costly in terms of public relations, for the telephone, in spite of its convenience and speed, has the power to convey a poor impression, not only of an individual, but also of the organisation that employs him. For these reasons, a chapter giving some guidance on telephone techniques is essential in any book dealing with business communication.

Conducting business by telephone – the individual within the organisation

Telephone communication is a two-way process and the techniques which assist in making and taking a call are perhaps best considered separately.

Making a call

As with any kind of communication, preparation and planning are an essential prerequisite. Before making a call the following checklist should be observed:

1. Define the purpose and objectives of your call.

2. Make notes in advance of the main facts, points or questions you wish to clarify, and any you wish to give.

3. Put these notes into a logical sequence; it is much easier for the receiver to understand them if they are in the correct order, and if everything that concerns one point or query is grouped together.

4. Make sure any relevant correspondence, files, records, invoices or reference numbers that you may need are on your desk at the time of making the call, so that there is no need to keep the person at the other end waiting while you search for them.

5. Be cost conscious – don't waste your time, or the receiver's, by leaving the phone to indulge in lengthy consultation with anyone else; state that you will call back if you have to seek further information. Also choose the timing of your call carefully – it is cheaper to 'phone after 1 p.m., for instance, and even cheaper if you 'phone after 6 p.m.

6. Try to ensure that you have the correct STD code, number, extension and preferably the name and position of the person to whom you wish to speak, before you make the call.

7. Have your prepared notes ready, and put a pad for note-taking next to these.

Once the preparation has been carried out, the call can be made quickly and efficiently within the minimum time needed to gain the information required.

When conducting a call, remember the following points:

1. Help your own telephonist or the operator by giving accurate codes and numbers; if you have a direct dialling system, make sure you dial correctly.

2. Help the telephonist of the company that you are calling, once having given a greeting, by stating your name, position and company, and the name, position and extension number of the person you are calling. Then wait to be put through.

3. If you are cut off, replace the receiver, wait, ring back and state what has just happened in a polite manner, requesting to be reconnected. (It may not be the telephonist's fault!)

4. If you speak to your contact's secretary first, give a greeting, state your name, position and organisation and the objective of your call. If her superior is not available she may be able to help you herself or know someone else who may be able to do so. (Incidentally, if you are ringing a male, and a female answers who does not announce herself as his secretary, don't assume that she is; she may be his colleague or someone in a senior position. This unwarranted assumption can cause irritation and resentment.)

5. When connected with the person who can deal with your call, announce yourself and your purpose again, and give the appropriate greeting. State the main points of your call, and proceed on the basis of your notes, to give the main points and queries in a logical order.

6. Pause to get the required feedback and note the information given, especially the name and number of the person to whom you speak eventually.

When spelling out words over the telephone, or when checking them, it is useful to use the official phonetic alphabet. This is used by NATO, the Post Office, the police, and by international air traffic control.

A	Alpha	J	Juliet	S	Sierra
B	Bravo	K	Kilo	T	Tango
C	Charlie	L	Lima	U	Uniform
D	Delta	M	Mike	V	Victor
E	Echo	N	November	W	Whisky
F	Foxtrot	O	Oscar	X	X-ray
G	Golf	P	Papa	Y	Yankee
H	Hotel	Q	Quebec	Z	Zulu
I	India	R	Romeo		

Fig. 30   The telephone, or phonetic, alphabet.

7. Check on spellings of names and addresses and any numbers that are (The telephone alphabet – Fig. 30 – is useful here.)

8. If you have to leave a message for anyone, help the receiver by dictating this so that the main points you require are included.

9. Be polite and courteous and thank the receiver for his help, even if it has not been all that you required. Remember that this is good public relations.

10. Be brief; this is not difficult if you have prepared adequately. Remember that it is the caller who should terminate the call, although this is not a hard and fast rule and will depend on the situation.

After the call has been made, remember to do the following:

1. Write up the notes you have made under queries or headings derived from your prepared notes so that they make sense at a later date and constitute a complete future reference.

2. Date the notes made and file in an appropriate place.

3. Note any dates and future actions which are required in your diary.

4. Write down any messages that concern others and pass them on immediately, with the date of the call and the name/company of the person who you have just called included.

If a call is planned, conducted and recorded following these rules, telephone communication can be rapid, cost effective and can establish a reputation for the efficiency of the caller and his company.

Taking a call

Taking a call courteously and responding to the caller's queries competently is equally important in conveying a professional approach and promoting good public relations. The major points to remember in this case are as follows:

1. Keep a message pad and pencil near the telephone.

2. Keep an internal directory near the telephone permanently, in case you have to transfer a call, plus your own appointments diary so that you can consult it as necessary.

3. Ask other people to be a little quieter, if possible, before answering if you work in an open plan office, and answer promptly.

4. If the call has come through the switchboard, and the name of the company has already been given, simply announce your name and/or position and department, give a cheerful greeting and ask if you can help. Try to sound as though you wish to do so. Some people only announce their surname which, while correct, can sound a little brusque. It is probably better to give both names in any case to avoid confusion. 'Clark' for example, sounds like a bark; the addition of a first name – 'Trevor Clark speaking' – not only sounds friendlier but also identifies the speaker more exactly.

5. Listen carefully and check any facts, numbers or spellings where necessary. Names and addresses, in particular, should be spelled out.

6. Take notes; do not rely on your memory.

7. If there is a message which you should pass to someone else, clarify the main points with the caller, note and read back what you have written.

8. Use phatic communication – 'mm', 'Yes, I see', etc. – in order to reassure the caller that you are still there and are concentrating.

9. Do not allow yourself to be distracted.

10. Be cost conscious – if there is someone or something which needs to be consulted, or is unavailable, do not leave the caller 'hanging on'. Ask if you can ring back, and try to agree a time when you can do so.

11. Always check figures, times and dates, and confirm any action that has been agreed – 'I will ring back Thursday at 9.30 a.m.', for example – before ringing off.

Once a call has been taken, it is essential to review, record and take any necessary action. Therefore, after the call, remember to do the following:

1. Write up the notes clearly so that they are understandable and are not a series of jottings.

2. Carry out any actions required immediately – tell any colleague who is concerned, enter any appointments or calls to be made in your diary with the exact times, write any memoranda or letters as soon as possible on the basis of your notes.

3. If you have taken a written message for anyone else, make sure it is recorded clearly with all the facts, numbers, etc., accurately noted and deliver it immediately.

If a call is taken and recorded in this way and messages are passed on immediately, the communication process will be well managed and effective. This always should be the outcome if a good public image and a successful communication network are to be maintained.

The receptionist/telephonist – the first line in public relations

The first impression of any company is derived, usually, from the receptionist and/or telephonist. Sometimes these roles are combined, although this can result in unwelcome pressure which may affect efficiency and therefore the image of the company. It is essential, therefore, that the staff chosen for these important positions are not the most junior and inexperienced members of staff. Their selection should be given very careful consideration. Let us examine the two functions of reception and telephone operation separately.

The receptionist

THE ENVIRONMENT

The reception area should be attractively designed and comfortably furnished, with any brochures or catalogues at hand for visitors who have to wait for a few moments. The environment itself will begin to communicate an image of the company's work, philosophy and attitudes. It should represent, therefore, its range of activities, as well as be as welcoming as possible.

Often it is deliberately prestigious, with models of products or pictures of overseas operations. Sometimes, too, it is a security area, designed to act as a barrier, through which all must pass, in order to be identified and directed to their correct destination.

SELECTING A RECEPTIONIST – QUALITIES AND CHARACTERISTICS

The receptionist needs to be carefully selected, for it is his or her appearance, voice, attitudes and manner which will determine how the caller begins to perceive the company as a whole. The non-verbal impressions are very important here in creating favourable reactions – the 'halo' or 'horned' effect referred to on page 144. A smart appearance indicates a businesslike approach, and a pleasant greeting, a smile, an enquiry as to how the caller can be assisted, establishes an agreeable atmosphere and an assurance that his query or visit will be worthwhile. A clear, audible voice is necessary. Everyone tends to make judgements about speech which extend, not only to that person's entire character, but also to his or her company. Careless appearance, ignoring the caller or giving a muttered answer to his query, and appearing indifferent to his needs, tend to create embarrassment, resentment and a total lack of confidence, not only in the receptionist but also in the management.

A good receptionist should be able to cope with difficult situations confidently. When interviewing people for this post, situational questions, or even small case studies, are useful to see if the receptionist will be able to act tactfully and diplomatically on her own initiative. If a caller asks to see someone who is not available and/or if he has a complaint of some kind, he is likely to become irate or aggressive and the receptionist needs to be able to calm him down and suggest alternative solutions. To do this, however, the receptionist, no matter what the qualifications, experience or training previously received, must be adequately briefed in all relevant matters relating to the organisation.

THE BRIEFING AND TRAINING OF A RECEPTIONIST

In order to help callers in the most constructive way, the receptionist should have a comprehensive knowledge of the following:

1. The range of products and services offered by the firm.
2. The roles of the personnel within the firm.
3. The names of the secretarial staff who hold information on the where-abouts of executive personnel and of their programmes of activities.

Organisation charts, company literature and house journals are useful sources of information which should be given to the receptionist, but anyone undertaking the role will also need a thorough induction training. This should include security procedures, since receptionists often issue passes to visitors, record who they are visiting and why, note times of arrival and departure, and register numbers of visiting vehicles. If the receptionist is to undertake the duties of a telephonist as well, either as a relief to a colleague or as part of a combined job, then other factors must be considered.

The telephonist

SELECTING A TELEPHONIST

The telephonist, too, plays a vital role in conveying initial impressions about the firm to the outside world. Here, however, the situation is somewhat different, for the telephonist has been called the 'faceless voice'. The non-verbal elements which assist someone concerned with the personal reception of visitors – appearance and expression, the smile of greeting – are absent over the telephone, and it is perhaps for this reason that many people have developed a dislike for this method of communication. The disembodied voice, deprived of other ways of conveying its message, may appear abrupt or brusque, which can be very off-putting to any caller. The telephonist, therefore, needs to be selected for the qualities her voice conveys. It must be clear, audible, intelligible, cheerful, warm and confident.

The telephonist, however, is not just a voice and is expected to do far more than act as an answering machine. Like a receptionist, she needs to be tactful and be able to cope with difficult callers. She must convey reassurance and calm by her telephone manner, and employ intelligence and initiative when putting through a call, if the person required is unavailable.

Recruiting a good telephonist involves choosing someone who is familiar with the technical operation of a switchboard through previous training or experience. She should be given adequate induction training in, and a careful briefing on, the type of system and the procedures expected within that specific company.

THE BRIEFING AND INDUCTION TRAINING OF A TELEPHONIST

Any new telephonist will need some initial help before she can operate a particular system without error and with confidence. This is a necessity if the first impression received by the caller is to be the efficiency of the company and if communications are to be quick and effective. In particular, the procedure for transferring calls (or, as is now possible in newer and more sophisticated systems, for connecting more than one extension so that conferences can take place), must be known. In addition to acquiring the required technical expertise to manipulate the system competently, the telephonist must, like the receptionist, be knowledgeable about the company itself.

An induction process will take account of this need. This will involve, firstly, instruction as to the kind of initial greeting preferred by the firm – the name of the firm should be clearly given obviously, and the telephonist should be reminded not to speak until the call is entirely connected, or over the top of the mouthpiece. Often, an incomplete final syllable '... Sons Ltd' is all that is heard by the caller. For this reason, and in order to be polite, it is probably better if the telephonist says 'Good morning' before announcing the firm's name. If a 'Can I help you?' follows, all the better – especially if the voice actually conveys the impression that the speaker would like to do so!

Secondly, the telephonist must have access to information concerning the activities of the firm and the roles of the various personnel within it, who may be approached if a certain executive is unavailable. Only then can incoming calls be rerouted successfully and incoming calls be connected correctly.

In addition, everything needed for reference to make outgoing calls quickly and accurately must be at hand. The telephonist will require an operating manual, a list of extension numbers, the necessary updated directories, code books and reference or trade directories and an organisation chart with names and positions of personnel, preferably with extension numbers for quick reference.

The following is a list of key 'do's' and 'don'ts' if the public relations function is to be kept constantly in mind.

1. Give the required greeting and announcement of the firm's name clearly, audibly and cheerfully.

2. Be courteous – ask how the caller can be assisted.

3. If someone is asked for by name or by number, and this is not clear immediately, check carefully – remember that numbers sound similar, e.g. five and nine, fifty and fifteen. If spelling or letters are unclear check the first by spelling back and check the second by using the Post Office telephone alphabet.

4. Reassure the caller as to what is happening – the words 'I'm putting you through' help to ensure that he is aware that the process has been set in motion and prevents him ringing off in despair.

5. If the extension number is engaged, say so, and ask whether the caller would prefer to hold the line or ring back. Remember that telephone time is money.

6. If the extension number is not answered, do not leave the caller connected endlessly. Interrupt, state that there is no reply at present, and ask whether he would prefer to call back or speak to someone else.

7. If the person concerned is unavailable, be constructive; try to suggest someone else who may help.

8. When rerouting a call, reassure the caller and tell him that you are doing so. Give him the name and position of the person to whom you are connecting him.

9. Never leave the caller, under any circumstances, hanging on interminably, apparently connected to a silent and echoing chamber!

10. Always be cheerful, polite, tactful and discreet. The last quality – that of discretion – is needed by telephonists, receptionists and by anyone within the firm.

The telephonist/receptionist is central to the communication processes of any company, and to its public relations with the outside world. This fact needs to be recognised, and appropriate care taken over selection and training; the receptionist/telephonist also needs to see that the firm regards that role as important, and that his or her work is valued. If this can be conveyed, then motivation will be high.

Conclusion

Telephone communication can be very cost effective, compared to the exchange of letters. The letter is slow and it has been estimated that each business letter sent costs approximately £7, in real terms, at the time of writing. The telephone is the quickest method of obtaining answers and information from anywhere in the world.

If the interaction it requires has been carefully planned and recorded, and is conducted with intelligence and courtesy, the outcome of a telephone call can be both productive and an asset to public relations. It is, therefore, the most widely used communication service in business today. Unfortunately, it can be misused, with resulting delays, frustration and waste of time and money. The observation of the basic principles and a mastery of the simple techniques discussed in this chapter are essential if this important medium of communication is to be used to realise its full potential and prove truly cost effective.

In the future, business telecommunication will become increasingly sophisticated. New methods, aided by allied developments in computers, already are being adopted by companies which realise the need to improve the accuracy, speed and capacity of their communication systems. A knowledge of the applications of the new technology will soon be a necessity in any career as it has an unprecedented impact on nearly every aspect of modern society. A book such as this can scarcely ignore what is effectively a revolution; consequently, Part 4 examines its implications for communications in the business world.

* * *

Suggested activities for interest and self-evaluation

1. Refer back to the suggested activity for self-evaluation at the end of Chapter 3.

2. Compile a check list which would be helpful to the junior who will be trained to operate a switchboard. The technical checks should be based on the telephone system which operates within your own firm and should include instructions for transferring calls, making internal connections, etc.; the other checks should refer to her task as a public relations representative of the firm.

3. List, over one week, the main faults that you have noticed in the telephone communications in your firm. Try to analyse the reasons why they occurred, being entirely honest about your own shortcomings! How could they have been remedied? What might you learn from these?

Part 4 | New directions in business communication – the expansion of information technology and its implications

12 | The rapid revolution – a review of the techniques now available for business communication

Introduction

'Information Technology (IT) is the fastest developing area of industrial and business activity in the Western world. Its markets are huge, its applications multitudinous and its potential for efficiency immense.' Mr K. Baker, Minister for Information Technology, made that statement in 1982 – Information Technology Year. Nowhere have developments moved so fast and the potential for efficiency been so great as in business communications. The next decade is likely to prove even more astonishing in the rapidity of its advance.

Two separate technologies have brought about this revolution. The first was the use of the silicon chip, on which highly complex electronic circuits could be etched in a minute space, reducing both the size and the cost of computers. The second was the accelerating pace of developments in telecommunications, which has taken us, in a few years, from the traditional (but unreliable) analogue telephone, carrying electrical signals representing human speech, to the modern digital systems, which can convey almost any type of information and carry a high volume of signals simultaneously. Already, further developments are taking place, exploring the possibilities of optical fibre and opto-electronic devices, which can convert light to electrical current and vice versa. These developments have meant that more than one signal can be carried at a time (known as multiplexing), thus reducing costs. In the case of fibre optics, very high reliability has been achieved, resulting in clear, accurate data transmission, free from distortion or 'corruption'.

The convenience of these two areas (the French have coined the word 'télématique' for them) have begun to transform business communications and, indeed, the very pattern of our lives. The 'information society', where information can be stored, processed, retrieved and communicated more speedily and accurately, yet at a lower cost that ever before, is already with us. The impact on the future of the business world will be significant.

Like the Industrial Revolution, information technology has met with resistance from many, especially where it has affected the sensitive area of employment. For better or for worse, however, its advantages and its dangers are here to stay, and anyone in business today would be well advised to become as familiar with the devices and systems available, if he or she is to select wisely those most appropriate to his or her company and its work, and to operate them competently and confidently.

For this reason let us review briefly the developments to date and their applications to business communications. It must be stressed, however, that what follows is in no way intended to be a technical manual; it is merely a short appreciation of the impact of the new technology on business and a discussion of the possible applications and potential problems which have become evident so far. It is meant for the layman, rather than the expert, and every effort has been made to keep this final part, which is believed to be essential in any book on modern business communications, as simple, clear, relevant and jargon-free as possible.

The development of computers and their relevance to business communication

Computers have been referred to as 'office clerks with no spark of imagination'. Certainly, in concept, they are just powerful tools which can store, process and output information in a very simple way based on a binary code (a number system with base 2), essentially a series of dots or spaces punched on to a tape. These are called 'bits' and, in order to make one letter or number, a combination of eight of these is required, known as a 'byte'.

The information which needs to be stored, processed or output at a later date then needs to be fed into the computer by a program. This might be in any one of a number of computer languages. These were originally very complex (yet known paradoxically as 'low level' languages), ensuring that only an expert could programme and use the computer. One of the most important developments has been the use of languages that are simpler ('high level'), which have particular relevance to the activities of different kinds of companies, e.g. Cobol, Fortran, PL/I, Pascal, Algol and 'C'. This last is becoming very popular. Software developed on a microcomputer can now run with little modification on a mainframe computer, too.

Perhaps the most important development is the use of languages, such as BASIC, which everyone can use easily because they are very near to normal English. This has meant that most people can be trained (or can train themselves) to use a computer quickly and easily. The result is that many offices and homes have computers installed in them. This move towards simplification has affected the actual design of the machines, particularly the keyboards. In the future, voice recognition will undoubtedly give immediate and unimpeded access to all.

Whatever advances are made, however, in order for the computer to understand its operator, it must have some means of translating normal English into computer terms. This is achieved by a program, called an Operating System, which is held by the computer and is its means of communicating with the outside world. In most small computers this is called an Operating System for Microcomputers (a CP/M) which allows input and output of information. To process it, however, a further program is needed which converts a list of procedures or facts into a form the computer understands. This program will be controlled always by the CP/M, but any number of programs, with any number of applications, can then be run.

Information which needs to be stored long term is usually stored on magnetic tape or magnetic disk. Tape is economical but needs to be read in sequence (e.g. for monthly statements); the disk has to be used when it is necessary to extract information from different places – known as 'Random Access'. Random Access Memory (RAM) means that information can be retrieved, in any order, from the internal memory. Typically, the larger mainframe computers use both tape and disks. Floppy disks are most in use, for they can store up to 130 A4 pages of information. Larger disks hold even more and are usually used in the mainframe computer. Information can be stored also short term in internal memory on the silicon memory chip, but this is too limited for mass storage. At present, therefore, a number of other solid state storage systems are being developed for this purpose.

Once the machine has been programmed, and the information stored, it can then be retrieved, manipulated or transmitted by 'keying in' specific words on the keyboard which have been incorporated into the program already, in order that the computer recognises the task required of it. An operator learns these – and again, efforts have been made to make operating manuals and procedures as simple as possible, as the necessity of training large numbers of staff to use the new techniques has become evident.

Computers have become cheaper and smaller with the advance of microchip technology, so they are used by all levels of personnel within companies. The first digital computer used large valves to store the memory, was big enough to require a whole room to accommodate it (often needing full air conditioning), needed experts to operate, it and was extremely costly. Today's small business computers can be constructed from a small number of integrated chips. (It is not inconceivable that the single chip will soon be developed.) They can communicate quickly and easily with the outside world, and vice versa through a simple arrangement of keyboards and visual display units, which can stand on a desk top, and their costs are being reduced constantly.

The company mainframe computer is still important today and is linked to a number of microcomputers, which in turn are often linked together. This is achieved through a 'local area network' (LAN) – a cable laid through a firm's premises, with sockets or 'jack points' at convenient locations. The pieces of equipment which need to communicate with one another, or the central computing facility, can be plugged into these. In this way, the microcomputer can communicate with the mainframe, and the various devices of the modern office can communicate with each other. These extra devices that are added to an internal system are called 'peripherals'.

In the past, there have been problems concerning the 'compatibility' of machines – that is, their ability to 'talk' to one another. Today, this problem is being overcome. Manufacturers have been compelled by market pressures to give priority to making systems and devices compatible.

Generally, within a local area network, each piece of equipment has an 'interface' – a device which 'interprets' its output before it transmits it and translates its input, as it receives it from other machines, into a form which can be understood and assessed by the operator. In this way, the various pieces of equipment available to modern business – word processors, graphics plotters, telex terminals, etc. – can be linked together as required. The microcomputer also can communicate with the company's mainframe computer or major database, interrogate it, store information and process it, so saving mainframe time, a facility that has given it the name of the 'intelligent terminal'.

These developments, which have allowed machines to communicate with one another, have created the concept of the 'integrated office'. With each 'work station' linked with others within a company, internal electronic mail has become possible.

The punch tape and computer print-outs which have characterised computers to date – although still in existence and very useful for record keeping or pre-recording telex messages – have largely been replaced (for storage purposes) by magnetic tape or disk. These take up little space, and can be displayed readily on a visual display unit (VDU). The local area network allows messages to be flashed from screen to screen. Bulky filing cabinets are being replaced by microfilm techniques. Computer-aided retrieval has made quick cross referencing and fast access possible. Computer Output Microfilm (COM) uses information already held in the computer memory. It uses a very high speed camera, held within the COM recorder, which interprets this on to microfilm in 'fiche' format. Microfilm has a vary large storage capacity in a very small space, making storage space minimal and the distribution of information very cheap. (One fiche can go into an envelope and replace 270 pages of computer print-out.)

External communication by letter could become obsolete, too. Electronic mail, already widely in use within companies via LAN, can now be extended outside the companies by the addition of a further link which gives access, via a dialling system, to all external telecommunication services. This link, known as a 'Modem' (Modulator-Demodulator), is a telephone receiver/transmitter which is a further interface converter.

In this way, companies are not only able to communicate and process internally all the information at their command, but also can take advantage of these facilities externally. Modem has direct access to data transmittted to it by other organisations or central databases. It can communicate with them directly, obviating the need to send contracts and letters by slow postal methods which can be unreliable. These electronic transactions are rapid, accurate and cheap, especially when they are international, since the charge is based on the amount, rather than the distance involved. Business communications, therefore, benefit immensely from the combination of the advances in computer technology and those achieved in telecommunications.

Developments in telecommunications related to business communication

The traditional analogue telephone does have faults – mainly its high cost, since only one signal can be transmitted at one time. The error rate can be high – according to a number of surveys, only 40 per cent of calls reach their destination. For large amounts of information, a low grade system such as this, designed for voice transmission only, is slow and costly.

Advances in digital systems, and most recently in fibre optics, have meant that it is now possible to carry vast amounts of information of various kinds – whether transmitted verbally, or in writing, since everything is converted into binary digital form prior to transmission. Because of the high volume sent, the cost will also be low. Some of the services, which have resulted from these advances, are already widely used, such as Datel and telex. Others, such as public packet-switched networks (notably Teletext), Viewdata systems and teleconferencing, are currently being developed and implemented. I will now describe briefly the major developments.

1. *Datel* This is already in general use for the transmission of data. It can use normal telephone lines, or specially leased high frequency lines for high transmission rates. It enables terminals in scattered work locations to communicate with central computer facilities or databases at a rate equivalent to several A4 pages per minute.

2. *Telex* This, too, is already in general use. Teletypewriters are used to transmit text messages, contact being established by dialling. The message is transmitted over normal telephone lines. Its advantages are that it is a 24-hour service and it is cheap for, unlike a normal telephone call, the charge is based on time taken, not distance. Using telex means that a permanent record of the message and the reply are kept. However, as it is a little slow, the message is often pre-recorded on to punch tape to save line time. When fed back, this automatically activates the teletype at the other end which records the message.

3. *Facsimile* Facsimile can transmit image, as well as text, over normal telephone lines and is cheaper and faster than telex. It maintains the exact state of the original and is thus the best method of communicating charts, graphs, designs and contracts. As it can produce hard copy, it is useful for record-keeping. In the past, there have been problems over the compatibility of the facsimile system, especially internationally, but these are fast disappearing. The new digital Group 3 machines can communicate with other electronic office equipment, as well as communicate externally. Transmission time and reception time from such machines is now down to 30 seconds approximately for one document, and British Telecom is planning a subscriber facsimile service which will make use of cheap telephone time at night. Documents transmitted in day time will be scanned, stored on magnetic tape, and transmitted automatically later.

The introduction of the new telecommunications network, known as System X, will mean a transmission speed of 3 seconds and the use of satellites could reduce this even further, making instant international communication a reality.

Facsimile is likely to be very widely used in the future, for it will be cheap, fast and precise, especially when the new services, now being developed by British Telecom and throughout Europe, are introduced. Let us now review these services and their current state of development.

Public packet-switched networks

These are now being implemented and will accelerate further the development of speedy and accurate communication on an international scale. Like System X (the network planned by British Telecom), they will employ laser transmissions by fibre optics, enabling a high volume of messages of any description – voice, text or image – to be sent rapidly and accurately at low cost. These networks will be computer controlled and messages will be sent in 'packets' to a coded destination address. The computer will work out the best route for the packet, will store it for a short space, if necessary, and automatically will assemble any number of packets in the right order at the correct destination.

There will be standardised interfaces enforcing compatibility of machines so that international communication will be extended and facilitated throughout the world and, since the user will be charged by volume and not by distance sent, it is likely to become even cheaper than at present.

Value-added networks, including Teletext

These will offer data transmission services, as well as giving 'value added' computer facilities, such as electronic storage and retrieval, access to information bases, text editing and multi-address mailing. Perhaps the most important of these is Teletext, a worldwide communication system now being implemented. This will operate on any network, including telephone and packet-switched networks. Its rate of transmission will be 50 times as fast as telex and it will be able to transmit images from facsimile machines, too – from anything, in fact, that has reduced its message into binary form, has the right interface and the right coding characteristics. Thus any word processor or facsimile receiver (providing they have these facilities) will be able to gain access easily to all the information processing services.

Viewdata or video text

Viewdata, or videotext, brings information into offices or homes by linking a television screen to a central computer via the telephone line. Any telephone subscriber can make use of the service – all that is required is an ordinary television, an adaptor to connect it to the telephone network, and a keyboard. Viewdata is an electronic filing system, storing 'pages' or frames of text which can be displayed on the network user's screen by keying in a code number. A comprehensive index, known as a 'menu', enables the user to locate any frame for which he does not know the code number.

Company viewdata systems, and those provided by computer bureaux, provide management information quickly and accurately and will doubtless assist management decision making in the future. The text held on any frame can be updated easily by keying in new information, and bureaux offer facilities for this. Manufacturers are now developing viewdata systems which can combine data and word processing so that all the information which needs to be processed by a business will be available to any of the electronic work stations which will form the basis of any commercial organisaion in the future.

In addition, British Telecom provide a public viewdata system known as Prestel. This provides government statistics and stock exchange information, as well as consumer information. It is interactive, messages can be sent between Prestel users, and hard copies of pages can be obtained by connecting the network to the printer. It has some 'closed' user facilities, that is, it allows some subscribers to rent space on particular computers or to have access to some private databases. Thus, companies can have access to relevant information for their particular business, and research information is also available. Again, a 'keyed in' code is needed to open up the 'gateway' that links the user to the database required. Hatfield Polytechnic, and the Institute of Electrical Engineers, for example, have such databases available for designated users.

The future is likely to see transaction services carried out by viewdata systems – teleshopping and electronic banking are already developing quickly. Copies of bills and statements can be obtained by connecting a printer. Point-of-sale transactions in supermarkets and Electronic Funds Transfer (as the banks are already calling this facility) may mean not only a paperless office, but also a cashless society!

Teleconferencing and confravision

If the necessity for paper and cash is being reduced in the business world of today so, too, is the need for travel. Teleconferencing is already widely used via the local area network within companies and the modern public telecommunication systems have also made intra-organisation teleconferencing possible.

Confravision, a facility at present only available in special studios, can link conference members via telecommunication networks and television screens, allowing simultaneous interaction by voice and image. At the moment this is expensive, but, in the future, especially with the development of fibre optics systems, it is likely to become cheaper and more universally accessible. The savings in terms of travel time, transport costs and security risks are likely to make this attractive to business executives and politicians alike. Undoubtedly, this kind of communication has enormous potential – for project planning and top level meetings of all kinds – in the business of tomorrow.

The future – satellites, cables and fibre optics

In the telecommunications of the future, satellites, coaxial cable and developments in fibre optics are likely to offer an enormous range of facilities. Satellites already carry all kinds of information, transmitting, internationally, voice, facsimile, image and data, as well as telephone calls and television broadcasts. British Telecom is now advertising Intelpost – 'the post box in the sky'. The Intelstat network today links 105 nations via 12 satellites, for we have come a long way since the single pioneering Telstar of 1962. Multi-national companies in the United States are beginning to put up their own satellites already and it has been predicted recently that a satellite link between London and New York will allow a page of information to be transmitted by facsimile in 2 seconds. At the same time, fibre optics using laser, infra-red and ultraviolet technology are advancing at a rapid rate, allowing a high volume of information, in any form, to be transmitted quickly, cheaply, accurately and free from corruption.

Finally, television networks are moving ahead with the development of coaxial cable, allowing the transmission of a high volume of signals (and, therefore, a wide choice of programmes and services), which are relatively free from interference. All these developments, particularly as they become interwoven with the rapidly accelerating computer technology of today, must lead to enormous improvements in business communications and will transform the office of the future.

The electronic office – tomorrow's business organisation

The offices of tomorrow are likely to be unrecognisable when compared with those of the past, containing less people and less paper. The 'digital desk', as it has been called, will not be cluttered with papers and trays but will contain a variety of electronic devices, linked to other work stations within the office, to executives and salesmen working outside, to relevant central computing facilities and databases, and to the rest of the world via its links with the telecommunications services.

The electronic devices within the office will reduce the lengthy paper-based methods of communication, the space-consuming storage systems, and the labour force. They will therefore cut costs and increase efficiency – every manager's dream. It will be worthwhile, now, to look at the potential, and the applications, of the electronic equipment at present being adopted by the most forward-looking companies.

Word processors and the alternatives

A word processor is a computer which is 'dedicated to' (or specialises in) processing text. Until recently, word processors were capable of little, except the storage and editing of words; now some models offer calculation and other storage facilities.

Unlike the traditional typewriter, where words typed on the keyboard are printed on paper simultaneously, the word processor stores the text in its memory, displaying the completed document on a VDU so that the operator can correct errors by using its special editing functions. Some now offer the facility whereby a document can be printed out while the operator corrects another, avoiding the frustration and time wasted between jobs.

When the text is perfect, it can be printed out, using (usually) a daisywheel printer. The costs and speeds of these vary, but any company that really needs a word processor needs a fast printer – some can type an A4 page in less than a minute. (The word processing and printing equipment, used by the *Reader's Digest* for its mass mail shots, produces 1,800 lines a minute.)

Apart from ease of editing and speed, the other main advantage is that all documents can be stored on floppy disk and retrieved, when necessary. Furthermore, information from more than one disk can be merged into a standardised letter with personalised names, addresses and salutation – ideal for circular letters.

Alternatives to the word processor include, firstly, the electronic typewriter. This has a limited memory but is less costly and is adequate to produce error-free text where typing is neither complicated nor repetitive. Some of the latest electronic typewriters can be upgraded, if necessary, to screen-based word processors, but at present the cost makes these uncompetitive.

The second possibility is an ordinary microcomputer system with a capacious memory, word-processing software and a printer. This is relatively cheap, and some systems even offer the simultaneous printing/editing option (or device which can be plugged in to give this facility, known as a 'Macrobyte').

At the moment, the word processor remains the easiest system to use although, with the arrival of more 'user-friendly' micro software (one program tested in a recent survey by *The Observer* could be learned in 90 minutes[25]), this advantage may lessen in future. Some new systems being produced will offer more business applications than the word processor and, before long, 'voice' typewriters will be able to convert dictation into typed text directly.

Whichever system is chosen, it means that many jobs will disappear at a lower level – a word processor which produces hundreds of documents in a day with one operator is bound to take the place of a number of typists. As such, it is not only efficient and accurate but also highly cost effective, especially with the prices of such equipment being reduced and the range of facilities offered being constantly improved.

Electronic mail and the microcomputer

These have already been described earlier – the microcomputer, when linked internally and externally into the electronic mail systems, saves both paper and time. A microcomputer, acting as a word processor, for example, can send and receive electronic mail, transmit telex messages, link into databases – all at a very low cost. Using a screen and keyboard, it is now possible to send letters over the telephone network, via the Modem, and these will reach their destination in seconds. Every microcomputer is a potential electronic mail terminal, and a new service called Micromail will be introduced shortly to give personal computer users access to the British Telecom 'Gold' system. As far as business is concerned, the packet-switched data service now offers speeds of up to 6,000 characters per second. Teletext is likely to offer even further facilities, if the cost can be kept low.

The microcomputer, linked to electronic local area networks and external telecommunications systems, as well as central databases, is likely to be at the centre of the office revolution, saving managerial time, reducing the costs of slower forms of communication and replacing the piles of paper on the executive desk with a keyboard, a VDU and instant access to information and transmission systems of all kinds. It may reduce also the need for attendance at the office! Suitcase microcomputers for salesmen, and portable keyboards for managers at home, will allow them to take decisions at any work station, since the information they require can be made available to them immediately. They can also communicate with other staff, receive and give messages, gain access to sales figures and orders and accounts, communicate with any relevant database, manipulate information, and even have access to their diary from any location.

Photocopiers and facsimile

The facsimile or 'fax' machine has been relatively slow to reach offices, while the photocopier has held its ground. This has been partly due to the past failure to agree on standards and compatibility. The advantages of facsimile have already been discussed at length. We are, therefore, likely to see, with the advent of advanced telecommunication systems and agreement on standards, far wider use of facsimile. With these advances, integration between facsimile, word-processing and photocopying equipment is likely to develop further, too, and the potential for producing and transmitting exact information and confirmation by precise record, cheaply and quickly, exists. The office of the future is likely to see the integration of all communication equipment, and thus advances in the accuracy and speed of its communication and information processing.

Telex and Teletext

Telex, too, is likely to be displaced by technological advances in telecommunications and Teletext is likely to become the most widely used service. The separate telex machine will probably disappear and the microcomputer, with access to telecommunication systems, will be used instead to transmit information via the Teletext system previously described. Teletext could become integrated with and/or take over from the facsimile machine, and video conferencing will become accessible and cheap.

The necessity for older methods of communication and for travel will be reduced inevitably and this may well have implications for an increasing amount of managerial activity taking place away from the office. Work will be located at the electronic work station, rather than in the accepted office premises of the past.

Viewdata

Although Prestel now has 50 per cent more users than a year ago and offers useful general information, private and business-based systems are likely to proliferate. These offer specific information to public and private enterprises.

Databases holding specialised information are increasing in number and sophistication already. Again, access and use are likely to become more widespread, and most offices of the future will use the viewdata system relevant to its business. The advantages for small businesses are particularly outstanding here, allowing access to a store of information which would have been impossible previously.

Conclusions – costs, benefits and delays in implementation

The office of the future is likely to consist of an integrated electronic system with machines and equipment through which the company's personnel can input, access, manipulate or transmit information, intra- and inter-organisationally, by microcomputer, from any location. Speed and accuracy of communication will be increased and cost reduced as manpower levels fall and hours are saved. The typewriter, the filing cabinet and the in-tray are likely to become obsolete. Expenditure on the electronic office has been low compared to other areas of industrial automation. This is in spite of the fact that most offices are overmanned and that managerial and administrative salaries are rising as fast as those of other white-collar workers. This is because computer costs are falling just as rapidly.

Although the market for automated office equipment is currently growing at a rate of 34 per cent per year, office integration is not being introduced universally at present. The reasons for this delay appear to be varied. Some are technical, such as the problems of incompatibility discussed earlier in this chapter; some are due to problems in development, such as the lack of suitable software, and some are financial – a lack of commitment by top management can result in too low a budget, possibly stemming from an understandable reluctance to risk high capital investment in an area which is developing so rapidly that obsolescence is likely, even within a year of the date of purchase. Then, too, there has been wariness after the tales of expensive mistakes and commercial disasters. These have occurred either because commission-hungry salesmen sell computers irresponsibly to businessmen who don't know enough about them, or because an inadequate evaluation of a company's needs by suppliers or purchasers has been made. Occasionally, past incompetence has been made the cause. A computer is logical and if it attempts to computerise inefficient manual systems this will lead, inevitably, to failure.

Most errors are human ones. Resistance to change has been shown by people's reactions – lack of planning or willingness to implement the system, or resentment owing to fear of job loss. Unions also are opposed to these changes. Such resistance can be overcome if the changes are introduced in the right way and communicated to everyone concerned after careful consultation, preparation and planning.

The next chapter looks at the importance of communication in the technological revolution. Its future direction will depend on how successfully it can accommodate the human factor and on how far people working in businesses can be convinced that they need, and are able to use, its products.

* * *

Suggested activity for self-evalution and interest

Try to make a list of your work activities during one week at work under the following headings:

1. Document related activities – mail, reports, letters, memos, etc.
2. Telephone calls – receiving and transmitting.
3. Meetings, formal and informal, including interviews.
4. General administration related to the storage or retrieval of information (filing, researching, preparation of references, etc.).
5. Analysis or decision-making – analysing information and solving problems.
6. Calculations.
7. Supervision or allocation of work to others.
8. Information seeking from others.
9. Training (undergoing training or giving training).
10. Unproductive activity – waiting, travelling, wasting time, etc.
11. Other activity (specify this).

Now note against each activity how any of the systems or equipment discussed in this chapter might help to save time or make your work more efficient; in particular, how could they reduce unproductive activity? Are there any activities which you could perform just as well at home, given access to electronic equipment?

13 | The human factor – the need to prepare for technological change

Introduction

This chapter has been deliberately slanted towards managers as they are responsible, usually, for choosing the new technology and for phasing it in gradually and, therefore, successfully. Although we will look at the problems of employees' resistance to technological change, we must bear in mind that some managers also resist it, and that some employees do exploit the communication advantages of the new technology.

Computers in industry have attracted high capital investment – sums of between £15,000 and £20,000 invested in capital equipment per worker, are quite common. Up to 75 per cent of total office costs are managers' salaries, yet they use only 30 per cent of the automated equipment[26]. These figures for the United Kingdom are supported by similar findings in the USA[27] where surveys have found that, although salaries for white-collar workers are increasing, only a small amount is spent on office automation; the office seems to be the last bastion of resistance to the technological revolution. What are the reasons for this and are there any ways in which this resistance can be overcome?

The first step in overcoming resistance is to understand the reasons for it and to analyse the reactions it produces. It will be valuable, therefore, to identify and describe these at each level, before discussing the ways in which such resistance might be reduced.

The resistance of white-collar workers and the unions

I have seen an advertisement for microcomputers that showed a group of tough workers carrying pickaxes, which was captioned 'The lads would like a word or two with your computer'. The image of unionists as machine breakers and Luddites is a rather unfair stereotype, however. The unions realise that the modern worker must come to terms with technological advance for reasons of economic survival. They do have very real fears for their members, however, and these need to be understood by any manager wishing to introduce new methods successfully. The main fear – and it seems to be justified – is of massive job losses.

183

Although, in 1979, the Department of Employment published a reassuring study on the effect of the chip on employment levels,[28] the evidence has been to the contrary so far. The picture has been one of constantly decreasing manpower levels, even within the electronics industry itself. In businesses and in offices the situation is no better than in industry. Incomes Data Services and the Equal Opportunities Commission have all demonstrated in studies that new technology inevitably will reduce white-collar jobs, especially those of women – the word processor, the use of the microcomputer to process information, and electronic mail will mean less typing and secretarial work.

This has caused unfavourable reactions from the unions, who have made efforts to protect their members and reach agreement on acceptable methods of 'phasing in' changes which they know will be inevitable. Their main areas for concern are, firstly, de-manning. Their aim, if possible, is to protect existing jobs and to ask management to redeploy personnel. Secondly, where jobs have changed as a result of technology, to negotiate new rates for these jobs. White-collar unions, such as NALGO and APEX, are asking employers to enter into new technology agreements to achieve these objectives as far as possible. Even the Civil Service and the Post Office and television news services, not usually noted for their militancy, are facing severe problems, and negotiations have been long and difficult.

The fear of unemployment has reduced morale nationally and has meant that people are less willing to implement technological change. When this occurs, systems that are imposed in the face of resentment will be blamed for anything and everything which goes wrong, for everyone has a vested interest in proving them to be unworkable. Often this creates a self-fulfilling prophecy and a company will find that its capital investment has been costly in other directions – those of industrial relations and poor productivity.

The situation, however, is not entirely hopeless. With an understanding management, careful consultation can be carried out which can solve the problems. The case of Bradford City Council was quoted in a television programme called *Managing the Micro*[29]. In it the council admitted that they 'forgot the people' when they first attempted to introduce technology into the council offices. Resentment and sabotage resulted and the situation became impossible. To their credit, Bradford City Council admitted their mistake, undertook a long series of negotiations with the unions, consulted and briefed their white-collar employees, and provided the retraining and preparation that should have been instigated in the first place. The results were acceptance of, and enthusiasm for, the changes introduced, properly negotiated rates and a co-operative union and workforce.

This showed that careful communication – gaining understanding and the required response – can be achieved. It is not always easy; management needs to identify the causes for resistance and should not dismiss its employees as old fashioned or pig-headed, and the unions, with which it has to negotiate, as aggressive and politically in opposition. The fears are real, therefore honesty and reassurance are essential qualities for management. Acceptance can come only through consultation about change and through thorough preparation for its impact – and not through its imposition.

There is no doubt that the nature of work, as well as the manning levels, will change and that the types of skills needed will be different. Some redundancies will be inevitable and some new recruitment of different types of employee necessary. However, some retraining and redeployment is possible. Management can avoid the worst evils of confrontation and can stand a real chance of gaining support if it consults carefully, implements the new technology after preparing, briefing and approaching the staff with understanding, and then supervises their work.

Managerial resistance

Technological change should change the quality of managerial decision-making – immediate access to relevant information and improved efficiency of communication should free managers from the frustrations of routine matters and allow them to get on with the real job of managing. Yet there have been reports of managerial resistance to altering working practice, apparently through fear of the unknown and a desire not to relinquish power or status.

Some managers are unaware of how routine clerical work is done. If they wish for information they shout at a secretary to find a file, or a telephone number, and rarely use office equipment themselves. This means that they do not have any knowledge of how long it takes to obtain information and, therefore, are unlikely to have any idea of what improvements are needed.

Unfortunately, many managers do not keep up with the rapid technological advances and, therefore, they avoid implementing them in their offices. This has been called, rather unkindly, 'computer paranoia – the new ageing executive's disease'.[30] The blow to their pride and self-esteem should not be underestimated. One managing director ruefully put it: 'I've sat behind this desk for 30 years, but a kid of 21 can come in and tell me anything about computerising my business and I have to believe him.' In this case disastrous errors could be the result, which would not advance the cause of change and may well result in other managers resolving never to lay themselves open to such risks.

The problem here is again lack of preparation. Managers are often too busy to acquaint themselves with the latest developments, yet they are responsible for purchasing systems. If managers are not familiar with the systems, expensive errors can occur. For example, a single-user system could be bought when multiple application will be necessary in the near future. There is a possiblity, too, that a manager will beome the prey of unscrupulous salesmen, using jargon he does not understand, or become a victim of his own computer staff, who may be 'empire building' when they assure him they need a mainframe computer and not a cheap minicomputer. Finally, choosing appropriate software, and computers that are compatible with other machines, will be a problem.

It is not surprising, therefore, that a manager prefers to continue with the practices with which he is familiar. If the efficiency of the business is to be increased by the introduction of technology, then sufficient time and effort must be set aside by the management concerned to ensure a wise choice of hardware and software, appropriate to the company's needs, and an informed approach to its planning and implementation. Only in this way will the required commitment and enthusiasm be forthcoming from management itself.

Resistance and other problems resulting from poor planning and implementation

Although the lack of expertise and training in the new technologies may be through no personal fault of the manager, lack of planning and poor implementation is more difficult to understand or forgive, since these are both fundamental managerial functions. Richard Pawson[31], editor of *Micro Computer Print Out*, has identified that these factors are common to many of the failures to introduce technology successfully. He lists the three key mistakes as trying to computerise a system which doesn't even work manually, trying to computerise too many functions, too fast, and failing to take the needs of the company into account. Let us now look at these major aspects in turn.

The need for accurate analysis of the present system – gaining co-operation

A system which does not work manually needs to be overhauled and re-organised first, for computerisation will not do anything to improve it. (You may discover that a computerised system is not needed – just an efficient manual one!) The system may need to be altered slightly so that it runs on logical lines suitable for computerisation. Even in a system which does work manually, careful analysis of the present content, volume, procedures and flow of work is essential.

It is at this early stage that the co-operation and help of the staff operating the existing manual system must be sought. They will have the clearest and most detailed view of what is involved in each job, and without accurate information from them, mistakes and omissions will be passed on to the computer programs, perpetuating inefficiency and confusion.

If technological change is planned, the staff should be consulted openly about their work practices and their daily procedures. Analysis is vital if a precise and comprehensive pattern of a company's activities is to be built up, and the best choice of hardware and software made. Any unions involved must be approached early, and full discussions need to be carried out at every level.

In this way, it is possible to plan for gradual implementation, to accommodate existing staff over a period of time more readily, and to identify retraining and redeployment needs. If negotiations begin at this stage, planning will be carried out for people, as well as for technology, so that they will adapt suitably and the change, when implemented, will be more successful. The degree to which implementation will be acceptable and successful will, in its turn, be affected by the rate which is planned for the introduction of change.

The rate of implementation

It is always easier to adapt to change if it is gradual, and it is easier to monitor and control it, for most innovations have teething troubles and side-effects that have not been foreseen. It is for this reason that industrial and scientific organisations rely heavily on pilot programmes before making a total commitment to invest capital.

Many consultants recommend that manual systems, even when suitably re-organised and thoroughly analysed, should be kept running alongside the computerised systems for at least a month or so, in order to help detect and solve any initial problems which may arise. This also gives existing personnel a sense of security, for there is a familiar source of reference if they feel uncertain or confused, as will happen inevitably over the initial period of change in work methods.

Some advisers recommend computerising one function at a time. This has the advantage that time wasted, or costly mistakes made, the first time can provide a learning experience and be avoided when changing the other functions. As far as people are concerned, it also means that some staff can see that implementation of change can be accommodated by their colleagues, and this may increase their confidence – provided that there have not been too many problems!

Gradual familiarisation by both management and staff will promote acceptance, as their fear – which is often based on lack of confidence – recedes, and their ability to handle the new equipment and systems increases. Once people have gained this new assurance – and it is because of this that good training courses insist on 'hands on' experience – the reaction is likely to be enthusiastic. As this tends to be infectious, it can be communicated to those in other departments. If implementation is 'phased in' in this way, it must be carried out within the framework of an overall plan which must take account of the firm's needs for the foreseeable future.

Taking the future needs of the company into account

Perhaps the most serious indictment of management planning is the failure to take the future needs (in terms of expansion) of the company into account. (Remember, two of the most important functions of top management are to 'forecast and plan'.[32]) It is only when the future direction of a company has been analysed carefully that appropriate choices can be based on appropriate budgets. If not, the company might find that the computer it buys becomes obsolete and has to be replaced, thus wasting a great deal of money. In addition, the frustration that unsuitable systems generate within a company tends to increase staff resistance to technological change and make further innovation even more difficult, so, once again, there are hidden costs, in terms of human relations.

187

Initiating technological change successfully – planning, consultation and communication

Initiating technological change successfully relies on good communication processes and adequate consultation. From the previous discussion in this chapter, it is now possible to identify some basic principles which any manager has to bear in mind when faced with the complex problems of choosing from a bewildering array of technology, and the systems and devices appropriate to his organisation's needs, and implementing them in the face of possible resistance. These principles are as follows:

1. The analysis of the present work of the company, based on consultation with all job holders. This will involve the communication of the objectives, the initiation of negotiations with any unions involved, the consultation with staff in order to identify the work content, load and flow, and the clarification of work procedures within the present manual system.

2. The analysis of record-keeping, flow charts and critical path analysis, in terms of job descriptions.

3. The re-organisation of the manual system (if necessary) into logical and more efficient procedures. Improvements are best achieved by consultation with staff.

4. The revision of flow charts, etc., in the light of this re-organisation.

5. The identification of the long-term needs of the company, especially those related to planned growth and expansion. These should be recorded as a projection for the next five-year period.

6. An approach to an impartial consultancy organisation and/or the attendance at training courses or exhibitions run by such organisations. Time should be set aside to read the literature and pricing available. A representative from such an organisation should be invited to look at the analysis of activity and future projections, and to recommend suitable systems/suppliers of compatible and appropriate hardware and software.

7. The identification of alternatives and the setting of budgets in the light of these suggestions.

8. The re-consultation of the representative, who should be invited to recommend the best alternative.

9. An approach to suppliers and/or analysts recommended. The analysis of activities and future projections should be made available to them.

10. The invitation to analysts/suppliers to observe or interview staff. (It is important to inform the staff beforehand of what is happening, and why, as this enlists their co-operation.)

11. Based on the reports of the analysts/suppliers, and discussions with them, a choice of the hardware and software, within the budgets previously decided, should be made, which will best meet the needs of the company and which will also be compatible with all the devices needed and with the mainframe computer.

12. The manuals which come with the software/hardware should be checked to see if they are understandable, and that staff can be trained easily to use the

machines and software. (Check particularly that there are clear instructions on codes and keywords.)

13. The software should be checked to see it is suited to the company's needs and is written in the appropriate commercial, technical or scientific language relevant to its operations. It should be as easy and 'user friendly' for the operators as possible.

14. Before ordering, a consultative session with the staff and analysts should be held, to tell them the reasons for the choice. Time should be allowed for queries and questions afterwards. The initial training and redeployment needs should be discussed with them.

15. Once all the communication and consultative processes listed above have been carried out, the order can be placed.

A useful warning at this point is that users should insist on a written specification from the supplier, stating what the equipment can do and how it will perform. In addition, it should list the facilities and provide an indication of the time scale, in accordance with the user's projected growth. This is a legal document or a 'contract' between both parties – and it may concentrate the mind of the supplier on suiting the company's needs precisely!

Of course, if the manager concerned with ordering systems or equipment is already knowledgeable, there will be less need to employ expensive consultants. If budgets are very limited, it may not be possible to carry out consultancy on a very large scale. However, even if budgets are small, and the knowledge of the manager concerned is inadequate, one reputable and impartial consultant can prove invaluable by preventing expenditure on totally unsuitable – and, therefore, useless – equipment.

Implementing technological change – training, supervision, 'phasing in' and review

Deciding on the right strategy for implementing technological change, in order to minimise resistance, may prove to be even more difficult than the initial planning already discussed. However, there are some principles which can be identified. These can be categorised as follows:

1. Sufficient initial training or retraining should be given to those who are expected to operate the system. Some suppliers send someone to explain the system. If not, someone must be designated, preferably the manager who chose and ordered the system, to consult the suppliers and study the manuals thoroughly. Training must include 'hands on' experience and plenty of practice time if the staff concerned are to become confident, competent and are to accept the equipment happily. It is worth remembering that adult learners may need to be trained at a slower pace because, unlike younger ones, their main concern is accuracy. This is commendable, and plenty of time must be given for them to experiment and familiarise themselves thoroughly with what the equipment can do. If this is done, and there is someone knowledgeable to whom they can refer, if in difficulty, most people respond by becoming

highly motivated towards the retraining process, and enthusiastic, rather than hostile about change.

2. Supervision must be carried out by someone who has studied the system and equipment at length. The first week or so will be vital in terms of continued training in the job situation. Correction of error is particularly important in the early stages, in order that poor working practices, or misuse of the equipment, do not occur. Anyone supervising staff during this time needs to act as a guide and mentor, who can be approached easily, and has sufficient time for every query, however small it may seem. For this reason, there must be *adequate* supervision. Depending on the scale of the change, this may mean that more than one manager will need to carry out this function, or it may mean that one manager should devote most of his time to doing so in this crucial period. This not only ensures the correct use of the expensive equipment purchased, but also shows the management's caring attitude. This involves recognising the staff's difficulties and being willing to help them. This approach communicates concern and will ensure that the staff support the company's decision.

3. 'Phasing in' or running the manual system alongside the computerised one, has been stressed already as a useful method of coping with the inevitable problems that arise in a new system, and communicating reassurance to the staff. It means that they still have a familiar source of reference if they feel unsure of anything. The usefulness of computerising one section at a time has been emphasised also, for this will enable the mistakes made in the first function to be corrected in the second – a saving in costs and wasted time.

4. After the initial period of implementation, a review of what has occurred is essential. Any outstanding faults should be identified and the necessary modifications carried out. It is vital that management is prepared to admit that there *are* problems, and attempt to solve them, rather than brush them aside and maintain the importance of the original ideas and decisions. This will lead to the faults perpetuating themselves and the situation deteriorating. It will also be seen by staff as arrogance and lack of concern for their difficulties.

Conclusion – future decisions

There is no doubt that the technological revolution will affect the whole nature of work in the business field in the future and, indeed, the whole occupational structure. In America the information industry has overtaken all other occupations, in terms of the percentage of the workforce it employs. The same trend is beginning to be seen in the United Kingdom.

The characteristic skills and abilities required in all business employees at every level, are changing, too. There is a high level of literacy (computers dislike errors of syntax!), numeracy, excellence in decision-making and analysis, and skill in processing information. The outcome of this is likely to be that lower grade jobs will disappear at an increasing rate and a very high level of expertise will be required at management level.

The environment from which work is conducted will become more varied –

many managers have already taken advantage of the new technology to work from the home, the car or even a suitcase. The international executive will be able to communicate directly with anyone in the world and to have access to crucial and accurate information from any location. The sales force will be more mobile and better informed. Financial transactions will soon be carried out and controlled by computerised systems, allowing safe transfer throughout the world without the need for cash or expensive security procedures.

Technology is altering the nature of other occupations too. Distance-learning systems in education, pioneered by the Open University and the National Extension College, have now spread to other 'open' institutions. The material available for learning at home now includes educational programmes for video recorders, and tape and software packages for home computers. The home is also increasingly likely to be a favoured location for work and education. Direct broadcasting is also possible. Within educational institutions, computer-aided learning and instruction have been found highly motivating. The teacher's role is now being changed to that of a guide. Such advances are reducing the need for expensive institutionalised learning, particularly for adults. Other public services, such as the police and the health service, have been quick to take advantage of systems which will aid the storage, retrieval and manipulation of the enormous amount of information needed in their work. Computer-aided design has become a valuable tool in engineering, science and architecture. The profession of estate agents is creating a database for its own specific needs.

Leisure activities have been affected, and not just by the television, the video recorder and the increasing number of home computers. Teleshopping and banking are likely to become the norm. Point of sale transactions in shops and garages will be controlled by computer.

New concepts and attitudes will be required of us all as the pattern of our lives changes. Central to the technological revolution are the speed and accuracy now possible in the telecommunications field and the versatility of the microcomputer. It is very easy to 'forget the people', yet it is the expertise and the motivation of staff within a company that will ensure its success, and it is they who must programme, operate, manipulate and communicate with other people.

The technological revolution has to be accepted and its advantages have to be utilised to the full if businesses are to survive. In any occupation, therefore, the ability to communicate effectively on an inter-personal basis, or remotely, via the electronic systems now available, will become an increasingly vital asset.

* * *

Suggested activity for self-evaluation and interest

Read the case study 'Core Chemicals PLC' and attempt the questions that follow it.

Case study

Core Chemicals PLC -- a problem of technological innovation.

BACKGROUND TO THE COMPANY

Core Chemicals Ltd was established in 1960 and continued to develop its range of products until, in 1980, it was selling up to 500 different chemical preparations and had 2,500 customers on its books. Products were ordered by post on the basis of standard formulations and, as it was not possible to manufacture exact quantities, orders were accepted with a quantity tolerance of plus or minus 5 per cent.

THE ORDER-PROCESSING SYSTEM IN 1980

Each week 200 orders were received. They were edited by a technical specialist who gave each order a product code and a price and noted the quantities or ingredients to be used. Orders were gathered together each week and no stocks of finished product were kept.

At that time, a product/delivery 'set' was headed by an addressing machine and the specification and other particulars were typed in afterwards. Product specifications were complex and averaged about 80 words in length. After delivery, invoices were prepared by similar means. Invoices were posted to ledgers, using an accounting machine; statements were prepared, by hand, monthly. Production was analysed weekly, by hand, from the invoice copies. This was done by the type of chemical used, and the information was used to reprovision the materials stock.

The office supervisor in charge of order processing has been with the company ever since its establishment and, although his order-processing system has never been documented, as far as management was concerned, it had worked efficiently. He has several clerks working for him and, although he is seen to be firm, he is fair, if somewhat 'pernickety' on occasions. He is well respected generally.

THE DECISION TO COMPUTERISE

In 1980, the managing director decided to computerise the company's system after attending a short course on the new technological systems available. He collected as much literature as possible, and purchased the system that seemed best. He directed that the order-processing system should be computerised first, as an initial step towards integrating the stock control and invoicing procedures. In order to facilitate the introduction of the new system, a young systems analyst (a graduate) was recruited. He had some experience already, having implemented a similar system in a larger company. He is technically 'bright' and very enthusiastic about his work, if a little immature and rather diffident.

This systems analyst finds considerable difficulty in obtaining the necessary information and data from the office supervisor, but eventually designs a system based on what he can glean from this grudgingly-supplied information, and tests it successfully. Within days of implementation, it was found that the new system could not handle the large variation in types of order and, in order to avoid the complete breakdown of the order-processing system, the office supervisor's manual system was re-introduced and the computerised scheme suspended.

Questions for syndicate discussion

1. What steps did the managing director fail to take before purchasing the system and before implementing the computerisation of the order-processing system?
2. What do you think were the major reasons for the office supervisor's reluctance to help the system analyst? What might have been effective in overcoming this reluctance?
3. What other steps might the systems analyst have taken to obtain the information he needed?
4. If you were in a position to advise the managing director, what would you suggest he should do about the office supervisor and the planned computerisation of the order-processing system?
5. How correct was the managing director in his belief that the firm would benefit from computerisation?

Part 5 | The use of English

It is vital that accurate English is used to compose business documents. The new technological systems demand a mastery of the language by anyone who operates them. It is for these reasons that Appendices A, B and C have been included. It is hoped that this supplement will assist those who are learning English as a foreign tongue, and that it might prove useful to those who wish to improve their knowledge of English grammar.

The parts of speech

Articles

The most common words in English are the articles. Unlike some languages, which have masculine, feminine or neuter articles, there is only one definite article. There are two indefinite ones.

1. **The** is the definite article. It precedes any noun or naming word where there is only one possible object, person or idea that could be referred to in that context.

e.g.   **The** Government (when it is clearly of one particular country).
         The managing director (when it is clearly one particular company).
         The report (when it is the only report being discussed or referred to at the time).

2. **A** is the most used indefinite article. It precedes any noun or naming word where the object, person or idea referred to could be *any* one and where the noun begins with a consonant.

e.g.   A company.
         A bank.   Where these might refer to any
         A report.   company, bank, report or manager.
         A manager.

3. **An** is the indefinite article used before any noun beginning with a vowel (a,e,i,o,u).

e.g.   An argument.
         An emergency.
         An institution.

It may be used also if the noun has an adjective in front of it which begins with a vowel.

e.g.   **An** urgent message.

Cases where articles are omitted – the exceptions

There are always exceptions to every rule. Articles can be omitted before some nouns. Usually, these are abstract or collective nouns.

e.g.　**War** always produces economic change.
　　　Justice is a basic principle of law.
　　　We need **information**.

The plural of articles

The only correct plural of articles is **some**. Although **many** or **several** can be used in the same way, these are adjectives. Rather confusingly, some can also be used as an adjective meaning 'certain' or 'particular'.

e.g.　I need **some** reports on this. ('Some' used as a plural article.)
　　　Some reports are badly written. ('Some' used as an adjective meaning certain.)

Nouns

A noun is a naming word; it names a person, place, object, idea, concept, feeling or work of art. Because it names so many different things, nouns are subdivided into several clear categories. These can be described as follows:

1. **Concrete nouns** These are nouns which name common objects or basic concrete concepts.

e.g.　**Report.**
　　　Desk.
　　　Company.
　　　Brief-case.

2. **Abstract nouns** These are nouns which describe abstract ideas, concepts or feelings.

e.g.　**Justice.**
　　　Efficiency.
　　　Communication.
　　　Happiness.
　　　Motivation.

3. **Proper nouns** These are nouns which name people, places, films, works of art, etc.

e.g.　**John Humble.**
　　　The City of London.
　　　The Dam Busters.
　　　The Mona Lisa.

4. **Collective nouns** These are nouns which name groups or categories of people or things.

e.g.   **The jury.**
          The staff.
          The information.

Singular and plural forms of the noun

Languages have different rules here and some nationalities may have difficulty with these. The rules are as follows:

1. **Regular nouns** These add an 's' when they are referring to more than one object, person or idea, that is, they are in the plural.

e.g.   **A book** (singular, meaning *one* book) becomes **some books** (plural, meaning *more* than one book).
          A report (singular) becomes **some reports** (plural).

2. **Nouns ending in a consonant followed by a 'y' in the singular** These change the 'y' to 'ie' before adding 's'.

e.g.   **A company** (singular) becomes **some companies** (plural).
          A jury (singular) becomes **some juries** (plural).
          A secretary (singular) becomes **some secretaries** (plural).

3. **Irregular nouns** These either change their form completely or they retain the same form in the plural, instead of just adding an 's'. There are only a few of these. The most common ones are as follows:

(a) Those that change their form.

e.g.   **A man** (singular) becomes **men** (plural).
          A woman (singular) becomes **women** (plural).
          A child (singular) becomes **children** (plural).

(b) Those that retain their form.

e.g.   **A fish** (singular) remains **fish** in the plural.
          A sheep (singular) remains **sheep** in the plural.

There are some irregular plurals where words have been derived from foreign languages. As English derives from many languages, it has a mixture of Latin, Greek and French plurals.

e.g.

Singular	*Plural*
Memorandum	**Memoranda**
Radius	**Radii**
Appendix	**Appendices**
Bureau	**Bureaux**

4. **Nouns which do not take a plural – the exceptions** Some nouns never take a plural form as they are collective already, e.g. information. Some, although they are collective, can take a plural, but only in exceptional cases, e.g the **staff** of this company (the most usual form) but, the **staffs** of several companies (an unusual context).

Pronouns

A pronoun is a small word which can be used instead of a noun ('pro' means 'for', thus, they stand in *for* a noun). They may refer to people or things; they may ask a question, or introduce more information about a noun. The form that they take depends on their position within the sentence. Pronouns, like nouns, fall into different categories according to their differing roles. They can be described as follows:

1. **Subject pronouns** These are as follows:

Singular	*Plural*
I	**We**
You	**You**
He, she, it	**They**

They should be used only when the noun has been used already, so that it is evident to what or to whom they refer.

e.g.   Thomas Jones is now managing director. **He** has had a very successful career.

The report has been prepared by a sub-committee. **It** has been circulated already.

2. **Object pronouns** These stand in place of a noun but they perform a slightly different role in the sentence, usually coming *after* the verb and acting as the *object* of the sentence.

Singular	*Plural*
Me	**Us**
You	**You**
Him, her, it	**Them**

Sometimes **this** and **that** (singular) and **these** and **those** (plural) can also be used in the same role.

e.g.   This year, the members of your project team will be John Evans and Carolyn Williams. Fortunately, you know **them** well.

Of the two cars, I prefer **this**.

I have met **him** before.

I like most kinds of vegetables, but I don't like **those**.

Sometimes this kind of pronoun is preceded by a preposition.

e.g.   Would you like to come in our car **with us**?

They are going to the conference. Would you like to go **to it**, too?

Have you had a letter **from her**?

Do you agree **with that**?

3. **Possessive pronouns** These are pronouns which denote possession, or that something belongs to an object or person.

Singular	Plural
My	**Our**
Your	**Your**
His, hers, its	**Their**

Because they are used to show that something belongs to someone or something, they perform the same role as adjectives that describe their noun.

e.g.　　This is **your** report.
　　　　This is **my** desk.

Other possessive pronouns stand instead of nouns, usually in the object position within a sentence.

Singular	Plural
Mine	**Ours**
Yours	**Yours**
His, hers, its	**Theirs**

e.g.　　This desk is **mine**; that one is **yours**.
　　　　This car is **his**; that is **hers**.

Possessive pronouns never have an apostrophe. (The only time it is correct for 'its' to have an apostrophe is when it is an abbreviation of 'it is' not when it means 'of it' or 'belonging to it'.)

e.g.　　This chair is broken. It has lost **its** back. (No apostrophe.)
　　　　It's time to go. (Short for 'it is' so it has an apostrophe.)

4. **Reflexive pronouns** These, used more rarely in English than in some other languages, are for stressing *who* is performing an action.

e.g.　　I washed **myself** this morning.
　　　　He wants to carry out that task **himself**.

Often it is preceded by the preposition **by**.

e.g.　　I taught him to perform this task, now he can do it **by** himself.

5. **Question pronouns and pronouns introducing more information concerning a noun** These are pronouns that can carry out either of the above functions. They are **who/whom**, **what** and **which**. 'Who' is used if it is the *subject* of a sentence. 'Whom' is used if it introduces, or acts as, the *object* of the sentence, when it is often preceded by a preposition.

e.g.　　**Who** is coming this afternoon?
　　　　To whom did you give this report?

The others do not change their form and can either introduce a question or introduce more information about a noun.

e.g.　　**What** do you want?
　　　　The report **which** describes the event.

In this they are being used as *adjectives*. These are described next.

Adjectives

These are essentially words which *describe* or give more information about a noun or a pronoun, although we have seen already that pronouns can sometimes fulfil this role, especially where they denote possession (e.g. **my** desk) or identify a particular object (e.g. **that** desk). Usually, however, an adjective describes a noun (e.g. The manager is **busy** today) or a pronoun (e.g. He is **happy** today). In these two examples, the adjective is separated, from the noun or pronoun it describes, by the verb 'is'. Adjectives usually *precede* nouns (and, in some contexts, pronouns).

e.g.   A **good** manager is able to motivate his staff.

Where there is more than one adjective preceding a noun, these are usually separated from one another by commas.

e.g.   The **well-lit, airy, open-plan** office was a **pleasant, friendly** place.

We have mentioned already separating the adjective from the noun or pronoun by a verb, as in this further example:

e.g.   The light is excellent in this office.

Next we must define the verb.

Verbs

The function of the verb

The main 'pillar' on which any English sentence is constructed is the verb. Verbs are described usually as 'doing' words, but they can be 'being' words also; that is, they can either convey an action or identify a state of being or, more precisely, a state of mind, feeling or situation.

e.g.   John Evans **wrote** the report and **gave** it to the manager. (Both 'wrote' and 'gave' are *doing* words conveying John Evans' actions.)
He **was** highly **motivated** because his job interested him. (Both words convey his state of mind or feelings.)

Verb tenses and 'moods'

Verbs in English are expressed in various tenses to convey whether the actions happen in the present, past or future. They have two major 'moods' – *active* or *passive*. A verb is used actively when it expresses *directly* the action or state of mind of the person involved (e.g. The managing director **dictated** the report). It is used *passively* when the action is shown as being carried out by an agent (e.g. This letter **was dictated** by the managing director). Here the sentence structure has changed. Often the passive sounds impersonal so it is used deliberately to convey unpopular messages, indicating that no human being is involved! In this case, even the the agent or 'doer' is omitted (e.g. Your job **has been terminated**). The subjunctive can also be used for expressing moods.

The various tenses are simple to formulate, once you have identified the infinitive, present participle and past participle, and provided you remember that English uses auxiliary verbs, plus the two participles, to make its present, past and future tenses. The auxiliary verbs are *irregular* ones – **to be** and **to have**. In the future tenses, **will** is used; in the *future simple*, this is followed by a part of the verb that is taken fom the main stem of the verb, i.e. the infinitive without 'to' in front of it (e.g. I **will dictate**). In the *future perfect tenses*, the past and present participles are used with the auxiliary verb. Occasionally, the auxiliary used is **shall** to emphasise an intention (e.g. (I **shall dictate** it as soon as possible). (This has a subjunctive sense sometimes – see page 204.) Similarly **should** may appear (e.g. I **should go** because I need to). (Again, 'should' can be used in a subjunctive sense.)

Regular verb patterns

Let us take the verb **ask** as our example. As stated earlier, the first step is to identify the infinitive (or name of the verb). In this case, the present participle (which in all regular verbs ends in 'ing') is **asking** and the past participle (which in all regular verbs ends in 'ed') is **asked**. Once these have been identified, the tenses can by formed be adding the necessary auxiliary verbs. We can now set out a pattern for these forms that all regular verbs will follow. For convenience these are listed with the subject pronoun, **he**, in the active and the subject noun, the **question**, in the passive.

Tense	*Active (subject pronoun – he)*	*Passive (subject noun – the question)*
Present		
Simple	**asked**	**is asked**
Continuous	**is asking**	**is being asked**
Past		
Simple	**asked**	**was asked**
Continuous	**was asking**	**was being asked**
Perfect		
Simple	**has asked**	**has been asked**
Continuous	**has been asked**	
Future		
Simple	**will/shall ask**	**will/shall be asked**
Continuous	**will/shall be asking**	
Future perfect		
Simple	**will/shall have asked**	**will/shall have been asked**
Continuous	**will/shall have been asking**	
Conditional		
Simple	**would/should have asked**	**would should have been asked**
Continuous	**would/should have been asking**	

Note: **Should** can also be used to express intention and thus can sometimes be used to indicate a subjunctive.

The subjunctive and the use of **may, might, shall** and **should**

The subjunctive is used very rarely in its pure form in English. When it is, the present tense is characterised usually by the word **may** before the main stem of the verb. It appears in rather unusual expressions such as '**May** he have a long life!' and 'Whatever that **may** be, it is not a report'.

May and **might** are used also to express an intention which is uncertain, and tend to be used interchangeably. Often, they are followed or preceded by a clause beginning with **if**, expressing a conditional sense.

e.g.   If he gets here early, I **may/might** be able to meet him, but I have to go soon.
I **might/may** be able to attend the conference if there are enough places.

This 'uncertain intention' idea is sometimes expressed by **should** or **shall** to give a future subjunctive sense, as opposed to a simple future idea, or to emphasise a definite intention. 'Should' and 'shall' are often paired with an 'if' clause and/or a conditional.

e.g.   I **shall** go **if** I am not too busy.
I **should** go, **but** I am not sure whether I could with the amount of work I have to do.

The other, more common, use of the subjunctive is in the past tense, usually **within** an **if** clause followed by a conditional.

e.g.   **If** he **were to go**, I would not be able to do so.

Colloquially, the subjunctive is often forgotten. It does exist, however, and I have given the most commonly used examples.

Irregular verbs

Unfortunately, there are many irregular verbs in the English language, and here the forms of the present and the past participle, in particular, need to be memorised. In most irregular verbs, the past tenses change too. Many, for example, change their middle vowel in the past simple

e.g.   *Present*   *Past*
I **write**   I **wrote**
I **speak**   I **spoke**

Some change their stem and add 'en' instead of 'ed' to form the past participle.

e.g.   **Written.**
Spoken.

Obviously, there are far too many verbs to list. However, I will list fully the past tenses of the three most common irregular verbs – **to be, to have** and **to go** – and will identify the other tenses.

1. The verb: **to be** (infinitive)

Present participle: **being**
Past participle: **been**

Present simple tense (irregular)

Singular	*Plural*
I **am**	We, you, they **are**
You **are**	
He, she, it **is**	

Past simple tense (irregular)

Singular	*Plural*
I, you, he, she, it **was**	we, you, they **were**

2. The verb: to **have** (infinitive)
Present participle: **having**
Past participle: **had**

Present simple tense (irregular)

Singular	*Plural*
I, you **have**	We, you, they **have**
He, she, it **has**	

Past simple tense (irregular)
All pronouns take **had**

3. The verb: **to go** (infinitive)
Present participle: **going**
Past participle: **gone**

Present simple tense (irregular)

Singular	*Plural*
I, you **go**	We, you, they **go**
He, she, it **goes**	

Past simple tense (irregular)
All pronouns take **went**

The *usage* of verbs sometimes varies, and now we need to turn to some exceptional uses of the verbs where they perform a different role.

Verbs used as adjectives and nouns

Two parts of a verb can be used occasionally to fulfil a different role (as an adjective) and be used as a different part of speech (a noun). The past and present participles can be used as an adjective, e.g. 'The boat has **running** water' (present participle) and 'The **typed** report is ready to be signed' (past participle). The present participle can be used occasionally as a noun, in which case is is called a gerund, e.g. 'His **writing** is excellent'.

Adverbs

Adverbs give information about verbs, in the same way as adjectives give information about nouns. Adverbs answer questions about the verb, limiting and extending their meaning by giving some qualification about the action or state of being they describe. The questions they answer about the verb are as follows:

> How? How many? How much?
> When? Where?
> To what extent? In what way or by what method?

They usually end in 'ly' and so are easily recognisable.

e.g. He wrote **quickly** (answering the question how or in what way did he write?)
He gave his report **orally** (answering the question by what method?)

Some irregular adverbs do not end in 'ly'.

e.g. The manager arrived **late** although he had driven **fast** to get there. (Late describes *when* he arrived and fast *how* he drove.)

Occasionally, adverbs can describe an adjective or another adverb.

e.g. We need an **extremely** quick answer (describing the adjective 'quick'). We need an answer **extremely** quickly (describing the adverb 'quickly').

Conjunctions

These are extremely useful words – such as **and, but, next, then** and **yet** – that are used, as their name implies, as a *junction* in a sentence, to link connected ideas, words or parts of sentences. They can be used in many different ways as follows:

1. To link parts of a sentence which could stand as independent sentences in themselves, but are connected by their topic, or main ideas.

e.g. The report was brief **but** it included all the important facts.

These two sentences can stand individually, however it is neater to link them.

2. To link dependent ideas to a main one.

e.g. He decided to read the Health and Safety Committee's Report first, **as** the Inspector was coming tomorrow.

The following conjunctions are most frequently used in this way:

> **So**
> **Since**
> **Because**
> **Though**
> **Although**
> **So that**
> **With the result that**
> **In order that**

> **As soon as**
> **After**
> **Unless**

3. To link more than one adjective or adverb.

e.g. The office was cool **but** light.
   He moved quickly **and** quietly.

But and **and** are the most used conjunctions in this case; **though** and **although** may be used also.

4. To link nouns, pronouns or verbs. The conjunction used will always be **and**.

e.g. Evans **and** Brown worked together on the report.
   He **and** she will go to the meeting together.
   The people came **and** went.

5. To make a contrast. The conjunctions used here always appear in pairs.

e.g. We can go **either** today **or** tomorrow.

The most common pairs of conjunctions, besides the one in the example, are **neither...nor, both...and**, plus **not only...but also**.

Prepositions

Prepositions indicate a location, position or relationship and thus precede a noun or pronoun.

e.g. The report is **on** the desk.
   Give the report **to** me.

When they are used with nouns, they are used usually with an article, as in the first example above. Sometimes, however, they precede a noun *without* an article. This is most usual when a form of transport is denoted or a proper noun/name is involved.

e.g. We went **by** train **to** London.
   He went **by** aeroplane to the USA and stayed **in** New York.

There is one other usage of prepositions which should be mentioned here. They are used sometimes as part of a verb.

e.g. He never **gets down to** work before 9.30 a.m.
   He was elected a trade union official because the work force thought that he could **stand up to** management.

Interjections

An interjection, only used in direct speech, conveys either feeling or emotion, and provides a pause while the speaker thinks out an answer, or the next phrase of a sentence.

e.g. The chairman began his speech: 'Ladies and Gentlemen, the first thing to say is – **Oh!** what was that?' (An explosion was heard in the room next door.)

'**Well,**' began the interviewee, as he searched for an answer, 'that is hard to say.' (The interviewer had asked a difficult question.)

Conclusion

In order to construct English correctly, it is important to be able to identify and use the various parts of speech in the right way. It is also necessary to be able to use vocabulary correctly and to have an understanding of English syntax.

Syntax and the use of vocabulary

Introduction

The rules governing the parts of speech are the foundation of the structure of English. We need to study how these are used in order to form sentences and paragraphs, and how their usage varies between written and spoken English.

The construction of sentences

A sentence in English is the most basic unit. It always begins with a capital letter and usually ends in a full stop, although it can end in an exclamation mark or a question mark. It must contain certain elements. These are as follows:

1. A **subject** (except in the very rare case of a direct command, where it is understood).
2. A **complete** or 'finite' **verb**; participles *alone* are not enough.
3. A **predicate** – that is the rest of the sentence. This may be made up of a variety of ways as follows:

(a) With another noun or pronoun.
(b) With another adjective or adverb.
(c) With a number of dependent clauses – or with a combination of these.

These elements now need to be examined further.

A subject

The subject of the sentence is that which initiates the action or state of mind described by the verb that follows it. Every sentence *must* have a subject, if it is not a direct command. The subject of the sentence may be any of the following:

(a) A noun.

e.g.   **John** gave the report to the manager.

(b) A pronoun.

e.g.   **He** gave the report to the manager.

(c) A verb acting as a noun (gerund – see page 205), in which it is usually preceded by a possessive pronoun.

e.g. What is the use of my **scolding** him?

In English, the subject comes *before* the verb *unless* a further qualification, or idea, is inserted concerning the subject.

e.g. John, who wrote excellent reports, gave a copy of his most recent one to the manager.

The verb

The role of the verb in describing an action or state of mind, and the formulation of various tenses and moods of English verbs, have been discussed earlier (pages 202-205). The usage of verbs within sentences, however, needs further explanation on some points, as follows:

1. Verbs are of two types which govern the type of predicate that follows them. *Transitive* verbs describe actions which need an object to receive the action.

e.g. John **wrote** the report.

Intransitive verbs complete their meaning without an object. (Objects and other predicates are described more fully on page 211.)

2. As we have seen, a verb can be a combination of a number of words in English. If this is the case, the complete verb should be used, i.e. a participle cannot stand on its own.

e.g. I **have referred** to your letter.
not
Referring to your letter.

This is a clause, *not* a sentence, having neither a subject nor a complete verb. It requires a comma, to be followed by the main part of the sentence.

e.g. Referring to your letter, I cannot find the information I require.

Other 'dangerous' participles, where people are often tempted to treat them as complete verbs, are 'hoping' and 'wishing'.

3. Any verb must agree in number and person with the noun that precedes it.

e.g. The manager and his assistant **are** going to the conference.

There are some collective words, such as 'everyone', which, although giving an idea of a plural, always take a singular verb.

e.g. Everyone on the committee **is** present tonight.

On the other hand, some collective words, such as 'people', take a plural verb.

e.g. People **are** more complex than machines.

In the case of some collective nouns that describe bodies of people, either the singular or plural of the word may be used, according to whether their unity as a body, or their characteristics as individuals, need to be stressed.

e.g.   The government **is** united.
         The jury **are** in disagreement.

The predicate

The predicate of a sentence may be made up of one or a number of elements of the following:

1. An **object**.

The object of a *transitive* verb may be one of the following:

(a) A **noun**.

e.g.   The manager attended the **conference**.

(b) A **pronoun**.

e.g.   He attended **it**.

(c) A **gerund**, in which case it is preceded by a possessive pronoun.

e.g.   The manager praised his **reporting**.

(d) A **clause**.

e.g.   The manager examined **what appeared to be the main weakness of the report**.

2. A **complement**.

Some *intransitive* verbs, usually those describing a state of being or feeling, take a complement. This can be an adjective describing the subject which comes after the verb.

e.g.   The manager is **competent**.

It can be a noun (or pronoun) which is another way of naming the subject.

e.g.   The managing director is **John Evans**.

It can be a clause or phrase naming the subject or describing it further.

e.g.   It is too early to leave.

3. **Phrases** and **clauses**.

The predicate can be made up of any number of phrases and clauses of different types, either in addition to the subject, or complement, or, as has been seen, as a substitute for them. There are several different types and these are defined further in the next section.

The clause and the phrase – differences and definitions

A clause is a group of words which forms a major part of a sentence and possesses a subject and a finite verb. A clause can stand as a sentence alone and is then called a *main* clause. Complex sentences consist of several main clauses, linked together by conjunctions or semicolons.

e.g.   He wrote the report and he gave it to the manager; the manager was impressed.

If a clause cannot stand alone, it is called a dependent clause. It is usually linked to the main clause by a conjunction.

e.g.   The report was accepted although it was late.

A phrase is a much shorter group of words which does not include a finite verb, is related to the main clause(s) of the sentence, and is introduced, usually, by a *preposition*.

e.g.   He stopped to see his secretary on the way to his office.

It can be introduced by a *conjunction*.

e.g.   He went to see the sales manager after his business trip.

It can be introduced, sometimes, by a *participle*.

e.g.   Coming into the office, he immediately saw the notice.

The role of dependent clauses and phrases in a sentence

Dependent clauses and phrases act instead of parts of speech, substituting for or extending a meaning usually given by nouns, pronouns, adjectives or adverbs. For this reason, they are often called *noun* phrases or clauses, *adjectival* phrases or clauses, or *adverbial* phrases or clauses.

e.g.   He did not know that the problem was so complex. (A *noun* clause, acting as an object to the verb 'did not know'.)

e.g.   The manager, who motivated his staff well, was promoted. (An *adjectival* phrase describing the manager further.)

e.g.   The manager was not present when the representative arrived. (An *adverbial* clause, qualifying the verb 'was not present' further by answering the question 'when?')

e.g.   People are always wise after the event. (An *adverbial* phrase, qualifying the verb 'are' by answering the question '*when are* they wise?')

The construction of paragraphs

Paragraphing will be discussed in more detail in the next section on punctuation, beginning on see page 215. The paragraph is an important unit in written English. It contains the sentences that relate to one topic area, therefore a fresh paragraph is needed for each new topic. In some documents, such as reports, or discussion papers, the paragraph has a topic subheading. In others, such as letters, the initial sentence of each paragraph should indicate the subject of the paragraph to follow. This is the 'topic sentence', which is a useful 'signpost' to guide the reader through the main divisions of the document.

Clear paragraphing promotes comprehension and is particularly necessary when a document deals with complex subject matter or a number of different topics. Paragraphs should not contain more than three to five related points, otherwise they become too difficult to follow. Paragraphs may be of varying lengths, but those which are extremely short, or very long, are to be avoided. Short introductory paragraphs may be used in letters, for example, where the writer refers briefly to previous correspondence or queries. A paragraph usually consists of several sentences and is concluded when the writer moves on to a new group of points related to a different topic.

Archaic phrases and jargon

Archaic phrases can still be found in many letters today which make them sound pompous, stilted and very outdated. Many organisations use intelligible jargon at the expense of clarity and conciseness. Chapters 1 and 5 give examples of outdated phrases, clichés and jargon. These must be avoided in order to communicate well and to write business letters and other documents in plain, clear, modern English.

Colloquialisms and slang – vocabulary differences in written and spoken English

Colloquialisms are common in speech. They avoid the impression of pomposity and promote informality and a friendly approach. However, they should be avoided in written English, particularly in formal documents, such as reports, minutes and most letters. They can be used occasionally in informal memoranda or circular letters that are designed to be persuasive. I will now give some examples of colloquialisms which can be used in written English when direct informal speech is being quoted.

1. Colloquial abbreviations.
These are used to show omitted letters.

e.g.   I'm, won't, doesn't, you're, 'phone. (I am, will not, does not, you are, telephone.)

2. Colloquial verbs.
These are used incorrectly to give a variety of meanings in spoken English. The most common are as follows:

(a) 'To get' is used to mean *to obtain* (e.g. to get the right results), *to buy* (e.g. to get some writing-paper in a shop), *to fetch or bring* (e.g. Could you get me a cup of tea?) and *to understand* (e.g. I didn't get the point).

(b) 'To do' is often used carelessly to mean *to complete a task* (e.g. I did the report yesterday).

(c) 'To make' is used colloquially to mean *to achieve* or *to succeed* (e.g. That man has made it; he is now President). To make should never be used in written English to mean anything other than *to manufacture* or *to create*.

3. Colloquial expressions or words.
The most common of these are as follows:

(a) A lot of or lots of – used instead of *many* (of a number) or *much* (of an amount).

(b) Stuff – used to mean *material*, or *a collection of objects*, or *information*. (e.g. 'What is all this stuff on the floor?').

(c) OK is an Americanism which is constantly used by English people to mean *all right*.

Slang should never be used in written English. It should not be used in spoken English to anyone who is not familiar with it as this is impolite. Many regions, occupations and commercial organisations have created their own slang which is not in common usage. This can lead to much misunderstanding.

Conclusion

As well as a knowledge of the correct use of the parts of speech, it is important to use the English language correctly. Having mastered this, you will be in a position to punctuate your writing, as the correct use of punctuation depends upon an understanding of English syntax.

Punctuation

Introduction

Punctuation is used in English for the four following reasons:

1. To ensure that what is written is comprehensible and unambiguous.
2. To denote direct speech, titles, abbreviations or quotations.
3. To indicate a pause.
4. To denote the beginning of a new topic.

There are 11 major punctuation marks that are used to achieve these functions, and, in addition, English uses capital letters and paragraphs to assist them further. The punctuation marks in general use are as follows:

1. The full stop.
2. The semicolon.
3. The colon.
4. The comma.
5. The apostrophe.
6. Inverted commas.
7. Brackets.
8. The dash.
9. The hyphen.
10. The exclamation mark.
11. The question mark.

I will begin by discussing the use of paragraphs and sentences since these divide the main topics in any piece of written English.

The paragraph

This is an extremely important method of indicating a topic. Occasionally, for example in reports or discussion papers, a paragraph may have a topic subheading. More usually, however, the first sentence of a paragraph in most documents will indicate the topic to follow; once the discussion of that topic is complete, a new paragraph should be started.

Paragraphing is crucial to clear communication, for it guides the reader through the written material which he must digest. Careful attention, therefore, should be given to the structure of the paragraphs of written pieces of English. Lack of paragraphing confuses the reader and can discourage him from reading further.

Paragraphs are indicated usually by indentation (as at the beginning of this sentence) but in the blocked style of letter writing, where open punctuation is employed (see Chapter 5), they are shown by missing a line.

The sentence

Within the paragraph, the main points should be contained in separate *sentences*. Each sentence has a subject (a noun or a pronoun) unless it is a direct order or request. Each sentence has a main verb and a predicate (that is, the rest of the sentence). This might be made up of an *object* (a noun or a pronoun), a *complement* (usually an adjective) or it might contain a number of *phrases* or *clauses*. These terms have already been discussed in Appendix B.

e.g.   The manager asked his assistant to investigate the problem.
'Investigate the problem, please.' (Direct order.)

A sentence must begin with a capital letter and it must end with a full stop. It must be the right length, too. Sentences that are too short often give a rather 'jerky' style and give the impression of poor fluency, although they can be used effectively to give the impression of a quick succession of events.

e.g.   He investigated the problem as asked. It was more difficult than he thought. Everyone he asked appeared to have a different view. Nothing was clear.

Generally, however, the use of too many very short sentences should be avoided.

On the other hand, sentences that are too long can be unstructured, imprecise and confusing. Research has shown that more than 30 words in one sentence leads to considerable problems of comprehension. The best principle to follow, is, if in doubt, or if your sentence is becoming clumsy, begin another.

The full stop

The main function of the full stop is to end a sentence. It is used also to indicate abbreviations or initials.

e.g.   Mr. K. L. Jones, B.Sc.

Here both parts of words which have been abbreviated (Mr. for Mister, Sc. for Science) are follwed by a full stop, as are the initials (K.L. – the initials for Kenneth Leonard, and B. – the initial for Bachelor). Full stops are omitted if open punctuation is used for a fully blocked letter (see Chapter 5). The style of some books allows the use of abbreviations without full stops.

Many common abbreviations in English have Latin origins and these, too, have full stops in the appropriate place to show that they have been shortened.

e.g.   *Et cetera* – etc. – 'and the rest'.
        Exempla gratia – e.g. – 'for example'.
        Nota bene – n.b. – 'note well'.

The semicolon

The semicolon is an extremely helpful punctuation mark. It is surprising, therefore, that many people seem unaware of its function. The semicolon can be used instead of a full stop or a conjunction, when the causes that it separates can stand as individual sentences, but are closely connected in thought.

e.g.   He worked hard; it was no surprise when he passed all his examinations.
        The board's corporate plan was excellent; the company has been very successful this year.

The semicolon can give variety to a writer's style, offering an alternative to the repetitive use of full stops and conjunctions. It therefore adds fluency and conciseness to written English.

The colon

The colon's function is to introduce a list, a quotation or direct speech.

e.g.   The following members of the committee sent apologies for absence:
        Mr. K. L. Rees
        Mrs. P. S. Brough
        Mr. J. R. West.
        The report contained all the usual main sections, as follows:
        a 'terms of reference' section, a methodology section, an analysis of information, some conclusions and recommendations.
        The Managing Director began: 'Ladies and Gentlemen, I am pleased to say that we have had a very profitable year.'
        In the play *As You Like It*, Shakespeare gave the following view of life: 'All the world's a stage, and all the men and women merely players.'

The comma

Commas can be used in the following ways:

1. After one or two words on which the rest of the sentence depends.

e.g.   However,...   As a consequence,...
        Just lately,...   Finally,...

2. To separate a short dependent clause, or phrase, from the main sentence.

e.g.   Although he worked hard, he did not receive the expected promotion.
        When he finished dictating, he sent the tape to the typing pool.

3. To interject a further thought or modification about a subject *before* the verb which follows it.

e.g.   The report, which was late, was so comprehensive that the manager gladly accepted it.
The presentation, which was excellent, did much to make the report acceptable.

4. To separate brief items in a list, usually introduced by a colon.

e.g.   The following items are in the stationery store: pens, pencils, rubbers, rulers, drawing instruments, lined A4 paper, graph paper and stapling machines.

5. To separate a list of adjectives.

e.g.   The report was rambling, inaccurate, ungrammatical, poorly presented and far too long.

Commas are not needed in the following cases:

1. Where a phrase between the subject and noun actually defines it, rather than gives a further thought or modifications about it (as in 3 above).

e.g.   The report that you requested is on your desk.
The brochure that you ordered has arrived.

2. Where there is a conjunction such as and, but or when.

The apostrophe

The rules governing the use of the apostrophe are peculiarly characteristic of the English language, and often create difficulties. There are two major functions of the apostrophe. The first is to stand in place of the word 'of' – either to denote possession or to indicate some expression of time. The second is to indicate abbreviations in spoken English, when letters are often omitted. It is important to note that this is very rare in written English, unless direct speech is being quoted.

THE APOSTROPHE USED TO DENOTE POSSESSION

The apostrophe, used instead of the word 'of' to denote possession applies to nouns only. Remember, pronouns *never* take an apostrophe to denote possession (its, yours, theirs, etc.). There are rules for the position of the apostrophe, according to whether the noun is singular or plural. These are as follows:

1. Regular nouns.
In the singular, the apostrophe comes after the noun and is then followed by an 's'.

e.g.   The manager's desk. (The desk of the manager.)

In the plural, the apostrophe is found after the normal 's' of the normal plural form.

e.g.   The managers' desks. (The desks of many managers.)

2. Nouns ending in 'y' in the singular and 'ies' in the plural.
These have already been discussed (see page 199) and the rule for regular nouns holds good.

e.g.   A company's corporate plan. (Singular – the corporate plan of one company.)
These companies' corporate plans. (Plural – the corporate plans of many companies.)

3. Irregular nouns.
Some irregular nouns, as we have already seen, make their plurals in a differ – ent way. The most common of these change their form. In this case, the apostrophe always precedes the 's', whether the noun is singular or plural.

e.g.   A man's shoe. (Singular.)
Men's shoes. (Plural.)

The form will be the same for women and children. The usual rule, however, holds true for those irregular nouns which do not change their form.

e.g.   A sheep's wool. (The wool of one sheep.)
Sheeps' wool. (The wool of many sheep.)

4. Nouns already ending in 's' in the singular.
Nouns which end in 's' in the singular have another 's' after the apostrophe.

e.g.   St. James's Square.

THE APOSTROPHE USED TO REPLACE 'OF' IN EXPRESSIONS OF TIME

The rules here are the same as those for the position of the apostrophe to denote possession.

e.g.   *Singular*   *Plural*
One month's pay.   Six months' pay.
One year's time.   Three years' time.

THE APOSTROPHE USED TO DENOTE ABBREVIATION IN SPOKEN ENGLISH

In this case, the apostrophe appears at the point where letters have been omitted. This is used in colloquial spoken English and should not be used in written English, unless direct speech is being quoted. It should never be used in a formal document.

e.g.   'I don't like it,' he said. (*Don't* is an abbreviation for *do not*.)
'This isn't right; you must 'phone and tell them,' she said. (*Isn't* is an abbreviation for *is not*; *'phone* is an abbreviation for *telephone*.)

It is worth noting here that *it is* can be abbreviated to *it's*.

e.g.   'It's a lovely day,' she remarked.

Possessive pronouns *never* have apostrophes.

e.g.   The car lost its wheel.

Inverted commas

These may be single or double. They are used to denote direct speech, direct quotations or titles of books, films, plays and ships. Single and double inverted commas may be used interchangeably.

INVERTED COMMAS TO DENOTE DIRECT SPEECH

Inverted commas are used to show direct seech and they encase only the words actually spoken. When a new person begins to speak, a new paragraph is required.

e.g.   The manager said: 'Well Jones, do you want to attend this conference?'.
'Oh, yes please, sir, it would be most useful,' replied Jones.

If a word (or words) within quotation has to have inverted commas, *double* inverted commas should be used.

e.g.   'Are you going to see "Hamlet" tonight?' she asked.

Note: The question mark, exclamation mark or full stop which ends the direct speech comes *inside* the inverted commas.

INVERTED COMMAS TO DENOTE TITLES

The titles of books, films and plays should appear in inverted commas.

e.g.   I read 'Moby Dick'.
She saw 'War and Peace'.
They went to see 'King Lear'.

Some proper names should be in inverted commas, when, for example, they are names of ships. The official titles of people do not take inverted commas.

e.g.   The S.S. 'Canberra'.
Lord Peter Wimsey.

Brackets

Brackets are used in two ways in English – to denote an additional idea as an aside or to give a reference.

e.g.   A training course for managers (though not recommended for junior levels) is beginning tomorrow.
A questionnaire method was used (see Appendix 2 for an example).

The dash

The dash is used in a very similar way to brackets – that is to insert a further idea into the sentence.

e.g.   The marketing strategy of this company – and the whole performance of the marketing staff – has been very successful this year.

The hyphen

The hyphen acts as a link between parts of a word – when two words have been used together for so long that they have become one word (e.g. a record-player), when parts of a word must be pronounced separately, usually when there is a prefix of some kind (e.g. co-operation), and when a word has been split into two because it cannot fit at the end of a line. When in doubt about hyphens, consult a dictionary.

The exclamation mark

An exclamation mark may stand in place of a full stop in a number of circumstances.

1. It denotes speech which is shouted, or an urgent command.

e.g. 'Look out!'
'Please get this done at once!'

2. It denotes approval or enthusiasm.

e.g. That display is marvellous!

3. It denotes incredulity, sarcasm or surprise.

e.g. You can't really mean it!
That man's performance is incredible!
Good heavens! I can't believe it!

The question mark

The question mark, as its name implies, ends a question in place of a full stop.

e.g. What do you think of his report?

Indirect questions (usually introduced by *if* or *whether*) do not need a question mark.

e.g. She asked whether the report had been good.

It is better to use indirect questions in formal documents; direct questions may be used effectively in writing articles.

Capital letters

Capital letters have certain specific uses in English. They are used at the beginning of words in the following cases:

1. To denote proper names or proper nouns.

e.g. John Humble.
London.

2. To denote the titles of books, films, etc.

e.g. 'The Human Side of Enterprise' by Douglas McGregor is an interesting book.

(Note that the major words only have a capital letter.)

3. To denote the beginning of a sentence after a full stop, exclamation mark or question mark, or direct speech beginning in the middle of a sentence.

e.g. The manager asked him whether he would come to the conference. 'Can he come to the conference? There is room for one more delegate,' said the manager.
'You may well ask: "What shall I do?"'

4. To identify the pronoun 'I'.

e.g. When I go to the conference, I expect to learn a good deal.

5. To give the title of someone.

e.g. The Lord Chancellor.
The Chairman.

6. To give initials of a person, award, qualification, country or organisation.

e.g. J. K. Galbraith, Ph.D. (John Kenneth Galbraith, Doctor of Philosophy).
U.S.A. (United States of America).
B.R. (British Rail).

Sometimes, where the initials have been used very often, they appear as one word, only needing a capital at the beginning.

e.g. Ernie (Electronic Random Number Indicator Equipment).

Conclusion

Choosing the correct punctuation is crucial to communicating clearly and unambiguously. There are clear rules for its usage which should be observed if misunderstanding is to be avoided and comprehension is to be promoted.

Notes to the text

Chapter 1

1. Fayol, Henri, *General and Industrial Management* (Pitman, 1949).
2. Burns, Robert, 'To a Louse, on seeing one on a Lady's Bonnet in Church', *Scots Airs with Poetry*, with George Thompson (1792).
3. Andersen, Hans Christian, *Fairy Tales* (translated by M. Howit, 1846).
4. Barnet, Correlli, 'Technology Education and Economic Strength', *Journal of the Royal Society of Arts*, No. 5271 vol. CXXVII (February 1979).
5. Peter, Dr L. J., *The Peter Principle* (Souvenir Press, 1969).
6. Stewart, Rosemary, *Managers and their Jobs* (Macmillan, 1977).
7. Ritchie, Barry, 'The art of gobbledegook' (*Sunday Times*, 1977).
8. *Managing the Micro*, BBC television series.
9. Mant, Alastair, 'The Experienced Manager: a Major Resource', *BIM* (1969).
10. Orwell, George, 'Politics and the English Language', *Horizon*, No. 76 (April 1946).
11. Bernstein, Basil, *Class Codes and Control* (Routledge & Kegan Paul, 1971).
12. Gowers, Sir Ernest, *Plain Words* (HMSO, 1948).
13. Morris, Desmond, *The Naked Ape* and *Manwatching* (Cape, 1967).
14. Betjeman, Sir John, 'Private Line', *Punch.*

Chapter 2

15. Wordsworth, Sir William, Preface to the *Lyrical Ballads* (1800).

Chapter 3

16. Townsend, Robert, *Up the Organisation* (Michael Joseph Ltd, 1971).
17. Ibid.

Chapter 5

18. Gowers, Sir Ernest, *Plain Words* (HMSO 1948).

Chapter 7

19. ICSA Examination Paper, 1982 – Personnel: Principles and Policy.
20. ICSA Examination Paper, 1982 – Management: Principles and Policy.

Chapter 9

21. Stewart, Rosemary, *Managers and their Jobs* (Macmillan, 1977).
22. *Meetings, Bloody Meetings* (Video Arts).
23. Ibid.

Chapter 10

24. 'Square Pegs', *Horizon*, BBC television.

Chapter 12

25. Allason, J., 'Technology Extra – the Key to the Taintless Text', *Observer Magazine* (11 September 1983).

Chapter 13

26. 'Switch on Time for the Electronic Office', (quoting F. Heys of Butler Cox, Office Consultants, the *Sunday Times* (23 January 1983).
27. Poppel, Harvey J., Vice-President of Booz, Allen and Hamilton Inc., 'Who needs the Office of the Future?', *Harvard Review* (November 1982).
28. 'The Information Society', *New Society* (December 1982).
29. *Managing the Micro*, BBC television series.
30. Oliver, Brian, 'Technology Extra – The Sting and How to Avoid It', *Observer Magazine* (11 September 1983).
31. Ibid.
32. Fayol, Henri, *General and Industrial Management* (Pitman, 1949).

Further reading

General communication

Adair, J., *Training for Communication* (Gower Press, 1979).

Ashman, S. and George, A. *Study and Learn* (Heinemann, 1982).

Stanton, N., *The Business of Communications* (Pan, 1982).

Wainright, G., *People and Communication* (Macdonald and Evans, 1977).

General behavioural and organisational reading

Argyle, M., *Social Psychology of Work* (Penguin, 1972).

Argyle, M., *Psychology of Interpersonal Behaviour* (Pelican, 3rd edition, 1979).

Handy, C.B., *Understanding Organisations* (Penguin, 1981).

Warr, P., (Ed.), *Psychology at Work* (Penguin, 1981).

Other subjects

Enright, D.J., *A Mania for Sentences* (Chatto and Windus, 1983).

Mitchell, E., *The Businessman's Guide to: Speech Making and the Law and Conduct of Meetings* (Business Books, 1977).

Orwell, G., *Collection of Essays* (Harbrace Paperback Library, 1970).

Official documents from the Ministry of Information Technology, 1982.

Index

References to illustrations are in *italic* type.

Abbreviations, 216–17, 219
Abbreviations, colloquial, 213
  see also Colloquialisms
Abstain, 126–27, *126*, 132
Acts of Parliament (re. Meetings), 112, 117
Addendum, 132, 134
Ad hoc committee, 118, 121, 122, 134
Adjectival clauses and phrases, 212
Adjectives, 197, 198, 201, 206, 207, 209, 216, 218
  as complements, 211
  used as verbs, 205
  use of, 202
Adjourn/Adjournment, 130, 134
Adjourned:
  by consent, 134
  sine die, 134
Adverbial clauses and phrases, 212
Adverbs, 209
  irregular, 206
  use of, 205–206
Advertisement (employment), 140-41
Advisory committee, 116
Agenda, 119, 120, 123, *124*, 128, 130, 133, 134, 136
Agenda members, *120*, 120-22, 129
Algol, 172
Ambiguity and the public, 75
Amendment, 119, 128, 130, 131–32, 134, 136
Americanisms, 214
Annual General Meeting, 118, 122, *124*, 131, 134
Apostrophe, 201
  use of, 218–19
Appendix/Appendices, 48-49, 51, 52, 59, 101, 199

Application forms, 27–30, *28–29*, 140-41, 142, 143
Appraisal, 27, 31–33
  forms, *32*, *33*
  interviews, 138, 146–49, 159
  records, 157
  reports, 44, 61
Aptitude tests, 145
Archaic phrases and usage, 72, 73, 74, 213
  see also Commercialese; Jargon
Articles:
  of Association, 112, 118
  definite and indefinite, 197–98
  (re. newspapers, journals, etc.), 47, 89–91, *90*, 221
Assignments, 81–82
Audio visual aids, 96, 97, 102–106, 109
  see also Visual aids
Automation (re. office and office equipment), 81, 181, 189
  see also Electronic office; Integrated office

Ballot, 132, 134, 136
Bankers, Institute of, vii
Banking, electronic, *see* Electronic banking
BASIC, 172
Bibliography, 49, 51, 52, 59
Binary code, 172, 175, 176
Bits, 172
Blackboards, 80, 103
Body language, 95
Brackets, 215–20
Brain-storming groups/meetings, 103, 115

Briefing meeting, 115
British Telecom, 175–79
  'Gold' system, 179
Business/Technician Education Council
  (BTEC), vii
Buzz group, 115
Byte, 172

'C', 172
CCTV, *see* Closed circuit television
COM, *see* Microfilm
CP/M, *see* Operating System for
  Microcomputers
Cables, *9*, 160, 177–78
  see also Coaxial cable
Capital letters, 209, 216, 221
Casting vote, 129, 130, 132, 134
Ceefax, *9*
Chartered Secretaries, Institute of, vii,
  85, 92
Chair, addressing the, 134
Chairman, 112, 113, 119, 120, 122, 124,
  126, 128, 131, 132, 134–37, 222
  duties of, 129–30
Chairman's agenda, 122, *124*, 130, 134
Circulars/Circular letters, *6*, *9*, 38, *70*,
  71, 179, 131
Civil Servants, 10
Clauses, 209, 210, 211–12, 216, 217
  adjectival; adverbial; noun, 212
Closed circuit television, *6*, 104–105
Closure (re. committees), 135
Coaxial cable, 177–78
Cobol, 172
Colloquialisms, 60, 79, 89, 204, 223
  and slang, 213–14
Colon, 215, 218
Comma, 202, 210, 217–18
Command meetings, 116–17
Commercialese, 73–74
  see also Archaic phrases and usage;
  Jargon
Committee, going into, 135
Committee terms, glossary of, 134–137
Committees, 117–137
  see also Ad hoc committee; Joint
  committee; Joint consultative
  committee; Standing committee;
  Subcommittee
Company law, 112–117
Company Secretary, *124*
Compatible/Compatibility/
  Incompatibility, 173, 174, 175,
  181, 185, 188

Complement, 211, 216
Computer, 6, 8, *9*, 14, 80, 160, 171
Computer-aided design, 191
Computer-aided instruction/learning,
  191
Computer languages, 172
  see also Algol; BASIC; 'C'; Cobol;
  Fortran; Pascal; PL/1
Computer Output Microfilm (COM) *see*
  Microfilm
Computer technology, 169–82
  resistance to, 183–93
Computers (re. business
  communication), 172–174
Conditional, *see* Verbs
Confravision, 177
Conjunctions, 206–207, 211, 212, 217,
  218
Constitution of committees, 112, 119,
  129–*31, 134, 136*
Consultative committee, 116
*Control Program for Microcomputers
  (CP/M), see* Operating System for
  Microcomputers
Co-opt/Co-option, 119, 135
Council meeting, 120, 134
Counselling/Counselling interviews, 16,
  138, 141, 149–52, 153
Critical path analysis, 188
Curriculum vitae, 66–68, *68*, 75

Daisywheel, *see* Teleprinters
Dash, 215, 220
Data base, *9*, 174, 175, 177, 178, 179,
  181, 191
Datel, 175
Digital desk, 178
  Group 3 machines, 175
  systems/computers, 171, 173, 175
Direct command, 209, 221
Direct order/request, 216
Direct questions, 221
Disciplinary action/interviews, 16, 138,
  152–54
Discussion papers, 77–80, 215
Disks, *see* Floppy disks, Magnetic disks
Distance learning, 8, 191
Disturbance (re. committees), 135
Division, going into (re. committees),
  135

Electronic:
  banking, 177

circuits, 171
filing, 176
Funds Transfer, 177
industry, 184
mail, 174, 179–80, 184
office, 174, 175, 178–81
retrieval and storage, 176
typewriter, 179
work station, 174, 177, 178, 179, 180
Employment:
Protection Act, 37
(re. selection interviews), 16, 138,
139–50, 148, 151
English, use of, 195–222
Essays, 81–92
Examination Technique - 4 (example of
an article), *90*
Examinations, answers for, 81–92
Exclamation mark, 209, 221–22
Exit interviews, 138, 152, 154, 158
questionnaires, *155–56*, 157, 158
Ex officio, 129, 135
Exposition, essay of, 81–82
Extraordinary General Meeting, 135

Facsimile, 8, *9*, 175, 176, 178, 180
Felt boards, 103
Fibre optics, 171, 175, 176, 177–78
Fiche, 174
see also Microfiche
Films, 80, 104–105
Flip charts, 80, 103, 114, 115
Floppy disks, 173, 179
Flow charts, 188
Formal meetings, 112–14, 117–37
Forms, *6*, 27–41
see also Application forms; Appraisal
forms; Order forms
Forms, reports on, *see* Routine reports
Forms, useless, *32, 33, 43*
Fortran, 172
Full stop, 209, 216, 217, 221, 222

'Gateway' (re. computers), 177
Graphics plotters, 174
Group control, 114–15
Group maintenance functions, 113, 117

'Halo' and 'horned' effect, 144, 164
'Hands-on' experience, 36, 187, 189
Hand-outs, 99, 101, 102, 105
Hardware, 186, 188

Health and Safety at Work Act, 37, *55*,
153
Health Service, 51, 191
House journals, 165
Human factor, the, 183–93
Human relations function, 113–14
see also Group maintenance functions
Hygiene factors, *85, 86–87, 88*
Hyphen, 215, 221

Incomes Data Services, 184
Indirect questions, 221
Informal meetings, 112–14, 115–17
Information:
industry, 190
reports, 44, 47, 48–51, *49*
society, 171
technology, 80, 169–93
Technology Year, 171
Infra-red technology, 178
Initials, 216
Ink blot test, 146
Institutes, professional, *see* Bankers;
Chartered Secretaries; Electrical
Engineers; Management Services;
Pension Management
Integrated office, 174, 181
see also Automation; Electronic office
Intelpost/Intelstat, 178
Interface, 174, 175, 176
Interjections, 207
Interviews, *6*, 10, 16, 18, 22, 23, 47, 50
see also Appraisal interviews;
Counselling interviews;
Disciplinary interviews;
Employment (selection interviews);
Exit interviews
Intra vires, 135
Inverted commas, 215, 220
Investigation reports, 44, 47, 50–51, *53–
57*, 61

Jack points, 173
Jargon, 213
see also Archaic phrases and usage;
Commercialese
Job analysis, 97
Job description, 97, 139, 140, 141, 142,
159, 188
Joint committee/Joint consultative
committee, 118

Kangaroo closure, 135

LAN, *see* Local area network
Ladder layout, *15*, 22, 83, *86–87*, *88*, 89
Laser, 176, 178
Leadership and group control, 112–15
Leading questions, 143
Letter layout:
  blocked, *65*, 66, 216
  indented/traditional, *64*, 66
Letter writing, 62–76
  as a public relations exercise, 62–63
Letters of:
  application, 66–67, *67*, 75
  collection (of debts), 69–70
  complaint/adjustment, 69
  enquiry/order/reply, *64*, *65*, 67–69
  introduction, 71
  invitation, 71
Lie on the table (re. committees), 135
Listening skills, note-taking, 16–19
Local area network (LAN), 173, 174, 180

Macrobyte, 179
Magnetic:
  boards, 80, 103
  disks, 173, 174
  tapes, 173, 174, 175
Mainframe, 172, 173, 174, 185
'Management: Principles and Policy', 92
Management by Objectives (MBO), 146
Management Services, Institute of, *90*
Mandate, 101, 118
Manpower levels/planning, 146, 148
Man-watching, 11, 145
Market intelligence, *9*
Market research interviews, 138, 141
Marketing, 17
  strategy, 115
Media of communication:
  internal, *6*
  external, *9*
Meetings, *6*, 14, 16, 20, 22, 23, 111–37, 182
  see also Annual General; Brainstorming; Briefing; Council; Extraordinary; General; Formal; Informal; Joint committee; Joint consultative committee; Private; Problem-solving; Public
Memoranda/Memorandum, 5, *6*, 7, 21, 34–36, *36*, 38, 39, 40, 41, 44, 47, 48, *49*, 116, 182, 199, 213
  (re. committees), 112, 117, 135
Menu, 176

Micro technology, 6, 169–81
Microchip, 183, 184
  see also Silicon chip
Microcomputers, 8, 172, 173, 174, 179, 181, 183
Microfiche, 174
  see also Fiche
Microfilm, Computer Output (COM), 174
Micromail, 179, 185
Minute book, 118, 123, 128, 131, 135
Minutes, 18, 119, 121, 123, 124, 125–129, 130, 131, 136, 213
  narrative/of narration, *126–127*, 128, 135
  resolution, 128, 136
Modem, 174, 179
Motion, 119, 121, 123, 127, *126–27*, 128, 130, 131–32, 134, 136, 137
  dropped, 135
  substantive, 132, 137
Motivation, theory of, 65, *85*, *86–87*, *88*
Multiplexing, 171

Narrative minutes, *see* Minutes, narrative
National Institute of Industrial Psychology, 139–40
Nem con/Nem Dis, 132, 136
Networks, 175–76
  see also Public packet-switched networks; Value added networks
Next business (re. committees), 136
Non-verbal communication/signs 145, 151, 154, 158, 159, 164, 165
  see also Body language; Halo and horned effect
Note-form summaries, 19–20
Note-making/Note-taking, 14–23
Note-taking (re. listening) 16–20
Notes, 97–98, 145
  for a talk, 22
Notice of meeting, 40, 119, *120*, 130, 136
Notice(s), *6*, 27, 38–40, *39*, *40*
Noun, 197, 200, 201, 202, 206, 207, 209, 210, 216, 218
  clauses and phrases, 210
Nouns, 198–99
  abstract, 198
  collective, 198–99, 210–11
  object, 211
  regular/irregular, 199, 218–19
  subject, 203, 209
  verbs used as, 205

Object (of a sentence), 210, 211, 216
Office, *see* Automation; Integrated
   office; Paperless office
Open questions, 143, 144, 148, 150, 151,
   154, 158
Open University, 8, 110, 191
Operating System for Microcomputers
   (CP/M), 172, 173
Opto-electronic device, 171
Oral communication, 93–168
   presentation, 95–109
   reporting, 95–109
   reports, 20, 96–100, 101
   forms, 27–31
Organisation:
   and method, 47
   charts, 165, 166
   development (OD), 117
   pyramid, *7*
Overhead projectors, 80, 104

PL/1, 172
Paperless office, 177
Paragraph, construction of the, 212–13,
   215–16
Paralinguistics, 144, 148
   see also Phatic communication
Participle, dangling, 66, 72, 210
   see also Verbs
Pascal, 172
Past tenses, *see* Verbs
Pension Management, Institute of, vii
Perception, 11, 17, 45, 106
Performance appraisal, *see* Appraisal
Performance tests, 145
Peripherals, 173
Personality tests, 146
Personnel department, 27, *52–56*, 142,
   149, 154, 157, 158
'Personnel: Principles and Policy', 85
Personnel specification, 139–40, 141,
   142, 145, 159
'Peter Principle', the, 4
Phatic communication, 144, 163
Phonetic alphabet, *see* Post Office
   telephone alphabet
Phrases, 211–12, 215, 216, 217, 218
   adjectival/adverbial, 212
   archaic, 213
Pin boards, 103
Plain Words, 10, 62
Planning meeting, 155
Point of order/Point of procedure, 129,
   131, 136

Point of sale transactions, 177, 191
Poll, 132, 136
Post Office telephone alphabet, 162, 166
Précis, 19, 98, 103
Predicate, 209, 210, 211–12, 216
Preposition, 200, 201, 207, 212
Prestel, 9, 177, 180
Private meeting, 117
Probing/Probing questions, 142, 143,
   144, 151, 154
Problem-solving interview, *see*
   Counselling interviews
Problem-solving meeting, 115, 149–52
Professional journal, 89
Program, 172, 173, 179, 186
Program, Control for Microcomputers,
   see Operating System for
   Microcomputers
Progress meeting, 115
Project, 20, 45, 47, 58–59
Projector, *see* Overhead projectors;
   Slide projectors
Pronoun, 202, 209, 212, 216, 218, 219,
   222
Pronouns:
   object, 200
   possessive, 200
   question, 201
   reflective, 201
   subject, 200, 203, 209
   use of, 200–201
Proposal (re. meetings), 119, 123, *126–
   27*, 131–32, 134
Proposer, 119, 121, 123, *126–27*, 130,
   132, 136
Proxy, 136
Public meeting, 117
Public packet-switched networks, 175,
   176–77, 179
Public relations, 27, 62–76, 140
   function (re. telephone/reception),
   160–68
Public speaking, 21, 22, 96, 106–109
   see also Oral presentation; Talks;
   Speeches
Punctuation, 215–22
   open, *65*, 66, 220
Putting the question, (re. meetings), 136

Question, direct/indirect, 221
Question mark, 209, 221, 222
Questioning techniques (re. interviews),
   143–58
   see also Leading questions; Open

questions; Probing questions;
  Reflective questions; Situational
  questions
Questionnaires, 47, 58, 101, 139, 220
  see also Exit questionnaires
Quorum, 119, 129, 136
Quotations, 220

Random Access Memory (RAM), 173
Reception, 164
  techniques, 160–68
Receptionists (re. selection, briefing and
  training), 164–65
Reference back (re. committees), 137
References (re. employment selection),
  141
Reflective
  questions/statements/techniques,
  144, 148, 151
Registrar of Companies, 118
Report writing, 42–61
Reports, *6*, 14, 16, 19, 20, 22, 77, 78, 79,
  121, 182, 213, 215
  see also Information reports;
  Investigation reports; Oral reports;
  Project; Short reports on
  memoranda forms; Technical
  reports
Research and development (R & D), 9,
  53–57
Resolution (re. committees), 136, 137
Resolution minutes, *see* Minutes,
  resolution
Revolution:
  Industrial, 171
  Technological, 181, 190, 191
Rider (re. committees), 132, 137
Right of reply (re. committees), 137
Routine reports (on forms), 43–44, 45,
  48, 60
Royal Commission, 44, 58

Satellites, 160, 175, 177–78
Scrutineer, 137
Seconder, *126–27*, 130, 132, 136, 137
Secretary, of a meeting, 119, 121, 122,
  123, *126*, 128, 129, 130, 136, 137
  duties of, 130–31
Secretary, Honorary, 131
Selection interviews, *see* Employment
Semicolon, 211, 217
Sentence, topic, 212–16
Sentences, construction of, 209–12

'Seven Point Plan', 139–40
  see also National Institute of
  Industrial Psychology
Short reports on memoranda forms, 44,
  49
Silicon chip, 171, 173
Sine die, *see* Adjourned *sine die*
Situational questions, 143, 159, 164
Slang, 213–14
Slide projectors, 104
Slides, 80, 97
Slot boards, 103
Society, *see* Cashless society;
  Information society
Software, 172, 179, 181, 185, 186, 188,
  189, 191
Speech:
  direct, 207, 217, 219, 220, 221, 222
  parts of, 197–208, 209, 212, 214
Speeches, 21, 60
  see also Oral communication; Oral
  presentation; Talks
Standing committee, 118, 121
Standing Orders (re. committees), 112,
  117, 136, 137
Star layout/plan, 15, *16*, 21, 83–85, *85*,
  89
Status enquiries and replies, 71
Statutory meetings, 117
Subcommittee, 118, 137
Subject (of a sentence), 209–10, 211,
  216, 218
  see also Nouns; Pronouns
Subjunctive, *see* Verbs
Substantive motion, *see* Motion
Summons (re. meetings), 120
Surveys, 16, 47
Synopsis, 58
Syntax:
  and the use of vocabulary, 208,
  209–14
  (re. computers), 190
System X, 175, 176

'T groups', 116
Talks, 22–23, 95–109
  see also Oral presentation; Public
  speaking; Speeches
Tannoy, *6*, 38
Tape, magnetic, *see* Magnetic tapes
Tape, packages, 191
Tape recorder, 98, 104, 105
Task functions, 113, 117
Technical reports, 44, *46*, 47, 51–58

Technological change, resistance to, 183–93
Technology (re. business communication), 171–82
Telebanking, 191
Telecommunications, 160, 171, 174, 179, 191
 (development related to business communication), 175–78
Teleconferencing, 175, 177
Telegraph, facsimile, *9*
Télématique, 171
Telephone, *6, 9*
Telephone alphabet, *see* Post Office telephone alphabet
Telephone, analogue, 171, 175
Telephone messages, 162–63
Telephone and reception techniques, 160–68
Telephonists (re. briefing, selection, training), 166–67
Teleprinters, *6, 9,* 178–79
Teleshopping, 177, 191
Teletext, 175, 176, 179, 180
Teletypewriters, 175
Telex, *9,* 160, 174, 175, 180
Teller, 137
Telstar, 178
Terminals, 174
 electronic mail, 179
 intelligent, 174
 telex, 174
Terms of reference, 48, 50, *55,* 58, 59, 78, 101, 118, 129, 137, 217
Tests, 143, 145–46
 see also Aptitude tests; Medical tests; Performance tests; Personality tests; Trade tests
Testimonial, 141
Topic sentences, *see* Sentence, topic
Trade tests, 145
Treasurer, *126–27,* 129, 137
 duties of, 131

USA, 4, 183, 190, 207, 222
Ultraviolet technology, 178
Ultra vires, 129, 137
Unanimous, 132, 137
Union (re. resistance to technological change), 183–85
Unions, white-collar, 183–85

VDU, *see* Visual display unit
Value added networks, 176
Verbs, 206, 207, 216, 217
 active/passive, 202–203
 as adjectives/nouns, 205–10
 auxiliary, 207
 colloquial, 213
 conditional, 203–205
 finite, 209, 211, 212
 future/future perfect, 203–205
 gerunds, 205, 210, 211
 infinitive, 202, 205
 intransitive, 210–11
 irregular, 204–205
 participles, present/past, 202–203, 209, 210, 212
 past/past perfect, 203–205
 present, 203–205
 regular, 203
 role in a sentence, 210
 simple/continuous, 203–205
 subjunctive, 202, 203, 204
 tenses and moods, 202–205
 transitive, 210, 211
 use of, 202–205
Vice-Chairman, *124*
 duties of, 130
Video, 8, 80, 104
 conferencing, 160
 (re. orders), 191
 telephone, 160
 text, 175–76
Viewdata, 175, 176, 180–81
Visual aids, 37, 80, 96, 97, 101, 102–105
 see also Audio visual aids
Visual display unit (VDU), 173, 174, 178, 180
Voice recognition, 172
Voice typewriters, 179
Vote (of no confidence), 136
Voting, 119, 131–32, 136, 137
 en bloc, 135

White boards, 80, 103
White-collar workers, 181, 183–85
Word processors, *6, 9, 49,* 174, 176, 178, 180, 184
Work station, *see* Electronic work station
Work study, 47